THE
INTELLIGENCE
WARS

THE
INTELLIGENCE
WARS

LESSONS FROM BAGHDAD

STEVEN K. O'HERN

 **Prometheus Books**

59 John Glenn Drive
Amherst, New York 14228–2119

Published 2008 by Prometheus Books

Inquiries should be addressed to
Prometheus Books
59 John Glenn Drive
Amherst, New York 14228–2119
VOICE: 716–691–0133, ext. 210
FAX: 716–691–0137
WWW.PROMETHEUSBOOKS.COM

12 11 10 09 08   5 4 3 2 1

Library of Congress Cataloging-in-Publication Data

O'Hern, Steven K., 1954–
    The intelligence wars : lessons from Baghdad / by Steven K. O'Hern.
        p. cm.
    Includes bibliographical references and index.
    ISBN 978–1–59102–670–9 (hardcover : alk. paper)
    1. Iraq War, 2003– 2. Intelligence service—United States. 3. United States—Politics and government—2001–. I. Title.

DS79.76.O54 2008
956.7044/38—dc22

2008038763

Printed in the United States of America on acid-free paper

D edicated to these men who gave their lives in Iraq while serving with the Strategic Counterintelligence Directorate and the Air Force Office of Special Investigations:

Special Agent Rick A. Ulbright, Air Force Office of Special Investigations, August 8, 2004

Staff Sergeant Shawn A. Graham, 124th Cavalry Regiment, 36th Infantry Division, Texas National Guard, attached to the Strategic Counterintelligence Directorate, September 25, 2005

Special Agent Daniel J. Kuhlmeier, Air Force Office of Special Investigations, attached to the Strategic Counterintelligence Directorate, February 20, 2006

Sergeant Jessie Davila, 2nd Battalion, 137th Infantry, Kansas National Guard, attached to the Strategic Counterintelligence Directorate, February 20, 2006

Special Agent Matthew Joseph Kuglics, Air Force Office of Special Investigations, June 5, 2007

Special Agent Ryan Andrew Balmer, Air Force Office of Special Investigations, June 5, 2007

Special Agent Thomas Crowell, Air Force Office of Special Investigations, November 1, 2007

Special Agent Nathan Schuldheiss, Air Force Office of Special Investigations, November 1, 2007

Special Agent David Wieger, Air Force Office of Special Investigations, November 1, 2007

CONTENTS

CONTENTS

AUTHOR'S NOTE

I have changed the names of all of the personnel at the Strategic Counterintelligence Directorate (SCID) who are mentioned in this book except for those who have been killed while serving in Iraq. Many of the soldiers, marines, sailors, airmen, and civilian employees who were at the SCID continue to serve our country, and although they deserve great credit, I have changed their names out of concern for their safety.

Only a handful of the people who served at the SCID are mentioned by their pseudonyms. Although I would have preferred to write about their service in great detail, I was stopped by two considerations: Most of the details of their work remain classified, and, more important, the experiences of the men and women at the SCID serve to illustrate issues more urgent than the details of the insurgents captured as a result of their intelligence work. While those who serve in the intelligence field are often unsung heroes, they are held back by a system that is defective and dangerous. That is the story of this book.

I am grateful for the opportunity to have served with the men and women of the SCID and the other military and civilian personnel with whom I served while I was in Iraq. I salute all of you. Generous praise must also be given to the people who supported the SCID's operations from the United States, especially the men and women at the headquarters of the Air Force Office of Special Investigations, which served as the executive agency for the SCID.

In conducting research for this book, I was heartened to find many articles in professional journals written by military personnel who were stationed in Iraq and who described their experiences and the lessons learned for others to read. This is a valuable service to your fellow warriors and I thank all who have done so. Valuable contributions to topics addressed by this book have been made by others who have written eloquently and comprehensively based on careers of scholarship. Even among such a group the words of some stood out. Col. T. X. Hammes, USMC (ret.); Col. Ralph O. Baker, USA; and Professor Steven Metz of the Strategic Studies Institute provided particularly valuable insights. I especially thank Colonel Hammes for sharing his time in conversations and e-mails.

This book is not intended for academics. Many have studied warfare and intelligence operations far more than I. This book is intended to inform the American public that the military intelligence system needs careful study. It was not prepared to fight an insurgency, and change is needed. If this book has the added benefit of assisting someone who deploys to Iraq or another war, then my wishes will have been exceeded.

I am grateful to my literary agent, Jodie Rhodes, for suggesting changes in the book and placing it with Prometheus Books. Steven L. Mitchell, the editor in chief at Prometheus Books, and Meghann French, who edited the manuscript, greatly assisted this new author and made the editing process enjoyable. I am indebted to both Douglas Flanders and another friend, who must remain unnamed, who agreed to read an early draft of the first several chapters. Their comments were very useful. Finally, I thank my wife, daughter, and stepchildren for their love and support during my deployment, my military career, and the writing of this book. Without their patience and love, this book would not have been written.

FOREWORD

Bart Bechtel

S teven K. O'Hern deserves recognition and thanks for his contribution to the ongoing discussion about and effort to
improve US intelligence. A book written by an officer who
directed human intelligence operations against an insurgency is
unique and offers a perspective rarely seen. In this book, readers will
be reminded of systemic problems within the intelligence community and, more specifically, within our military intelligence in this
new era of the global war on terrorism (GWOT) and insurgencies.
O'Hern's book should be required reading for all officers of the
armed forces, noncommissioned officers (NCOs), civilian intelligence employees, law enforcement, and members of both the US
Senate and House of Representatives armed services committees.
Additionally, the book should be read by every citizen who cares
about our national security, in order to become educated about the
shortcomings in the practice of intelligence and its impact on our
fighting forces and mission successes and failures. In the author's
words,

> This book is not intended for academics. Many have studied warfare
> and intelligence operations far more than I. This book is intended to
> inform the American public that the military intelligence system needs
> careful study. It was not prepared to fight an insurgency, and change is
> needed. If this book has the added benefit of assisting someone who
> deploys to Iraq or another war, then my wishes will have been exceeded.

Within O'Hern's book, one finds eerie reminders of what the
9/11 Commission report contained. Years after the report, we see a
continuation of unappreciation for human intelligence (HUMINT),
stovepiping, lack of information sharing, failure of imagination,
and risk aversion. Clearly, some in the military intelligence community failed to read the 9/11 Commission Report, and because of
the continuation down the wrong paths, America paid more of a
price in Iraq than it might have otherwise.

Reading this book reminded me of problems I saw among too
many (not all, thank God) colleagues at the CIA. Too many were
more concerned with reading the political winds than serving their
ultimate employer, the American citizens and taxpayers.
"Careerism" is the term for conducting one's professional life in
order to advance rather than actually striving to do the best and
most complete job possible. It is seen in quotas on the numbers of
reports or recruited agents versus the quality of the same, and in
taking only those actions that have the least chance of causing problems or possibly failing.

This book tells, in more detail than has been told before, the
background of the explosively formed penetrator (EFP) weapon and
how it was shipped into Iraq by Iranian forces. Most troubling for
me, in the first chapter, was learning that senior military intelligence officers knew Iran was supplying the EFPs but chose not to
direct intelligence operations that would interdict the weapons.
Was this a case like the line in Phantom of the Opera: "Close your

eyes, for your eyes will only tell the truth, and the truth isn't what you want to see"?

In the author's words: "Why was each new threat a surprise? Well, one simple answer is that many things are a surprise to a blind man. Our intelligence system has blinded our military and political leaders when they face an evolving, multifaced insurgency" (p. 48).

During the time when the United States did not act, the Iranian Revolutionary Guard Corps (IRGC) imported many weapons and trained many Shiite militiamen to use the more sophisticated roadside bomb, costing the lives of many US service members whose armored vehicles could not protect them against the EFPs. Senior military intelligence officers wanted efforts focused on the Sunni insurgency and ignored Iranian contributions to the overall multiparty insurgency. One of the primary purposes of intelligence is force protection, yet those responsible for this effort are concerned only with protecting forces against one enemy. If I were a relative of a soldier killed or wounded by an EFP supplied by the IRGC, I would be mightily angry.

Every chapter of this book is worth reading and thinking about. The author illustrates, through examples, the consequences from both positive and negative procedures and their impact on operations in Iraq. To his credit, O'Hern does not only critique military intelligence doctrine, which is written primarily for large-scale ground warfare and not counterinsurgency combat; he also offers suggestion for improvement—networking. He recognizes that the status quo is unacceptable. Our nation cannot afford the blood and treasure wasted because of failure of imagination and systemic inflexibility. Rapidly changing and adapting enemies must be combated with equally imaginative, flexible, and nimble defenses. It is clear that O'Hern is deeply concerned about making improvements to how intelligence must be conducted for maximum benefit in the GWOT and counterinsurgencies in order to shorten conflict, minimize casualties, and achieve mission success.

In closing, I want to state how important it is for our military leaders (officers and NCOs) to take the time to do what O'Hern did. It is important to write down observations—good and bad—so they may be read by those who come after. Lessons from history cannot be studied if they are not recorded. The result of doing so will be to provide the foundations for good decision making and leadership among our armed forces of tomorrow.

Chapter 1

GETTING ACQUAINTED

The war in Iraq has lasted much longer than we were promised. The number of men and women killed and wounded has been high. The war has left its mark on the more than half a million men and women in the US military who served in Iraq, many for multiple tours. Civilians numbering in the hundreds of thousands went to Iraq to drive trucks, provide security, and handle myriad other jobs.

Despite the impact of the war on those who have been to Iraq, back in the United States most people are not personally affected. Only a fraction of our population serves in the military, and most Americans don't have friends or neighbors who have gone to Iraq.

Despite their lack of personal involvement, most Americans have opinions about the war. Regardless of their support for or against the decisions to go to war and to continue an American presence in Iraq, most people are mystified about why the war has lasted so long. The United States Army and Marine Corps captured Baghdad in a matter of weeks. But a few months later resistance to US forces began to build.

By 2004 it was clear that an insurgency against the coalition forces was growing. The opposition to the coalition was a collection of disparate groups that were not centrally controlled. Despite that lack of organization, the insurgents were fighting the same army and Marine Corps that had tossed Saddam Hussein's regime out of power—and they were fighting our army and Marine Corps to a standstill.

The insurgency is the reason the war has lasted so long. The "shock and awe" war became a fourth-generation war. The United States military was not built to fight an insurgency, but has adopted new techniques and relearned forgotten lessons from past wars. The intelligence system that supports our military, however, has not adapted.

I served in Iraq for six months during 2005 as the leader of an intelligence unit that hunted for insurgents. I was on the staff of the military's senior intelligence officer in Iraq. I worked with the Central Intelligence Agency (CIA), the Defense Intelligence Agency (DIA), and the National Security Agency (NSA). From those experiences, I took many lessons. The chief lesson is that our military's intelligence system does not work well for fighting an insurgency.

Knowing that the world's finest military is not well served by its intelligence apparatus when it fights an insurgency scares me. I am troubled because the "long war" against terrorists, especially Islamic terrorists, that President George W. Bush and others have predicted is likely to be a series of wars similar to the wars in Iraq and Afghanistan. The Horn of Africa, the Philippines, and

Indonesia all have large populations of poor Muslims who are displeased with their governments. We will see more insurgencies.

My lessons about our intelligence system began when I was assigned to be the director of the Strategic Counterintelligence Directorate (SCID) of the Multi-National Force–Iraq (the name of the military force operating in Iraq, abbreviated as MNF–I). The SCID has members from the army, navy, and air force, plus civilian contractors provided by the Defense Department's Counterintelligence Field Activity (CIFA).

Counterintelligence is the part of intelligence work that defeats an adversary's attempt to collect intelligence about our plans and capabilities. In the most glamorous sense, counterintelligence means catching spies. But it can also mean something as mundane as investigating people who work with classified information to make sure they do not present a security risk. Because of its source networks that helped identify insurgents, the SCID's work focused on identifying and fighting insurgents instead of other counterintelligence duties.

The work of intelligence can be divided into broad categories based on how intelligence is gathered. Signals intelligence (SIGINT) concerns collecting, decoding, and translating information gleaned from eavesdropping on conversations or messages (telephones, radio transmissions, etc.). Another broad category is the intelligence gathered from satellites or reconnaissance aircraft, which is broadly labeled imagery intelligence (IMINT). Another "-int" is HUMINT, or human intelligence. This is the work described in spy novels as fraught with danger and beautiful women. In real life, human intelligence is more often the work of identifying and recruiting someone else to acquire information.

In Iraq the SCID had four counterintelligence teams, each with counterintelligence agents from the army, navy and air force. There were two teams in the Green Zone, the Blue Team and the Black

Team. A third team was in the city of Irbil, in Kurdish territory in northern Iraq, and the fourth team was in Iraq's second largest city, Basra, in southern Iraq. All of the teams had army military intelligence personnel, Naval Criminal Investigative Service (NCIS) special agents, and Air Force Office of Special Investigations (AFOSI) special agents. Each team worked with a squad of Texas National Guardsmen who served as the security element for the SCID.

The SCID was a human intelligence operation. Intelligence from imagery and intercepted communications added to our picture, but our main method of collecting information was from Iraqis who we recruited and trained. Of course, we were not alone in relying on HUMINT. Several units in the army, Marine Corps, and air force conducted human source operations that focused on areas near their bases or areas of operations in order to better protect US bases or operations. This intelligence collection was one aspect of "force protection" work that consumed large numbers of people in Iraq.

With the capture of Baghdad, the Iraq War entered a new phase, one that wasn't recognized at first. In order to reduce the frequency and severity of attacks on US forces and the process of rebuilding the Iraqi government, the thousands of troops searching for insurgents had to be told where to look. Identifying the people who carried out attacks, built bombs, and provided logistical support to the insurgency may have been the most difficult task in protecting US forces. The insurgents lived and worked among neighborhoods of apparently peaceful Iraqis. Satellites, reconnaissance aircraft, and the interception of radio and cell phone signals were useful, but alone these methods of collecting information could not defeat the insurgency.

Sunni insurgents who were loosely linked in shifting and hard-to-identify networks were carrying out attacks against coalition forces daily. Fighting them was like a never-ending game of whacka-mole. As soon as insurgents were knocked down, others popped up. Collecting intelligence to locate and capture insurgents and to defend coalition forces from future attacks was critical to success in Iraq. We could not eliminate violence, but reducing it enough to allow orderly life to return to Iraq would be essential to a successful Iraq government friendly to the United States.

On my second day in Iraq, Frank Brown, the army civilian intelligence officer I was replacing as the director of the SCID, took me to a house we called the White House. Like the other SCID houses in the Green Zone used to house and office our personnel and vehicles, it was named after a color. The Blue and Black houses were named for the teams they housed. The White House, named for its exterior color, was the main office for the SCID and housed several interpreters, civilian analysts, soldiers, the operations officer, and the director.

As I walked toward the White House I saw the additional challenge the SCID would face. Black and gray, not white, were the dominant hues. A fire two days before my arrival had nearly destroyed the building. Frank had discovered the fire in a storeroom near his office. The few people in the house at the time had used fire extinguishers on the growing blaze while the fire department was responding. The fire department had just begun to fight the fire when ammunition in the storeroom began detonating from the heat, forcing the firefighters to pull back. Part of the building was a total loss. Smoke and water damage were present throughout most of the building.

On my third day in Iraq, I made the second of many trips up and down Route Irish to meet my boss, who worked at Camp Victory, one of the many bases in the Baghdad International Airport (BIAP, pronounced "bye-app") complex. Route Irish was one of several highways in Iraq named by the army as main supply routes

(MSRs). The highway that ran east from BIAP into the heart of Baghdad was part of MSR Irish, better known as Route Irish. The divided four-lane highway was the only direct route from BIAP to the Green Zone; any other route forced you to travel through dangerous territory for a much longer distance.

The area around BIAP was host to several army bases and camps, including Camp Victory, Camp Liberty, and Camp Slater. In addition, the air force operated a passenger terminal on the west side of the two north-south runways at the airport, at Sather Air Base. The BIAP complex of bases was home to thousands of army soldiers and the headquarters of the Multi-National Force–Iraq and Multi-National Corps–Iraq (MNC–I).

Large numbers of soldiers were required to secure the miles of walls and fences around BIAP. Within the BIAP complex, separate forward operating bases (FOBs) and camps were secured by their own checkpoints. In addition to supporting the 3rd Infantry Division and the many FOBs in and around Baghdad, the BIAP complex also provided the logistics that supported the US Embassy in the Green Zone and provided a location for the United States to train Iraqi military and police personnel. Civilian workers performed countless other services, such as operating several dining facilities, a well-stocked Post Exchange, and the passenger terminals for airplane and helicopter flights, and constructing and managing quarters to house the military and civilian personnel.

While Frank and I were at Camp Victory, he introduced me to my new boss, Brig. Gen. John DeFreitas III. He had been selected for promotion to major general and I was told that he would become the commander of the army's Intelligence and Security Command when he left Iraq. The general was running late so our conversation was brief. He shook my hand, welcomed me to Iraq, and then left to go to another meeting.

The next day, Frank departed for the Baghdad airport. Because of the fire in the White House, I spent the next week sharing the deputy director's office in the embassy with Mark Johnson. I asked Mark dozens of questions a day. Five days later Don Everest arrived to replace Mark as the deputy director.

Possessing a wealth of experience, Don was showing up for his third or fourth war. He spent multiple tours of duty in Vietnam as a soldier before being recruited into the army's military intelligence. Ending his military career after twenty years, Don was immediately hired as a civilian military intelligence agent. He came to the SCID after being operations officer of a unit at the army's Foreign Counterintelligence Activity.

Another key member of the SCID was Tom Reid, a Naval Criminal Investigative Service agent who was the SCID's operations officer. Tom had one of the most critical jobs at the SCID. He was responsible for supervising our team chiefs, agents, and analysts as they recruited and handled sources, reported information in intelligence information reports, and analyzed the information received from sources.

Nothing had prepared me for the level of detail I needed to know about Iraq's political factions, the history of Saddam's regime, and the operations of several insurgent groups in order to understand what we were doing and what we needed to do. I spent hours reading classified reports and talking with intelligence analysts.

The civilian intelligence analysts at the SCID were a big asset. At the time I arrived at the SCID, they were a mix of men ranging from their late twenties to their fifties who came from varied backgrounds. Later in my deployment, several female analysts arrived. Some were retired from the army or Marine Corps; others had separated from the military after a few years service. The SCID was supposed to have fifteen analysts, but the agency that supplied them, the Counterintelligence Field Activity, was not replacing analysts who were leaving after a one-year tour of duty. One of the problems Frank Brown briefed me about was his fight to get CIFA to honor its commitment to supply fifteen analysts. As a short-term solution for our analyst shortage, CIFA had recently sent four analysts on sixty-day tours.

This illustrated another problem that existed throughout the Iraq theater. It takes about four to six weeks for someone to acclimate to the environment, the climate, the numerous hostile groups in play, and the current situation in order to be effective. That time line was the same for all of the people at the SCID, whether the director, operations officer, team chief, agent, analyst, linguist, or member of our security element. Turnover was a constant battle for all elements of the military and the State Department. At the SCID we faced turnover in waves. The army sent all of its counterintelligence agents to the SCID in one rotation every six months, while the air force's agents also served six months but came in four rotations per year. NCIS agents served three months and rotated all at once, except for the polygraph examiner, who was on his own schedule. The army supplied a platoon of infantrymen to serve as our security element for a one-year rotation. Linguists and analysts came over as we hired new ones and generally served a one-year tour.

My boss, Brigadier General DeFreitas, was the deputy chief of staff for intelligence of the Multi-National Force–Iraq for a one-year tour. In army jargon he was the DCSINT (pronounced "des-scent") of MNF–I. The DCSINT was also called the C-2, the chief intelligence officer for a coalition operation.

Iran had been a sensitive topic in discussions between Frank Brown and my new boss. Frank and Mark Johnson told me that DeFreitas believed the attacks on US forces by the insurgency required our attention and he didn't want the intelligence issues caused by Iran's involvement in Iraq to distract us from that primary task. Even as a newcomer to the theater, I thought the Iranians were going to have a lasting effect on our presence in Iraq, so I was surprised to hear that the senior military intelligence officer in Iraq didn't want us to focus any attention on Iran. I would soon learn how serious the general was about that.

The SCID had been instrumental in uncovering Iran's involvement in unleashing an increasing number of deadly bombs known as explosively formed penetrators against US forces in Iraq. Combat casualties in Iraq came from three main sources: direct fire such as gunfire or rocket propelled grenades, indirect fire such as mortars or rockets, and bombs such as the ones that the military labeled as improvised explosive devices (IEDs). Bombs were set up beside roads, buried under roads, and placed in parked cars, and a triggerman watching the area would detonate the bomb. Another type of bomb frequently used was the suicide bomb carried on the bomber's body, often in a vest, or in a car driven by the bomber.

In Iraq roadside bombs have caused most of the deaths in the war. Most of the roadside bombs experienced in 2003 and 2004 were IEDs made with unused ordnance such as artillery shells attached to some type of detonator and a triggering device. Because most Iraqi ammunition storage areas were not guarded after the Iraqi army abandoned them, explosives were not hard for insurgents to acquire. IEDs could be set off using a cell phone or garage door remote control. Another way to set off an IED was to run a wire from the detonator attached to the explosive to a control held by the triggerman. Either method required someone to be able to view the IED's kill zone in order to activate the bomb.

IEDs that used artillery shells or homemade explosives sent their blast in all directions. In response to IEDs, US forces began using more armored vehicles. At the time of the invasion of Iraq, most of the Humvees in Iraq were unarmored. Similarly, the State Department and the military also used unarmored SUVs that lacked protection from IEDs or gunfire.

As more armored vehicles, such as light armored vehicles (suburban utility vehicles with armor) and armored Humvees were used, US personnel were better able to survive IED attacks. In 2003 a new kind of bomb, the explosively formed penetrator, began to appear. The EFP was constructed to channel the force of the explosive through a tube that was capped by a copper plate, creating an antiarmor cannon. The explosive formed the metal plate into a molten projectile that penetrated armor and caused severe damage inside the vehicle.

The technology for the EFP was developed by Lebanese Hezbollah, a group sponsored by Iran's Revolutionary Guards. The SCID's counterintelligence agents and analysts had developed an excellent source of information that not only described how EFPs were made, but also described how Iran was providing EFPs and instructing insurgents in their use. These deadly weapons were being used against US armored vehicles with devastating results. An attack by an IED was often survivable; an attack with an EFP was more frequently fatal to the occupants of the vehicle.

The military's explosive experts had deduced the nature of the weapons, but that only answered the "what" question. The patient and methodical work of SCID agents and analysts in 2005 provided detailed information that addressed questions of who was behind the EFP attacks and how EFPs were introduced to Iraq. The technology was not revolutionary. An EFP is essentially a platter charge that has been described in army field manuals for many years. Lebanese Hezbollah successfully used EFPs against Israeli targets in the past.

The fact that Iranian-backed groups were using EFPs and had

been taught how to disguise, aim, and trigger them against US forces was new information. At least some of the training and most, if not all, of the bomb making was taking place in Iran. For some time, however, only the SCID and a few analysts in Iraq paid much attention to the wealth of information the SCID had gathered.

In 2005 Iran's intervention in Iraq was not a topic about which my boss, the senior military intelligence officer in Iraq, wanted to hear. Less than two years later, senior members of the Bush administration and Gen. David Petraeus, commander of US forces in Iraq, would be openly discussing the EFP threat brought to Iraq by Iran.

The issue of Iran would be central to my first extended conversation with my new boss. Our discussion would be loud and would set the tone for our relationship.

A source handled by Evelyn Fine, an AFOSI agent on the Blue Team, reported information about a possible plan to attack a US facility in Syria. The source was untested, but the information was relatively specific, and we reported it in an intelligence information report to US Central Command (CENTCOM) and the DIA. Soon we received a request from the US defense attaché in Syria for permission to release details of our report to a Syrian security agency.

Syria was a pipeline for jihadists coming to Iraq and a refuge for pro-Saddam Iraqis who had fled after the war. I was astounded that an intelligence officer wanted to turn over information to the Syrian intelligence community, which would potentially reveal the identity of our source.

Evelyn, Tom Reid, and I agreed that the best course of action was to let the information develop, to further test the source, and to not reveal specific information to Syrian intelligence officers who might compromise the source. We wanted to protect the source's identity because he was supplying information about Iranian activities in Iraq that were hostile to the United States. The defense attaché in Syria insisted on disclosing nearly every detail, including the identity of the people named by the source as likely perpetrators of a future attack. Disclosing that information was tantamount to disclosing the source's identity because, according to the source, only a few people knew of the plot.

I resisted disclosure to Syria's security service because I believed the identity of the source would be communicated to Iran's intelligence services. The cooperation between Syria and Iran was legendary. Syria was the only Arab country to support Iran during the Iraq-Iran War in the 1980s.

My attempts to convince DeFreitas's staff to agree with my recommendation were unsuccessful. As the director of the unit reporting the information, my decision to not allow disclosure could only be overruled by DeFreitas. I had tried to schedule a meeting with the general, but instead received a call from him on my cell phone while I was driving to the SCID's embassy office. I told him my reasons shouldn't be discussed on a cell phone, so he told me to call him on a secure voice-over-Internet protocol (VOIP) telephone. Because our office didn't have a VOIP telephone, I had to go to the special security office in the embassy. Secure telephones are present in command posts and security offices throughout the US military and often are located in a small cubicle or phone booth to prevent being overheard. No such luck in this security office. I sat at a table in the middle of the small office next to another officer, who was reviewing some classified documents, and placed the call to the general.

To say we had a dialogue would wrongly suggest there were two people talking. My orientation to my new boss quickly became a lecture. When the general asked why I didn't want to disclose the information to Syria, I first mentioned a regulation addressing the procedure for disclosure of classified information to nonallies and my belief that Syria, a country declared by our State Department to be a sponsor of terrorism, was definitely not an ally of the United States. The general angrily told me to not rely on that rule. He had the authority to disclose the information to the Syrians.

After figuring out DeFreitas didn't agree with my reading of the regulation, I went on to explain why I was concerned about sharing the information. When I got to the word "Iran," I realized the first eruption had been a warning. In no uncertain terms, the general told me Iran was not the problem in Iraq. The problem in Iraq was the Sunni insurgency. Every asset needed to be directed at that issue. Agitated, the general shouted that Iran and foreign fighters weren't killing US troops. According to him, Iraqi Sunni insurgents were killing our soldiers and marines. Two years later, Shiite militias associated with Iran were killing more US troops than Sunni insurgents were. But at that moment, the senior military intelligence officer in Iraq was dismissing Iran as a threat. In a sarcastic voice DeFreitas asked if I wanted to be responsible for more American deaths.

Even if I had a good answer to that question, I would have shut my mouth. Any suggestion that we should consider the effect of Iranian interference in Iraq was met with louder and more emphatic statements. At one point, DeFreitas started reciting the methodology for how to recruit, test, and handle a source. I knew that the general's background did not include any time as a HUMINT specialist and I recognized his recitation to be something from some manual he had read.

Near the end of our call, my jaw dropped when he told me, "Now, don't think this is a bad conversation." *Holy cow*, I thought, *if this isn't a bad conversation, I don't want to have one of those.* Continuing on, he said, "You and I just haven't had a chance to get to know each other." When I got done with my call, the officer who had been sitting next to me said nothing but gave me a look that said, "It sucks to be you."

I came back to Don Everest's office shaking my head. When I told Don about my conversation, he wasn't too surprised, since he had been in the army intelligence world for about thirty years. Then I told Evelyn that the information was going to be shared and to handle the source accordingly. Finally, I got ready to "get to know" my new boss some more, as he had accepted my invitation to come to our office and get a briefing on our current operations.

In the next few days, as I prepared to brief DeFreitas on the SCID's operations, I reflected on the mindset I was encountering. It was a decision to focus on the ten-meter target instead of the one-hundred-meter target. When soldiers and police officers train on a firing range with multiple targets, they are generally taught to shoot at the nearest target. The theory underlying that technique is that the nearest target (ten meters away) is more dangerous than a target farther away (one hundred meters). But some firearm and tactics instructors acknowledge another principle—rapid evaluation of the threat. If the far target poses a substantial danger, even if the threat is not immediate, do not fail to engage the far target.

In the early years of the Iraq War, we did not engage the one-hundred-meter target, Iran, because our senior leadership chose to ignore it instead of evaluating it as a threat. In the early stages of an insurgency, there will be a never-ending supply of ten-meter targets. By ignoring Iran's activities, the United States allowed Iran to increase its influence in Iraq and pose threats to US forces in Iraq. Our leaders failed to recognize that a protracted insurgency was in the best interests of Iran.

Already stunned by our rapid defeat of Iraq, a feat Iran could not accomplish in its eight-year war with Iraq, Iran feared the precedent of an easily won war that resulted in regime change in an "Axis of

Evil" country that bordered Iran. If Iraq developed into a functioning democracy and there was not a serious insurgency, US forces that had quickly toppled Saddam's government would be available to focus on containing Iran's nuclear ambitions. On the other hand, if sectarian violence made the US-supported Iraqi government appear weak and the efforts of the US military to fight insurgents and militias eroded the US will to fight, Iran would benefit.

Decisions by the US policymakers to focus exclusively on the Sunni insurgency made it easier for Iran to appear strong and defiant as it developed the capability to build nuclear weapons. Two years later, the one-hundred-meter target was much closer.

I learned several lessons from my experiences in Iraq. Chief among those lessons is that our nation's intelligence community does not work well against an insurgency or fourth-generation warfare, a type of warfare described in chapter 3.

Reduced to its simplest requirements, intelligence operations have only three elements: Collect information, understand the information you collect, and act on the information. Failure to perform any of these three steps dooms an intelligence operation.

This book discusses why our intelligence system has difficulty doing all three steps. Understanding our mistakes is important because we will face other insurgencies and attacks that require us to learn and adapt. In the following chapters, this book discusses how our intelligence community failed to recognize and react to changing threats that US forces faced in Iraq.

Fourth-generation warfare and insurgencies require special attention that has been lacking. The evolution of warfare is driven by changes in society, and those changes are having a significant effect on the United States. Historically, insurgencies take many years to fully defeat. The war in Iraq has demonstrated why US leaders will have difficulty fighting such wars in the future. As a nation we are reluctant to devote the time and expense to such wars, yet such wars are the nature of the "long war" for which our leaders have warned us to prepare.

Improvement in intelligence operations can be a large part of the solution for our problem of facing an insurgency, a type of war the United States historically does not like to fight. Improved intelligence can reduce casualties, shorten wars, and give our leaders more flexibility in our nation's foreign relations.

But there are many roadblocks in this path. Our intelligence operations are bureaucratic and severely hampered by turf wars. Nearly anyone who has worked in intelligence will admit that the "stovepipes" caused by lack of cooperation among military units and intelligence agencies are common and hurtful. But the general public doesn't understand how bad it is.

Human intelligence is the most valuable intelligence tool we have against an insurgency. But it is poorly managed, it takes a back seat to the military's fascination with technology, and it is ground zero for turf battles.

The following chapters describe these problems in more detail and offer some solutions. I can't predict that my suggestions will be acted on or, if acted upon, that they will solve every problem. But I can predict that if we do nothing, our past problems will be insignificant compared to future failures.

Chapter 2

A LONG WAR

I magine you enter a boxing ring where your opponent is waiting for you. Both of you are wearing the uniform for boxers—shorts, shoes, and regulation boxing gloves. Shortly into the first round you knock your opponent to the floor several times, but each time he manages to return to his feet to avoid a knockout. As the second round of the fight begins, your opponent comes out of his corner dressed in street clothes. Not knowing what to do, you let him get close—and he punches you in the side and the back and then runs out of the ring.

In later rounds, your opponent remains in street clothes as you continue to fight, but you are now surprised when other men, some with masks over their faces, hop over the ropes, briefly join the fight, and then depart. In some rounds, your opponent is replaced by one or two of the men who have attacked you from behind. A couple of times, the men in your corner seem to have joined your opponent in kicking, biting, and punching you. None of the blows is fatal, but you are beginning to fatigue.

Eventually you realize the fight is lasting much longer than the fifteen rounds you were told it would last. Your fans, who had predicted you would score an early knockout to conclude the fight, are now busy explaining to reporters why it is clear you are prevailing even though it is taking longer than they anticipated.

During the fight, you notice another boxer who dislikes you very much. The other boxer, who you may fight in the future, is sitting in the audience in a ringside seat. During the fight you see some of the masked men talking to this other boxer. He seems to be instructing them in how to fight you and even gives them equipment. At times, some of the men you're fighting use clubs they have received from the boxer in the stands. Maybe it's because you've been dodging punches and kicks for a long time, but you continue to be confused about exactly who you're fighting and what is going on.

As you probably guessed, the boxer in the ring is the United States in the Iraq War. Like that boxer, our military and political leaders have been confused as to who we are fighting and the intentions of those who oppose us.

In Iraq, our foes should not be a mystery to us. But they are. The United States and its allies have faced a variety of threats in Iraq, but our military has been slow to recognize and counter new threats that emerge. Throughout the war, we have received clues but we have failed to understand and act on them.

Saddam Hussein's regime and the threat of weapons of mass destruction constituted the first threat our military encountered and was the one it planned on fighting. But even during the invasion and our drive north toward Baghdad, our forces encountered irregular forces in addition to Iraq's regular army units. Members of Saddam's Fedayeen, a paramilitary force formed in 1995,[1] attacked our forces using guerrilla tactics. Dressed in civilian clothing, driving civilian vehicles, and using hit-and-run attacks, the Fedayeen provided significant resistance to the invasion force.

The authors of *Cobra II: The Inside Story of the Invasion and Occupation of Iraq* wrote that following the hard-fought battle for Nasiriyah, the commanders of the units moving north into Iraq realized the Iraqis would be fighting differently than expected:

> The enemy faced by U.S. forces would be largely amorphous, not in uniform, and rarely part of an organized military force. This enemy would level the battlefield by ignoring the rules of conventional warfare; it would fight using guile, deception, and ambush.[2]

Although Saddam's Fedayeen is interpreted as Saddam's Men of Sacrifice,[3] the senior intelligence officer in the invasion force noted that many of those fighting as irregular forces were forced to do so. Maj. Gen. James A. "Spider" Marks was handpicked by invasion commander Lt. Gen. David McKiernan to be the senior intelligence officer for the invasion. Marks recalled in an interview that the intelligence the army had on Iraq's conventional forces was very good.[4] He was surprised, however, that members of Saddam's Fedayeen operated in "regime death squads" at the lowest levels of military formations. So an Iraqi private in a conventional army unit suddenly had a gun at his back and was forced to put on civilian clothing and fight as an irregular combatant or face the threat he and his family would die.[5]

The United States invasion force crossed the Iraq-Kuwait border expecting to encounter a conventional army. Instead, within days, a significant force of irregular troops fighting in civilian clothing formed much of the resistance to the invasion. Like our boxer's foe entering the second round dressed in street clothes, it was something we did not anticipate to the degree that it occurred.

Although Marks has said that prewar intelligence disclosed the presence of the Fedayeen, the resistance mounted by the Fedayeen and other paramilitary forces was significant enough that Lt. Gen.

William S. Wallace, the commander of the army's V Corps, told the *New York Times*, "The enemy we're fighting is a bit different than the one we war-gamed against, because of these paramilitary forces. We knew they were here, but we did not know how they would fight."[6]

One of the first examples of Fedayeen resistance was in the city of Nasiriyah, a city in southern Iraq on the road to Baghdad. Task Force Tarawa, commanded by Brig. Gen. Rich Natonski of the 2nd Marine Expeditionary Brigade, was assigned to capture two bridges in the eastern sector of Nasiriyah.[7] The bridges were critical to moving US forces north. After days of fighting in and near Nasiriyah, Task Force Tarawa had secured the bridges, but the Fedayeen were still operational in the town monitoring the marines' movements and attacking US checkpoints. But with orders to continue moving north as rapidly as possible, no marine units were available to track down the bands of Fedayeen fighters who had moved into the nearby countryside.[8]

Some within the invasion force recognized the threat the Fedayeen posed, particularly in view of the strategy the invasion force was pursuing. Lt. Col. Joseph Apodaca, the intelligence officer for Task Force Tarawa, was concerned the Fedayeen would return to Nasiriyah to engage coalition forces and threaten Iraq stability after the war. Apodaca, a counterinsurgency specialist, drafted a classified assessment for Natonski that was forwarded to higher headquarters. In his assessment, Apodaca compared the Fedayeen attacks to insurgencies in Nicaragua, El Salvador, and Columbia. He predicted that unless the United States used forces to track down the Fedayeen in smaller towns, hit-and-run attacks would continue and would hamper the stabilization of Iraq after the war.[9]

But there were insufficient troops to stabilize areas as the invasion force passed through them on the way to Baghdad. In fact, Gen. Tommy R. Franks, the commander of US Central Command, threatened to fire Wallace for not moving rapidly enough. Soon after Wallace told reporters that his soldiers needed to delay their advance on Baghdad in order to put down the Fedayeen threat in the south, Franks telephoned Lieutenant General McKiernan, the commander of the allied invasion force, to warn that he might relieve Wallace of his command of the V Corps. To emphasize his point, Franks flew from his headquarters in Qatar to McKiernan's headquarters in Kuwait on March 31, 2003. During a meeting in Kuwait, Franks criticized the pace of the advance and questioned whether US troops had encountered serious resistance.[10] This meeting took place after the difficulty Task Force Tarawa had encountered in Nasiriyah.

Despite Franks's concern about the pace of the advance by US forces, by April 15, 2003, Baghdad had fallen. A day later, Franks convened a meeting at McKiernan's new headquarters at a captured palace in Abu Ghraib, on the northwest outskirts of Baghdad. Franks instructed his staff that the combat forces that had captured Baghdad and other cities in Iraq should prepare to pull out within 60 days. New units would arrive to relieve them, but most of those new units would stay no longer than 120 days.[11]

Several days after Franks gave instructions to prepare to rapidly draw down forces, McKiernan learned that he would not receive the additional forces the original war plan had promised him. After discussing the issue for several days with Secretary of Defense Donald Rumsfeld, Franks gave in to the defense secretary's desire to cancel the deployment of the sixteen thousand troops of the 1st Cavalry Division.[12] This decision was based on Rumsfeld's vision of the Iraq War. He wanted to avoid continuing commitments like the United States had experienced in Bosnia and Kosovo and was determined to withdraw the vast majority of the American forces from Iraq within four months.[13]

Before the invasion, Jay Garner, a retired army lieutenant general, had been selected to run the force that would get Iraq's government back on its feet. His organization was known as the Office of Rehabilitation and Humanitarian Assistance (ORHA). Quickly assembled as an afterthought to the invasion plan, ORHA was to be run by the Defense Department because Rumsfeld believed the State Department had been inefficient in its postwar administrations in Bosnia and Kosovo.[14] Garner was soon replaced by Ambassador Paul Bremer and ORHA was renamed the Coalition Provisional Authority (CPA).

Despite concerns that the United States had deployed too few troops to stabilize the country after quickly defeating Iraq's combat forces, the first few months after the fall of Baghdad were relatively peaceful. Within weeks after the capture of Baghdad, members of the US military felt safe enough to leave their camps and have dinner at Baghdad restaurants. While I was in a training course preparing to deploy to Iraq, I spoke with Robert Anderson, a fellow Air Force Office of Special Investigations agent who had arrived in Baghdad in May 2003 as the deputy chief of a contingent of air force and navy counterintelligence agents assigned to the CPA. Anderson and others who were in Baghdad at that time told me that during much of 2003, they traveled in pairs when leaving the Green Zone or a military camp, often carrying only handguns for protection. That level of law and order has yet to return to Baghdad.

As Lieutenant Colonel Apodaca predicted, the failure to press the attack against the Fedayeen and other irregular forces came back to haunt US forces. Lawlessness in Baghdad and other Iraqi cities was rampant. Iraqi police officers had abandoned their jobs in droves. US troops were not instructed to stop looters; keeping law and order wasn't part of their mission. Years later, keeping the civilian population safe would become the hallmark of US counterinsurgency policy in the military. But in 2003 and early 2004, when establishing law and order could have made a huge difference, the military commanders had too few forces and were planning for a rapid withdrawal from the country based on direction from the Defense Department.

The level of violence against US troops began to grow after the fall of Baghdad. During late 2003 and early 2004, the insurgency continued growing. Members of the Bush administration resisted labeling the attacks as an insurgency or guerrilla war. Rumsfeld asserted that troops in Iraq were not engaged in a guerrilla war and disputed that the Iraq occupation was comparable to the US experience in the Vietnam War.[15]

In 2004 the insurgency grew, its growth aided by several factors. Iraqi citizens were reluctant to turn in neighbors or acquaintances they suspected of participating in the insurgency because there was no assurance their cooperation would be kept secret or that they would be kept safe. In the spring of 2004, news of the abuse of prisoners in the Abu Ghraib prison circulated widely in the Western and Arab news media. Because 95 percent of the detainees at Abu Ghraib were Sunnis, the news of the prisoner abuse solidified the perception that the coalition was targeting Sunnis in an exclusive and indiscriminate manner.[16] The Abu Ghraib prisoner abuse and the growing perception that US forces were unable to secure Iraqi citizens or deliver basic services such as electricity reduced support for the United States and encouraged support for insurgents.

During 2004 and into 2005, the army focused on fighting an insurgency it believed was composed primarily of Sunni Muslims. The Sunni insurgency was perceived by the intelligence staff of the Multi-National Force–Iraq to be composed of three categories of Sunnis. The primary targets were former members of Saddam's regime. US military intelligence leaders believed these former members of the regime were directing many of the insurgent attacks. Known within the military community as the former regime elements (FREs), these Iraqis were Sunnis who had derived wealth, power, and status from serving in Saddam's government.

A second category of Sunni insurgents was comprised of persons who had not been members of Saddam's regime but who resisted the American occupation because it represented a reversal of fortune. These Sunnis included leaders of some Sunni tribes in provinces west and north of Baghdad, who rejected the US occupation in part because it deprived them of the benefit they derived from Sunni rule in Iraq. Sunnis, a sect of Islam that constituted 15 or 20 percent of the population of Iraq, had ruled the Shiite Muslim majority who comprised about 60 percent of Iraq's population. Lost financial power and a long-held dislike of Shiites fueled Sunni attacks on the United States and the new Iraqi government led by Shiite politicians. The split between the Sunni and Shi'a sects of Islam is centuries old. The sects practice the Islamic religion differently, and their differences began with a dispute about who should replace the Prophet Muhammad upon his death. In order to understand the violence in Iraq it must be recognized that some Sunnis and Shiites have hated each other for centuries. As long ago as the tenth century, Sunnis, who were the majority of the population in what is current-day Iraq, imprisoned and killed Shiite religious leaders and burned the houses of Shiites.[17]

But the US invasion unseated a Sunni minority that had viciously ruled over the majority sect for decades. Although Shiites are a minority of 10 to 15 percent of the world's 1.3 billion Muslims, they account for the majority of the Iraqi population.[18] When the disenfranchised majority suddenly took power, Shiites joined the new Iraq government and its security forces in large numbers. Even for Sunnis who had not been members of Saddam's regime or his Baath political party, historical dislike for Shiites and the sudden reversal of fortune motivated many to take up arms against the coalition ruling Iraq.

Hatred for Shiites was most easily seen as a motivation of a third, very potent portion of the Sunni insurgency: a network run by Abu Musab al-Zarqawi, a Jordanian terrorist whose real name was Ahmed Fadil al-Khalaylah. Zarqawi took his nom de guerre from the Jordanian town of Zarqa, where he was born.[19] Zarqawi, who had fought Soviet troops in Afghanistan, seized upon the decision of military commanders to place very few troops in Anbar Province, west of Baghdad. In that province, which includes Fallujah and Ramadi, Iraqi troops had deserted before their commander formally surrendered to US forces—the only Iraqi army unit to formally surrender.[20]

The lack of any authority, Iraqi or American, in Anbar Province made the region an ideal base for Zarqawi. Fallujah and Ramadi are both on the banks of the Euphrates River, which runs southeastward into Iraq from Syria. The Euphrates River valley became a conduit for Sunni jihadists from other Muslim countries who entered Iraq to join Zarqawi's group. These non-Iraqi terrorists became known as "foreign fighters."

Zarqawi was behind much of the violence in Iraq in 2003 and 2004. His hand was seen in the 2003 assassination of Ayatollah Sayed Mohammed Baqir al-Hakim, the leader of the Supreme Council for the Islamic Revolution in Iraq, one of the largest Shiite political parties in Iraq, when his associate Sami Mohammed Ali Said al-Jaaf (also known as Abu Omar al-Kurdi) was later arrested for Hakim's assassination.[21] Zarqawi's network became so robust that the battle of Fallujah in October 2004 was intended to eradicate it.[22] Even earlier, in February 2004, the Zarqawi network had built a reputation for spectacular attacks, many directed at markets, cafés, and mosques where Shiites gathered. The spokesman for the MNF–I, Brig. Gen. Mark Kimmitt of the US Army, said in February 2004 that Zarqawi was a suspect in all of the major bombings in Iraq.[23]

Of the three main factions of Sunni insurgents, the military made fighting the former regime elements the priority target for conventional military forces in Iraq, which included most of the American troops assigned to Iraq. Such army and Marine Corps units included infantry, armored cavalry, artillery, and aviation organizations. All of those US organizations, plus military units from other coalition countries, worked for the commander of the MNF–I.

The MNF–I had three main components. The Multi-National Security Transition Command–Iraq was responsible for training, equipping, and mentoring Iraqi security forces contained in the Iraqi Ministry of Defense and Ministry of Interior. The second component was an office of the US Army Corps of Engineers helping rebuild Iraq's infrastructure. But most of the troops in Iraq were conventional forces in the third component of the MNF–I, the Multi-National Corps–Iraq. Under the MNC–I, responsibility for the country was divided by geographic location. For instance, Multi-National Division–Southeast (MND–SE) was headquartered in Basra and encompassed coalition forces in four provinces in southern Iraq. British Forces constituted most of the troops of MND–SE, but that division also included troops from Italy, Japan, Norway, and several other countries. Another division, Multi-National Force–West (MNF–W), was composed mostly of Marine Corps units and covered Anbar Province, including the cities of Ramadi and Fallujah.

In the two paragraphs above, I referred to conventional forces. The other kind of combat forces were the special operations forces (SOF) supplied by the US Army, Navy, and Air Force, and some coalition countries, especially England. And there were a lot of them in Iraq. The SOF headquarters in Iraq was at Balad Air Base, north of Baghdad. The special operations forces included troopers from the army's Delta Force, and many other special operators, including Special Forces and Rangers from the US Army, the US Navy SEALS, and the British Special Air Service and Special Boat Service. The SOF operated throughout the country. The troop strength of the SOF is not publicly known, but it is a small percentage of the approximately 130,000 to 150,000 US troops stationed in Iraq since 2003.

Although the SOF were pursuing Zarqawi in 2004, the conventional forces under the MNC–I had focused their efforts on the former regime elements. The MNC–I had lists of former regime members it wanted to capture. Intelligence officers in the MNF–I believed the former regime members were leading the insurgency and could provide evidence of weapons of mass destruction. The initial deck of playing cards that had photographs of senior members of Saddam Hussein's regime was replaced with new lists of "high-value targets." The high-value target lists became the guides for efforts by intelligence and infantry units. Former regime members made up most of the names on the high-value target lists.

As if the efforts of the MNF–I were not enough, US Central Command, which is headquartered at MacDill Air Force Base in Florida, created the Joint Interagency Task Force–Former Regime Elements (JIATF–FRE) to coordinate the hunt for members of Saddam's regime in and out of Iraq. This task force was commanded by a brigadier general who reported to CENTCOM headquarters, not to the commander of forces in Iraq.

Despite frequent raids by special operations forces that killed or captured many of his followers, Abu Musab al-Zarqawi continued to be very active in Iraq. Zarqawi operated through an organization known as Jamaat al-Tawhid wa'l-Jihad (Unity and Jihad Group), which we called TWJ. Although Zarqawi had worked with al-Qaeda in the past, he did not formally pledge his allegiance to Osama bin Laden until October 2004.[24] On October 17, 2004, a statement attributed to TWJ that was posted on an Islamic forum Web site announced that Zarqawi and TWJ had joined al-Qaeda. Al-Jazeera television broadcast a statement by TWJ on October 20, 2004, identifying itself as Tanzim Qa'idat Al-Jihad in Bilad al-Rafidayn (Organization of Jihad's Base in the Country of the Two Rivers). That name refers to the Tigris and Euphrates rivers that run through much of Iraq before merging in southern Iraq. For several months, Zarqawi's organization was referred to as QJBR, but in the summer of 2005, the MNF–I began referring to QJBR and TWJ as al-Qaeda in Iraq (AQI). That name has stuck.

There was no mystery to Zarqawi's goals. Iraqi Kurds intercepted a letter from Zarqawi to bin Laden.[25] In that letter, Zarqawi labels the Shi'a as "the lurking snake, the crafty and malicious scorpion, the spying enemy, and the penetrating venom." Zarqawi further declared that Shiites have been "a sect of treachery and betrayal throughout history and throughout the ages."[26]

Zarqawi's letter explained his plan for the Shi'a. By targeting Shiite religious, political, and military targets, Zarqawi sought to provoke them to fight: "If we succeed in dragging them into the arena of sectarian war, it will become possible to awaken the inattentive Sunnis."[27]

There was Zarqawi's plan. As early as February 2004, the US intelligence community knew that Zarqawi planned to begin a sectarian war in order to cause such a reaction from the Shiite community that Sunnis within Iraq and from other nations would rise up and crush the Shiites.

Zarqawi's implementation of his strategy was not very discriminating. Many Sunnis were killed in attacks aimed at Shiites. But the attacks on mosques, markets, cafés, police and army recruiting centers, and other targets associated with Shiites were all according to Zarqawi's plan. The attacks had the added benefit for Zarqawi of embarrassing the United States and the Iraq government it supported.

In July 2004 the United States posted a $25,000,000 reward for Zarqawi's capture. Despite that reward, during 2004, Sunni jihadists flowed into Iraq and suicide bombings increased. Car bomb factories operated on the outskirts of Baghdad. Zarqawi's group posted its successes on Arab Web sites. In order to ensure the attacks were publicized, Zarqawi's group selected targets that allowed Western news media to cover the attacks. Targets that ensured mention in Western news reports included the front gate of the Baghdad International Airport, hotels across the river from the Green Zone, entrances to the Green Zone, and restaurants near the Green Zone.

By 2004 Franks's idea of a quick departure had become laughable. Lt. Gen. Ricardo Sanchez, the most junior three-star general in the army, had been left in charge of all military forces in Iraq under an organization designated as Combined Joint Task Force 7. In the fallout of the Abu Ghraib prison debacle and the increasing insurgency, Ricardo and his organization were replaced. The Multi-National Force–Iraq was created on May 15, 2004, and Gen. George Casey arrived as its commander in June 2004. Casey had served as the director of operations for the Joint Chiefs of Staff, where he had recurring contact with Rumsfeld and other senior Defense Department officials.

But despite a change in leadership of the MNF–I, the US strategy for countering the insurgency remained the same. Conventional forces continued to hunt former regime elements as their priority target. Meanwhile, the CIA and special operations forces were hunting for Zarqawi, who had become their number one target after Saddam Hussein's capture on December 13, 2003.

The priority of targets for the United States changed after April 29, 2005, when a string of car bombs exploded in Baghdad and other cities.[28] Fourteen car bombs were detonated that day, including ten suicide bombs. Zarqawi's group issued a statement on the day of the bombings promising more attacks. The bombings, which came four days before Ibrahim al-Jafari was sworn in as Iraq's interim prime minister, were aimed at disrupting and challenging the new government.

By the time I arrived in April 2005, much had changed from two years earlier, when Robert Anderson and my predecessors were able to enjoy a meal at a Baghdad café with little fear of attack. When I arrived most travelers entered and left the Green Zone in armored vehicles and large convoys. An armored bus that transported personnel from BIAP and Camp Victory to the Green Zone, known as the Rhino, had stopped making trips during daylight. Now the Rhino traveled only late in the evening—and only if it was protected by helicopter gunships. The six-mile route between the Green Zone and the airport was one of the most dangerous stretches of highway in Iraq.[29] During April 2005, thirteen people died on Route Irish between the Green Zone and the airport.[30]

Following the string of attacks on April 29, Casey made Zarqawi's group, Al-Qaeda in Iraq, the top target for the MNF–I. Less than a month after Brigadier General DeFreitas lectured me about the importance of not getting distracted by Iran and foreign fighters, he and Casey were quoted in a front-page *Washington Post* story with the headline "U.S. Officers in Iraq Put Priority on Extremists—Hussein Loyalists Not Seen as Greatest Threat." In the article, both generals admitted that foreign fighters and jihadists such as Zarqawi were a bigger threat than former members of Saddam's regime.[31]

But by the time senior military and intelligence leaders in Iraq recognized the threat posed by Zarqawi and the foreign fighters he was importing, another threat was emerging. By early 2005 there was much evidence indicating that Iran was seeking to influence events in Iraq, both overtly, through political means, and covertly, by sponsoring and enabling attacks on US forces. As discussed earlier, Iran had many reasons to influence the outcome of America's intervention in Iraq.

But the effect of Iran's involvement in Iraq and the threat of future Iranian action were discounted by senior military intelligence officials. Although there were military intelligence officers posted in Iraq who focused on tracking and analyzing Iranian activities, they worked for CENTCOM. The MNF–I intelligence effort did not treat Iran's involvement as an important issue. Since that time, as we have seen, the war between the United States and the Sunni insurgency became a war between the United States, the insurgency, and Shiite militias trained and equipped by Iran.[32]

As we look back we can see an evolution of threats our forces have faced in Iraq. The US military in Iraq has been opposed by many foes, including Iraq's army, the Fedayeen, a Sunni insurgency believed to be led by Saddam's loyalists, the Zarqawi network that became al-Qaeda in Iraq, Shiite militias, and Iran. Yet identifying and recognizing the danger of each opponent was a learning experience that took too long.

Our military possesses the capability to detect evolving threats. But our military and political leaders must rely on information collected at ground level instead of trying to make the facts fit a political prediction or a mission statement. We also must dramatically improve our ability to collect and use human intelligence.

We didn't anticipate the impact of the Fedayeen on the invasion or the growth of an insurgency that began soon after Baghdad fell.

Our strategy of using too few forces and not providing security for the population of Iraq played into the hands of those who opposed us. We created fertile ground for an insurgency.

Then, in fighting the insurgency, we focused on finding members of Saddam's regime. Our tactics of patrolling from large bases instead of living among the population reduced our ability to collect information about our enemy and to obtain the support of the Iraqi citizens. While we focused our forces on the former regime elements, Zarqawi's network grew in strength and began its campaign of attacks against the Iraqi population and security forces. After pledging his allegiance to Osama bin Laden and renaming his organization Tanzim Qa'dat Al-Jihad in Bilad al-Rafidayn (QJBR), Zarqawi continued his campaign of assassinations and car bombs aimed at igniting sectarian warfare. Zarqawi had spelled out his plan in a letter to bin Laden that was intercepted by the Kurds, but our intelligence system didn't appreciate the threat such a strategy posed.

And then, after the conventional military forces in Iraq finally began to focus on AQI, they largely ignored the Shiite militias and the Iranian influence upon those militias for another year or two.

Why was each new threat a surprise? Well, one simple answer is that many things are a surprise to a blind man. Our intelligence system has blinded our military and political leaders when they face an evolving, multifaced insurgency. As I mentioned earlier, there are three steps to intelligence operations: We have to collect information, we have to understand the information, and we have to act on the information. Everything about intelligence falls under those three steps. Intelligence officers argue over how to collect information. Is a human source more reliable than a satellite image or an intercepted telephone call? Intelligence professionals argue about the meaning of intelligence, especially when piecing together information from different sources. And sometimes there is disagreement about whether or how to act on information. But all of those disagreements can take place only after we actually collect some information. As later chapters explain, the best tool for collecting information in an insurgency, human intelligence, is poorly handled. That must change.

The United States claims to be fighting the long war against terrorism, but our political, military, and intelligence leaders have regularly failed to take a long view of the problems they face. By focusing only on short-term threats and devoting our intelligence systems to address those threats, the United States plays into the hands of an enemy that benefits from the American desire to do all things quickly.

In order to take the long view, military commanders facing an insurgency must understand and appreciate the politics of the situation. The new counterinsurgency manual encourages military officers and NCOs to be politically aware. The good ones have been for centuries. Often, however, their advice is ignored by their masters.

We can't afford to ignore the ground truth any longer. In a fourth-generation war, the leaders of frontline operational and intelligence units are in the best position to see the political and military landscape affecting the insurgency and to act upon it. In Iraq military priorities were based on satisfying political needs or ideas of how to run the war in the United States, not on the military and political situation in Iraq.

In the next chapter, we will take a more in-depth look at the type of warfare we are facing in Iraq and Afghanistan. We will also look at why this type of warfare attacks our will to fight and how societal changes increase the likelihood that we will face such wars in the future and at the same time increase the difficulty of combating insurgencies.

NOTES

1. Sharon Otterman, "Iraq: What Is the Fedayeen Saddam?" *Council on Foreign Relations Backgrounder*, March 31, 2003, http://www.cfr.org/publication/7698/ (accessed January 26, 2008).

2. Michael R. Gordon and Bernard E. Trainor, *Cobra II: The Inside Story of the Invasion and Occupation of Iraq* (New York: Pantheon Books, 2006), p. 259.

3. Otterman, "Iraq."

4. Donald Sparks, "Former Huachuca Commander Reflects on Tenure as Senior Intel Officer in Operation Iraqi Freedom," TRADOC News Service, July 2, 2003, http://www.tradoc.army.mil/pao/people_portraits/seniorintelofficer.htm (accessed April 6, 2008).

5. Ibid.

6. Jim Dwyer, "A Nation at War: In the Field—V Corps Commander; A Gulf Commander Sees a Longer Road," *New York Times*, March 28, 2003, Foreign Desk section, p. 1.

7. Gordon and Trainor, *Cobra II*, pp. 234–35.

8. Ibid., p. 258.

9. Ibid.

10. Michael R. Gordon and Bernard E. Trainor, "Dash to Baghdad Left Top U.S. Generals Divided," *Washington Post*, March 13, 2006, Foreign Desk section, p. 1.

11. Gordon and Trainor, *Cobra II*, pp. 458–59.

12. Ibid., p. 461.

13. Ibid., p. 464.

14. Ibid.

15. Vernon Loeb, "No Iraq Quagmire, Rumsfeld Asserts," *Washington Post*, July 1, 2003, p. A09

16. Nicholas I. Hauser, "Third Generation Gangs Revisited: The Iraq Insurgency," (master's thesis, Naval Postgraduate School, 2005), p. 145, http://www.ccc.nps.navy.mil/research/theses/haussler05.pdf (accessed April 7, 2008).

17. Vali Nasr, *The Shia Revival: How Conflicts within Islam Will Shape the Future* (New York: W.W. Norton, 2006), p. 53

18. Vali Nasr, "The Shia Revival," *Military Review*, May–June 2007, p. 9.

19. Jeffrey Gettleman, "Attacks in 5 Iraqi Cities Leave More Than 100 Dead," *New York Times*, June 25, 2004, p. A6.

20. Gordon and Trainor, *Cobra II*, p. 462.

21. "Iraq Captures 'top Zarqawi ally,'" BBC News, January 24, 2005, http://news.bbc.co.uk/2/hi/middle_east/4202421.stm (accessed January 28, 2008).

22. Steve Fainaru, "As U.S. Forces Pound Fallujah, Fighting Rages on City's Edge," *Washington Post*, October 18, 2004, p. A14.

23. Edward Wong, "The Struggle for Iraq: Combat—Up to 80 Killed in Bomb Blasts at 2 Iraqi Sites," *New York Times*, February 11, 2004, Foreign Desk section, p. 1.

24. "Jamaat al-Tawhid wa'l-Jihad/Unity and Jihad Group," GlobalSecurity.org, http://www.globalsecurity.org/military/world/para/zarqawi.htm (accessed January 28, 2008).

25. "Profile: Abu Musab al-Zarqawi," Council on Foreign Relations, http://www.cfr.org/publication/9866/ (accessed January 28, 2008).

26. "February 2004 Coalition Provisional Authority English Translation of Terrorist Musab al Zarqawi Letter Obtained by United States Government in Iraq," US Department of State, February 12, 2004, http://www.state.gov/p/nea/rls/31694.htm (accessed January 28, 2008).

27. Ibid.

28. Naseer Nouri and Bassam Sebti, "String of Explosions Kills 50 in Iraq—Secondary Blasts Place Rescuers at Risk—3 U.S. Soldiers Among Dead," *Washington Post*, April 30, 2005, p. A1.

29. Jill Carroll and Dan Murphy, "Toughest Commute in Iraq? The Six Miles to the Airport," *Christian Science Monitor*, April 26, 2005, World section, p. 1.

30. Jackie Spinner, "Easy Sailing along Once-Perilous Road to Baghdad Airport—Army Steps Up Presence to Quell Attacks," *Washington Post*, November 4, 2005, p. A15.

31. Bradley Graham, "U.S. Officers in Iraq Put Priority on Extremists—Hussein Loyalists Not Seen as Greatest Threat," *Washington Post*, May 9, 2005, p. A1.

32. Ibid., p. 11.

Chapter 3

FOURTH-GENERATION WARFARE

Failing to study and prepare for insurgencies is one of the main reasons why our military and intelligence community have not fared well in Iraq. Insurgency is a political movement that uses armed conflict against an existing government. The type of warfare seen in an insurgency is known by various terms, including low-intensity conflict, guerrilla war, unconventional war, and irregular war. Throughout history thousands of insurgencies have occurred and most were successfully, sometimes brutally, put down with military force.[1] In the twentieth century there were more than fifty insurgencies ranging from the Second Anglo-Boer War to Iraq.[2] Other examples of insurgencies in the last century include the Philippine Insurrection in which the United States battled Filipino nationalists, the Chinese Communists' war against Chiang Kai-shek and the Nationalist Army, and the US struggle against the Vietcong and North Vietnamese Army.

The United States has historically not liked fighting insurgencies. Insurgent tactics often neutralize our advantages in firepower, communication, and mobility. Counterinsurgency is costly, difficult, and time consuming. It forces the United States to operate far away from its shores against foes that don't appear to be a direct threat to our national security such as the Filipino Moros and the Vietnamese.

In the mid-1970s, after fighting an unconventional war in Vietnam for several years, the US military was facing a significant conventional threat in the Soviet Union, a foe that was fielding a new generation of tanks, aircraft, and other equipment. As the army faced this new threat, it also had to rebuild a force that had been weakened by the Vietnam War. In order to face the Soviet conventional threat and because of a historical uneasiness with irregular wars, the army walked away from the counterinsurgency mission. The effect of the Vietnam War reinforced an American military culture that preferred not to fight unconventional wars. The Vietnam War cost the army many lives and significantly affected its relationship with the American people. During the Vietnam War, the US military lost much of the respect the American people had for their armed forces during most of the nation's history. Even after the Vietnam War, the military continued to suffer decreased respect and appreciation by the citizens it served.

As the army prepared for a conventional war, it abandoned the institutional knowledge of counterinsurgency war it had gained in Vietnam. But even after the Soviet Union collapsed in 1991, the army persisted in ignoring the counterinsurgency mission. The distaste the US Army had for such warfare was reflected in the way the army equipped and trained itself in the post-Vietnam era. When the US military confronted the Iraq insurgency it found itself ill prepared following a sixty-year preoccupation with high-tech conventional war.[3] That lack of preparation was later recognized by some of its senior officers. Gen. Jack Keane, the former vice chief of staff of the army, said, "We put an Army on the battlefield that I had been a part of for 37 years. It doesn't have any doctrine, nor was it educated and trained, to deal with an insurgency. . . . After the Vietnam War, we purged ourselves of everything that had to do with irregular warfare or insurgency, because it had to do with how we lost that war. In hindsight, that was a bad decision."[4]

In short, the entire US military, not just the army, spent the years after the Vietnam War preparing to fight a war against another nation on a large battlefield away from civilian populations where it could best use the high-technology weapons it spent the last fifty years developing and buying. The Desert Storm phase of the Gulf War in 1991 was the type of war for which the US military had prepared. But the Iraq War has presented a much different type of war.

FOURTH-GENERATION WARFARE DEFINED

Although many soldiers and academics have advanced theories and opinions about the current state of our nation's ability to fight an insurgency, one framework for analyzing the difficulties we face with insurgencies is the concept of "fourth-generation warfare." The idea of fourth-generation warfare has been debated within military circles for nearly two decades. Four generations of warfare were first identified in an article by William Lind and four other authors in a 1989 *Marine Corps Gazette* article.[5] This theory classifies stages of the evolution of warfare and theorizes that fourth-generation warfare is the latest generation of warfare.

The essence of fourth-generation warfare (abbreviated by some as 4GW) is to carry the battle to the homeland of the opponent. Although the weapons of 4GW can be bombs or diseases, the most potent weapon and the central strategy of 4GW is the communication of a message of hopelessness that changes the minds of the enemy's leaders. While prior generations of warfare sought to destroy the enemy's armed forces and its capacity to regenerate them, an insurgency facing a stronger, better-equipped foe can use 4GW to convince the leadership of the nation opposing the insurgency that its goals are too costly or can't be achieved.[6]

Realizing that a 4GW insurgency seeks to convince our leaders that their strategic goals are either unachievable or too costly is the key to understanding this new warfare.[7] When we face an opponent employing 4GW, we are facing a strategic communications campaign that employs a variety of tools, including military, political, economic, and social actions. From that understanding of the type of attack we face, we can recognize the changes in intelligence operations that are needed. But in order to understand the needed changes in intelligence, we must understand 4GW and the challenges it poses.

The Evolution of Warfare

Lind and his fellow authors defined four generations of warfare primarily based on the type of weapons and tactics employed in those wars. First-generation warfare employed smoothbore muskets and used the line-and-column tactics that the British used in the American Revolutionary War.

Second-generation warfare was based on heavy firepower provided by more advanced weapons such as rifles, machine guns, and artillery. As Lind notes, the French military maxim "the artillery conquers, the infantry occupies" captures the essence of second-generation warfare.[8] This style of warfare is exemplified by the early years of World War I, when hundreds of thousands of troops engaged in trench warfare featuring fierce artillery battles.

Third-generation warfare changed the focus from firepower to movement.[9] In third-generation warfare, a military force uses its ability to move through the enemy's lines and strike rapidly to cut off the enemy from its logistical support and reinforcement. The tank was the key weapon in developing this new style of warfare. Elements of third-generation warfare were seen at the end of World War I, but it wasn't fully developed until the German army employed its blitzkrieg strategy during its invasion of France. The most recent example was the Desert Storm offensive in the Gulf War of 1991 when the US Army and Marine Corps rapidly attacked through and around Iraqi lines.

Attacking through or around an enemy's front lines and striking at the rear of the battle area cuts off and reduces the effectiveness of the enemy's combat forces by making them less relevant to the ultimate outcome of the battle. Fourth-generation warfare further reduces the importance and effectiveness of frontline forces. Lind and his coauthors observed changes that would expand the battlefield. Instead of striking at the rear of the battle area, Lind predicted that fourth-generation warriors would strike at the enemy's society.[10] That strategy includes the goal of causing the enemy to collapse from within instead of physically destroying it.[11]

People's War

Col. Thomas X. Hammes was the first author to write a comprehensive study of fourth-generation warfare in his book *The Sling and the Stone: On War in the 21st Century*. Hammes is a retired US Marine Corps officer who not only studied insurgencies but, as part of his duties in the Marine Corps, trained insurgents. Hammes identified the originator of fourth-generation warfare—Mao Tse-tung. Mao was one of several Communist Chinese leaders who opposed the Nationalist Chinese led by Chiang Kai-shek in the 1920s. Soviet advisers had

urged the Chinese Communists to use city workers in urban upris-
ings, a strategy that Mao had not favored.[12] Mao and another Communist Chinese leader, Chu The, decided they had to abandon the
strategy based on city workers, the industrial proletariat in Marxist
terms, and base the Chinese revolution on the peasants.[13] After the
failure of the Communists' offensive against the cities, Mao's strategy
of relying on peasants in the rural areas yielded success.[14]

According to Hammes, Mao developed a style of warfare that we
now call fourth-generation warfare. Mao called his strategy
"People's War" and described it in a folk rhyme in 1927:

> Di jin, wo tui, [When the] enemy advances, we withdraw,
> Di jiu, wo roa, [When the] enemy rests, we harass,
> Di pi, wo da, [When the] enemy tires, we attack,
> Di tui, wo jui, [When the] enemy withdraws, we pursue.[15]

Hammes credits Mao with providing a strategy that "moved
guerrilla warfare from a subordinate effort to support a conventional
army to a war-winning approach."[16] In other words, using Mao's
strategy, the use of guerrilla warfare by itself could defeat a larger,
stronger enemy.

Mao wrote that there were three phases for a successful insurgency.[17] In phase one, insurgents would focus on building political
strength while pursuing limited military actions such as political
assassinations. In phase two, after insurgents gained strength they
would consolidate their control of areas to be used as their base of
operations and begin to govern some portions of the consolidated
area. During this second phase insurgents would conduct military
operations to capture arms (a function that was important to an ill-
supplied Mao) and to wear down government forces.[18]

In the third and final phase of Mao's People's War, insurgents
would commit regular forces in a final offensive. Mao believed that

an insurgency would eventually have to fight a conventional war to complete its victory. The first two phases provided the insurgents the strength and experience to finally confront their opponent in a conventional war.[19] Mao followed this strategy and, in 1949, employed the Red army in a conventional offensive that defeated the remnants of the Nationalist army, forcing Chiang to Taiwan.

The Enemy's Message to Our Homeland

According to Hammes, the next use of fourth-generation warfare was by the Vietnamese against France and later the United States.[20] The North Vietnamese modified Mao's People's War to include an aggressive attack on the national will of their principal enemy. This took the political war to the enemy's distant homeland in order to destroy the enemy's will to continue the struggle. Although Hammes and Lind disagree on several aspects of fourth-generation warfare theory, the North Vietnamese attack on the American national will described by Hammes fits well with Lind's observations that fourth-generation warfare would strike at the enemy's society and seek to collapse the enemy internally.

North Vietnam demonstrated the effectiveness of the new style of warfare. Despite military losses that included a decisive defeat in its 1968 Tet Offensive, the North Vietnamese convinced the US leaders to terminate the war. They did this by communicating a story of continuing victory over US forces that wasn't supported by the facts. For instance, the North Vietnamese portrayed the Tet Offensive as a great victory, not the military defeat it was.[21] The North Vietnamese made extensive use of the Western media to send its message of the Tet "victory" and other claimed successes to the American people, causing sufficient discontent and weariness to be felt by members of the US Congress.

The message that the United States was not winning the war combined with years of American casualties in a distant land to achieve the result desired by the North Vietnamese. By not losing, the North Vietnamese won. After the withdrawal of US forces from South Vietnam, the North Vietnamese Army began an offensive in 1975, pursuing the conventional war that is the third phase of Mao's People's War. Trained by the United States to rely on heavy firepower, the South Vietnamese needed resupply in order to survive.[22] But the North Vietnamese campaign directed at the US leadership had been effective. President Gerald Ford, new in office following the resignation of Richard M. Nixon, sought the funding needed to supply the South Vietnamese government. But the US Congress refused financial support to the South Vietnamese government, causing the government to collapse.

SOCIETAL CHANGES

But fourth-generation warfare is more than the use of different tactics and weapons. Hammes theorized that 4GW results from change "across the spectrum of human activity"—including political, economic, technological, and social.[23] Understanding fourth-generation warfare requires us to identify and appreciate the changes in society that make 4GW so potent. The intelligence community and military of the United States have difficulty fighting 4GW opponents because they have not adequately adapted to the changes that have occurred.

Societal changes at work in the United States are making our nation more vulnerable to successful attacks by opponents using fourth-generation warfare. In order to understand the societal changes that are driving the adoption of fourth-generation warfare and the threats to our country, let's first briefly look at some of the changes that caused previous modes of warfare to evolve. Changes in politics (the creation of the nation-state) and economics (the colonization of America that produced an economic boom) were key factors in raising the large armies of the Napoleonic era that marked the creation of first-generation warfare.[24] Similarly, second-generation warfare came about after the industrialization of western Europe and North America. Second-generation warfare required significant wealth that was not possible before the industrial age.[25] The growing industrial base allowed the warring nations to build the transportation and communication systems that were essential to move large armies and their supplies. Factories could mass produce the weapons and supplies needed for large-scale warfare.

A critical social change, patriotism toward one's nation, also aided the evolution of second-generation warfare.[26] During World War I millions of men went to war and both sides sustained tremendous losses. Without its people feeling a strong allegiance to their country, a nation-state could not raise the large armies needed for such warfare.

Social change was also a notable factor in the evolution to third-generation warfare. The hallmark of third-generation warfare was the blitzkrieg of World War II. After World War I, the decisions made by British and French leaders reflected the will of their populations—to avoid the staggering loss of life seen in that war.[27] For that reason, there was little popular support for reorganizing and reequipping their armies. In Germany, however, the population was devoted to their armed forces despite suffering even larger proportional losses than the British and French.[28] The German people supported rebuilding their army and that army began developing a new strategy: the blitzkrieg.

Fourth-generation warfare is driven by changes in the same

political, economic, technical, and social factors.[29] Hammes analyzes these changes in detail, but the key societal changes that affect the intelligence community's response to a 4GW insurgency are changes that erode the power of the nation-state while increasing the power of individuals and transnational organizations. One of the major changes allowing this shift is the growing power of information and the manner in which it is created and distributed. Information is especially significant in fourth-generation tactics directed against our homeland because it is the only medium that can change a person's mind.[30]

Changing minds was central to Mao's People's War. In 1961 Brig. Gen. Samuel B. Griffith II, the translator of Mao Tse-tung's *Yu Chi Chan (Guerrilla Warfare)*, recognized that attacking the will of the enemy was central to Mao's strategy, which we now call fourth-generation warfare. In his introduction to the translation of *Yu Chi Chan*, Griffith said, "[T]he mind of the enemy and the will of his leaders is a target of far more importance than the bodies of his troops."[31]

Recall the North Vietnamese propaganda that attacked the will of the American people and through them the willingness of their leaders to continue that war. Consider how much easier it is for a present-day insurgency to attack the will of our nation's decision makers than it was for the North Vietnamese. With the advent of video cameras, cheap laptops, and the Internet, insurgents can feed edited video of staged events to the news media or publish such video directly online. Al-Qaeda and Shiite militias have videotaped their attacks for posting on the Internet. Even the most respected news media carry sensational photos or video with a quickly forgotten disclaimer about the source of the video. Al-Qaeda in Iraq has chosen to attack targets with the intent to deliver the most horrific news to the American public in order to cause American leaders to choose to abandon the war.

This rapid exchange of information reduces the power of the nation-state. The availability of international travel and communication has broken down barriers to information and relationships. With the Internet available in nearly every part of the world, people can develop strong relationships with those in other nations. Hammes uses the example that a Greenpeace member living in the American Northwest may have more in common with a Greenpeace member in Germany than with the logger who is his neighbor.[32]

In addition to the information age there are other factors that contribute to breaking down citizens' allegiance to their country. Governments have ceded some sovereignty to international organizations such as the United Nations, the World Bank, the International Monetary Fund, and the International Atomic Energy Agency.[33] Regional organizations and trade agreements such as the European Union and the North American Free Trade Agreement (NAFTA) have also eroded the sovereignty of nations.[34] Nations are limited in what they can charge as tariffs and don't totally control the construction and safety standards that apply to their people and the goods they import and export. US companies and their employees are increasingly affected by new requirements and restrictions that result from international agreements and market forces. The control foreign bodies have over how US companies are organized, how large they are, and how much of the market they can have continues to grow. Microsoft, General Electric, and other US corporations are forced to shape their operations to accommodate European and other foreign regulatory bodies. These changes have the effect of reducing the loyalty and patriotism of these corporations and their employees to their government.

Another key political change is the increase in the number of and the role of transnational entities, which are organizations or movements that are not controlled by a single nation. As Hammes states, transnational groups "are literally free agents on the international scene and will interject themselves into international relations where and when they see fit, to meet their goals."[35] Transnational groups include the peaceful, such as Greenpeace, and the violent—such as al-Qaeda.[36]

SHIFTING LOYALTIES AND THE DECLINE OF THE NATION-STATE

The international distribution of the ownership of public corporations as well as the debt of nations and companies further divides the loyalty of the citizens of a nation. Because a nation's political position may be detrimental to the financial position of some of its citizens, owners of stocks and bonds may have much less interest in politics than what benefits their portfolios.

Lind and two coauthors identify other social changes they believe contribute to 4GW. Nations that can't protect their citizens will lose power as those citizens switch their loyalty from their nation to an organization that can protect them.[37] Lebanese Hezbollah and Moqtada al-Sadr's militia, the Jaysh al-Mahdi, are recent examples of organizations competing successfully against nations for the loyalty of people. For years, Lebanese Hezbollah has been more than an armed force fighting against Israel. It also distributes food and aids the poor. Soon after the 2006 Israel–Lebanese Hezbollah war, Hezbollah began assisting people with cash and physical assistance.[38] The Jaysh al-Mahdi has duplicated this strategy in the slums of Baghdad and in southern Iraq by protecting Shiites from attacks by al-Qaeda and by replicating some of Hezbollah's social assistance programs.

We can see evidence of this phenomenon in our homeland. The

need for protection can influence the decision of an urban youth to join a gang, whether that gang is in Los Angeles, New York, or Omaha. If society can't protect or feed a person or a group, that person or group will transfer loyalty to those who can.

In the United States, Lind sees multiculturalism as a major threat to the nation.[39] Lind argues that as the United States abandons its Western Judeo-Christian culture, its status as a nation-state weakens. Lind predicts that multiculturalism will cause American culture to be fragmented into groups based on ethnicity, race, gender, sexual identity, and class.[40] As this happens, Americans will have less in common with each other, further weakening the national identity of the United States.

The decline of the nation-state makes the attack on the national will by a 4GW opponent more powerful. A nation whose people have very different interests from their fellow citizens will find it difficult to develop policies that will retain support in the face of the 4GW strategy of making the government's foreign policy appear hopeless.

Democracies will be challenged to prevent societal changes from significantly reducing the power of their nation-states. Love of a cause, not love of a nation, is the theme of the future. The sense that patriotism is on the decline is not just sadness or annoyance at people who ignore the playing of the national anthem at sporting events: It is a threat to a nation's ability to remain a nation.

The United States is doubly affected by this trend. First, it faces enemies who are feverishly devoted to a cause, not a country. And, second, an increasing number of people in the United States feel more devotion to a cause or group rather than to the country in which they live. The combination of these two factors complicates the task of the leaders of the United States to act as a nation. A nation of many homogeneous groups with conflicting beliefs and values is more vulnerable to the propaganda of a 4GW enemy that seeks to have that nation abandon a war.

TRANSNATIONAL OPPONENTS

In addition to facing a decline in support for national policy (regardless of what the policy is), the United States and other democracies must confront ghostlike groups that have no base that an adversary can strike. In the years leading up to September 11, 2001, the Taliban openly hosted al-Qaeda—and paid for it when it was driven from control of Afghanistan. Nations in the future may not openly support a transnational group, giving another nation an easy target for retaliation after an attack by that group. Nations will continue to confront other nations, but with increasing frequency nations will be forced to fight transnational groups such as al-Qaeda or smaller movements that have even less central direction.

Nations such as the United States will face tribes, clans, religious groups, and criminal societies that may operate in several nations and that are immune to sanctions and attacks against their host nation's economy or infrastructure. These groups rely on the very committed as their warriors. As Hammes points out, there is a substantial difference between fighting soldiers and fighting warriors.[41] Soldiers don't receive financial or societal benefits from continuing to fight. No American soldier or marine got rich from serving twenty or thirty years of active duty. But a warrior thrives on war and receives money, food, property, and women as a result of his role. To such a warrior, starvation is a bigger threat than death from battle.

A single sentence in the postscript of Martin Van Creveld's book *Transformation of War*, entitled "The Shape of the Things to Come," sums up the decline of the nation-state and the resurgence of war among groups: "As war between states exits through one side of history's revolving door, low-intensity conflict among different organizations will enter through the other."[42]

CRITICISM OF 4GW THEORY

The concept of fourth-generation warfare is controversial among military writers and academics. Not only do those who advocate the usefulness of such a theory argue among themselves as to the nature of 4GW, but many argue that 4GW is not a valid theory. In a monograph entitled *Fourth-Generation War and Other Myths*, Antulio J. Echevarria II, of the army's Strategic Studies Institute, criticizes 4GW as a flawed theory not supported by history.[43] Echevarria argues that attacking an opponent's will rather than his ability to wage war is not new and has taken place throughout history.[44] With a doctorate in history and having written extensively about Carl von Clausewitz and other military theorists, it is understandable why Echevarria criticizes 4GW as a theory that doesn't comport with scholarly theory.

Despite the criticism of Echevarria and others,[45] fourth-generation warfare theory has much value as a tool to use in discussing deficiencies in military doctrine. Using 4GW to explain to politicians and the American public why insurgents win by simply not losing is very useful. The 4GW theory also explains to those who lead our nation to war why a clock starts ticking when a war begins—especially an insurgency. American citizens expect to see a war executed competently and to see progress. If two, three, or four years of war appear to have been fought with no progress, the clock will expire. Americans will begin to withdraw their support from such a war. The analysis of social, economic, and political changes contained within 4GW—including the reduction of power of the nation-state in favor of transnational groups and the decline of allegiance to a nation in favor of allegiance to other personal, economic, and ethnic interests—help explain why the United States is vulnerable to 4GW attack.

NATION-STATE FOES AND WOES

Regardless of whether or not you believe in 4GW as a theory to explain current insurgencies, it is clear that in addition to preparing for more unconventional war with transnational groups, the United States must be able to fight nations such as Russia, China, North Korea, and Iran. In those four nations, we face opponents that are very different from our democracy. Those four nations are held together as states by force. The rulers of those nations use their power to slow the flow of information, whether from the Internet or satellite television, and to reduce the ability of their citizens to align themselves with interests that are contrary to their nation. The citizens of those nations can't freely travel out of their countries. They can't communicate freely with people who oppose their government. And citizens of those nations don't have the freedom to move their capital to banks or investments that would reduce the power of their nation.

The restricted flow of information and capital enforced by China, Russia, North Korea, and Iran strengthens the leaders of those countries because such restrictions retard the loss of nationalism that is being experienced in Western countries. China, and to an extent, Russia, will also be able to more easily preserve citizen loyalty to their nation-states because of their improving national economies. China's large population ensures that it will have significant economic impact in the world. Russia has demonstrated its capability to use the distribution of its natural gas and other natural resources as tools to assert its power. Poor and marginalized countries that experience an improvement in economic fortunes also experience a rise in nationalism.[46] Increased national pride and demand for national recognition can result in support for military operations or isolationist economic and trade policies.

On the other hand, the openness of democracies encourages citizens of those nations to create and maintain ethnic, social, and financial ties to groups that detract from the power of their nations. Residents of the United States are increasingly divided into groups with widely divergent interests. The major political parties and the labels "conservative" and "liberal" only begin to describe divisions in our society. Some political and social issues—such as abortion, gay rights, immigration, and the environment—attract persons who are willing to focus nearly exclusively on one issue and ignore the positions of politicians on nearly all other issues. Members of ethnic groups who don't integrate into the social fabric of the nation are more likely to view domestic and foreign policy through the prism of their own ethnic identities.

More divisions are created by financial differences. The distinction between poor, middle income, and wealthy has always influenced political views. But now Americans are further divided between those who benefit from international trade, such as people who manufacture products or produce services that can be sold in foreign countries, and those who don't benefit from international trade, such as manufacturing workers whose jobs have been transferred to other countries. Another example of economic division is the financial services industry that caters to the aggregation and investment of capital and the spreading of risk through insurance, collateralized debt obligations, and credit default swaps. People who work and invest in these sectors want the least restrictive policy on international transactions. Financial services companies seek to invest their capital in whichever markets, countries, or industries will return the most profit with least risk. Restrictions on investments or transactions that protect consumers or workers who might lose jobs, while supportive of national policies, are not in the best interests of financial services companies or their owners.

Our country has always had divisions based on ethnicity, wealth, and political positions. But cable television and the Internet provide an abundance of information for those interested in their particular communities. The Internet also provides a cheap and easy way to organize people with similar interests into groups that can exercise their right to influence our legislators and those in the executive branch, or those who desire to join government service as legislators or executives.

One group whose influence continues to shrink, however, is veterans and other citizens who are focused on national defense issues. The primary responsibility of any government is not to feed the hungry, provide shelter for the homeless, or educate the youth. These are all admirable roles for government, but as a nation we forget the basic reason for the existence of the nation-state: to defend the nation and its people and to maintain law and order within the land. These duties must be carried out in order to provide any other service, yet there are few interest groups that focus on these essential duties.

Make no mistake—there are powerful groups that lobby for their version of a strong defense. But the views of such groups are based on the economic interests of defense contractors and states that host manufacturing facilities.

The United States and other democracies must recognize that the openness of their societies places them at a disadvantage in dealing with both transnational movements like al-Qaeda and non-democratic countries such as China, Russia, Iran, and North Korea.

4GW'S EFFECT ON FOREIGN POLICY

A nation—especially a democracy—that has many groups with divergent interests will experience difficulty in determining and implementing its domestic policy. It is differences among citizens that massively complicate national security for a democracy.

The increasing number of differences in our society and the willingness of people to be more loyal to a group or an interest than to the nation will change US foreign policy. The United States will be forced to operate on the international stage more swiftly and decisively than it has in the past. The decision to go to war may not be as difficult for our leaders as the decision to finish the war will be. Our experience fighting insurgencies in Vietnam and Iraq has demonstrated one fact: The citizens of the United States are willing to commit their forces to faraway battles when their leaders tell them that such wars are necessary to the interests of the nation, but they won't give their leaders unlimited time or budget to complete such a war. In Vietnam and Iraq, the US military fought protracted wars that allowed 4GW opponents to sap our national will by bleeding our army and Marine Corps and by overextending our sea power and airpower. The cost of war as we have fought it in Iraq—in terms of casualties, tax dollars, and fatigue to our military's people and equipment—may soon be viewed as a threat to our national defense.

The need to operate quickly and decisively in foreign matters will require a different approach to 4GW. In order to be successful at 4GW, the United States must have an intelligence system that functions much differently than the current system. One change in 4GW already under way is the new counterinsurgency manual jointly written by the US Army and Marine Corps.[47] The new manual was written by staffs supervised by Lieutenant General David Petraeus, who was commander of the Army Combined Arms Center, and Lieutenant General James Mattis, who was the commander of the Marine Corps Combat Development Command. Petraeus and Mattis both served multiple tours in Iraq leading large forces and were committed to improving the military's approach to counterinsurgency.

Instead of launching into a list of "how-to" tactics like many military manuals, the first chapter of the new manual summarizes the history and politics of insurgencies, sets forth new and old principles for counterinsurgency, and outlines practices that have been successful and unsuccessful. Rejecting the "mailed fist" strategy of brutally putting down insurgencies,[48] the new manual adopts the British style of counterinsurgency.[49] This approach focuses on neutralizing armed insurgents, separating the insurgents from "the people," and promoting political and economic reforms.[50]

But the counterinsurgency strategy described in the military's new counterinsurgency manual requires time and large numbers of troops. The manual warns that counterinsurgency is a long-term commitment that requires "considerable expenditures of time and resources."[51] The manual also tells soldiers and marines that establishing security for the civilian population is the cornerstone of any counterinsurgency effort.[52] In order to successfully establish that security, soldiers and marines must, at least in the short term, assume more risk to themselves.[53]

More risk means more casualties, as the United States experienced when it implemented the strategy outlined in the new counterinsurgency manual. Promoted to four stars and sent to his third tour of duty in Iraq, Petraeus was placed in command of all coalition forces in Iraq. Although Petraeus was not given the number of troops the new manual prescribed for counterinsurgency operations, the Bush administration increased troop levels in Iraq by approximately thirty thousand in 2007 during operations known as the "surge."

Just as important as the increase in troop strength, troops began to live in and secure specific neighborhoods. Previously, nearly all troops patrolled from large forward operating bases. Troops would leave their FOB, drive on patrol through neighborhoods in their assigned sectors, and return to their base. The increased number of troops and new tactics placed the troops in contact with insurgents more frequently and caused 2007 to become the year with the highest number of US casualties in the Iraq War. But by the end of 2007, troop casualties and attacks on the civilian population were sharply reduced. The strategy of accepting more risk and securing the civilian population appeared to have worked—at least while troop strength was at the increased level.

But the surge came only by extending combat tours from twelve to fifteen months and by sending some troops back to Iraq one year after their previous tour in Iraq was completed. For many units in the surge, it was their third tour in Iraq.

The new counterinsurgency doctrine enormously improved upon the strategy (or lack thereof) that was in place before. But the new strategy doesn't recognize the effect of fourth-generation warfare and the deteriorating power of the nation-state. Counterinsurgency, as fought historically and as viewed by the new manual, is an expensive and lengthy fight.

A strategy that requires long-term commitment and expense collides with our country's nature to be easily influenced by casualties and news reports of terrorist attacks. Professor Colin S. Gray of the University of Reading, England, has written that the United States is averse to suffering a high rate of casualties and that American society is no longer tolerant of bloody ventures in foreign affairs.[54] Col. Robert M. Cassidy has a different point of view. He argues that the American public does not have an aversion to casualties; instead, US military and political leaders *perceive* that the public will not accept casualties. Cassidy believes the public will tolerate casualties if the public is convinced its political leaders believe the endeavor is in the national interest and the leaders' support of the operation remains strong until a successful conclusion.[55]

The effect of both theories is the same: Whether the American public has an aversion to casualties or American political leaders become indecisive because they perceive such an aversion to casualties, our 4GW enemies operate on the assumption that America will not tolerate casualties. Recent history has not given our enemies reason to doubt that strategy. Al-Qaeda in Iraq has pursued a strategy of attacking targets designed to influence our leaders. It has exploded car bombs at the entrances to the Green Zone and the Baghdad International Airport. It has bombed mosques, police recruitment centers, markets, and bridges with the intent to cause large numbers of casualties. It pursued the use of chlorine bombs, which caused more fear than casualties. Although AQI would like to kill as many coalition troops as possible, it was not important that such attacks killed or injured few troops. The number of civilians killed by such attacks was important to AQI only because large numbers of casualties are more likely to be reported by Western news media.

Widespread awareness of such attacks caused the people of Iraq to view the US-supported Iraqi government as ineffective. Recall the above discussion about people shifting their loyalty away from a government that can't protect them. We must recognize that the insurgent attacks directed against Iraqis gathered to worship, shop, or seek employment also strike at the American heartland. Continued attacks that seem to have no end weaken the resolve of the American citizens and their leaders. That is the nature of fourth-generation warfare.

IMPROVED INTELLIGENCE CAN COUNTER 4GW'S EFFECT

So what connection do counterinsurgency doctrine and the theory of fourth-generation warfare have to intelligence operations? Improving our intelligence operations, especially improving our human intelligence operations, can significantly reduce our vulnerability to protracted insurgencies and the attack upon our decision makers that is the heart of 4GW.

The cornerstone of effective counterinsurgency is securing the civilian population. This requires reducing terrorist violence against civilians. Such violence takes the form of al-Qaeda-style bombings directed at Shiite targets and sectarian violence against Sunnis by squads of men wearing Iraqi police uniforms.

A rapid reduction in violence has significant benefit to the United States when it is fighting an insurgency and is vital to US strategy during counterinsurgency.[56] A lower level of violence would reduce the number of US soldiers, marines, airmen, and sailors deployed to foreign lands. There would be fewer casualties. Because of lower troop levels and reduced costs for supplies, equipment, fuel, and medical costs, taxes could be redirected to domestic expenditures and to maintaining the military force available to combat other threats. US leaders and citizens would see less violence and more progress and would be less vulnerable to a propaganda message claiming the US effort would fail. Fourth-generation warfare opponents facing the United States would be less successful.

Violence can best be stopped by knowing who is committing the violence and by capturing or killing those persons. The best way to identify who is committing violent acts is through human intelligence operations. But the US intelligence community has not focused on human intelligence operations in insurgencies. And the US military's poor management of human intelligence provides much less information than is possible.

"Intelligence is king," according to Gray—intelligence is the key to gaining the upper hand in counterinsurgency.[57] Improving human intelligence operations will not only make our troops safer; such an improvement is the best solution to avoiding and reducing protracted counterinsurgency operations once our leaders have decided to commit military forces against an insurgency.

But this is not just about the Iraq War. Our military leadership foolishly abandoned the lessons for which we paid a high price in Vietnam and in a century of small wars before Vietnam. We will face more insurgencies in the future as more militant Muslims in other countries fixate on the belief that the United States is the reason for their poor lot in life. And China, which has a sizable inventory of conventional and nuclear weapons, has already demonstrated that it would rather attack us by supporting others who despise us. By funding and encouraging others, China incurs little risk and expense, but achieves the goal of challenging the United States.

That is the case for improving intelligence operations. The rest of this book explains what is broken and how we should fix it.

NOTES

1. Ralph Peters, "Progress and Peril," *Armed Forces Journal*, February 2007.

2. Kalev I. Sepp, "Best Practices in Counterinsurgency," *Military Review*, May–June 2005, p. 8.

3. Jeffrey Record, "Why the Strong Lose," *Parameters* (Winter 2006–2007): 26, http://carlisle-www.army.mil/usawc/Parameters/05winter/record.pdf (accessed April 6, 2008).

4. General Jack Keane on the *Jim Lehrer News Hour*, April 18, 2006, as quoted by John A. Nagl, foreword to *The U.S. Army/Marine Corps Counterinsurgency Field Manual* (Chicago: University of Chicago Press, 2007), p. xv.

5. William S. Lind, Keith Nightengale, John F. Schmitt, Joseph W. Sutton, and Gary I. Wilson, "The Changing Face of War: Into the Fourth Generation," *Marine Corps Gazette*, October 1989, http://www.d-n-i.net/fcs/4th _gen_war _gazette.htm (accessed April 6, 2008).

6. Thomas X. Hammes, *The Sling and the Stone: On War in the 21st Century* (St. Paul, MN: Zenith Press, 2004), p. 2.

7. Ibid.

8. Lind et al., "The Changing Face of War."

9. Ibid.

10. Ibid.

11. Ibid.

12. Hammes, *The Sling and the Stone*, p. 49.

13. Samuel B. Griffith II, introduction to *On Guerrilla Warfare*, by Mao Tse-tung (Urbana and Chicago: University of Illinois Press, 2000), p. 17.

14. Hammes, *The Sling and the Stone*, pp. 49–50.

15. Ibid., p. 46.

16. Ibid., p. 51.

17. Griffith, "Introduction," p. 21.

18. Hammes, *The Sling and the Stone,* p. 52.

19. Ibid.

20. Ibid., pp. 56–75.

21. Record, "Why the Strong Lose," p. 18.

22. Hammes, *The Sling and the Stone*, p. 67.

23. Ibid., pp. 33–43.

24. Ibid., p. 17.

25. Ibid., p. 19.

26. Ibid.

27. Ibid., pp. 25–26.

28. Ibid., p. 25.

29. Ibid., pp. 32–43.

30. Thomas X. Hammes, "Fourth Generation Warfare Evolves, Fifth Emerges," *Military Review* (May–June 2007), p. 15.

31. Griffith, "Introduction," p. 23.

32. Hammes, *The Sling and the Stone,* 39.

33. Ibid., pp. 33–34.

34. Ibid.

35. Ibid., p. 35.

36. Ibid.

37. William S. Lind, John F. Schmitt, and Gary I. Wilson, "Fourth Generation Warfare: Another Look," *Marine Corps Gazette*, December 1994, http://www.d-n-i.net/fcs/4GW_another_look.htm (accessed April 6, 2008).

38. Hammes, "Fourth Generation Warfare Evolves," p. 15.

39. Lind et al., "Fourth Generation Warfare."

40. Ibid.

41. Hammes, *The Sling and the Stone*, p. 41.

42. Martin Van Creveld, *The Transformation of War* (New York: Free Press, 1991), p. 224.

43. Antulio J. Echevarria II, "Fourth-Generation War and Other Myths," Strategic Studies Institute, November 2005 http://www.strategicstudiesinstitute.army.mil/pdffiles/PUB632.pdf (accessed April 6, 2008).

44. Ibid., p. 10.

45. Colin S. Gray, "Irregular Enemies and the Essence of Strategy: Can the American Way of War Adapt?" Strategic Studies Institute, March 2006, p. 3, http://www.strategicstudiesinstitute.army.mil/pdffiles/PUB650.pdf (accessed April 6, 2008).

46. Fareed Zakaria, "The Rise of the Rest," *Newsweek*, May 12, 2008, p. 24.

47. Army Field Manual 3–24, *Counterinsurgency* (2006; designated by the US Marine Corps as Marine Corps Warfighting Publication 3–33–5).

48. Steven Metz, *Rethinking Insurgency*, Strategic Studies Institute, June 2007, p. 6, http://www.strategicstudiesinstitute.army.mil/Pubs/display.cfm?pubID=790 (accessed January 21, 2008).

49. Sarah Sewell, introduction to *The U.S. Army/Marine Corps Counterinsurgency Field Manual: U.S. Army Field Manual no. 3–24:Marine Corps Warfighting Publication no. 3–33–5* (Chicago: University of Chicago Press, 2007), p. xxiv.

50. Metz, *Rethinking Insurgency*, p. 6.

51. FM 3–24, para. 1–134.

52. Ibid., para. 1–131.

53. Sewell, "Introduction," p. xxvii

54. Gray, "Irregular Enemies and the Essence of Strategy," p. 47.

55. Robert M. Cassidy, *Counterinsurgency and the Global War on Terror* (Stanford, CA: Stanford University Press 2008), pp. 29–30.

56. Metz, *Rethinking Insurgency*, p. vi.

57. Gray, "Irregular Enemies and the Essence of Strategy," p. 20.

Chapter 4

IRAN'S SHADOW FALLS OVER IRAQ

In the last chapter I mentioned that other nations could use fourth-generation warfare as a tool against the United States. China, for instance, has used private military companies in Africa to advance their interests when deploying Chinese soldiers. Chinese operations in Angola involve 850,000 armed and unarmed contractors engaged in construction and security activities.[1] If the international community challenged the Chinese involvement as a significant intervention in African affairs, China could claim its companies are simply engaged in business operations by providing security for the Angolan government.

But in Iraq there is a better example of a nation using fourth-generation warfare than China's activities in Angola. In Iraq, Iran has been using Shiite militias and political parties to engage the United States in an insurgency designed to convince our leaders to change their policies affecting Iraq and Iran.

One key piece of evidence of Iran's intervention is its smuggling of explosively formed penetrators into Iraq, mentioned earlier. As early as 2005 the SCID reported that Iran was the source of the

EFPs that were used against US forces. The US military did not decisively act on the information and EFPs continued to flow into Iraq in even higher numbers, causing more deaths. Emboldened by a lack of action by the United States, Iran's Islamic Revolutionary Guard Corps stepped up its intervention in Iraq.

This chapter tells the story of Iran's shadow falling across much of Iraq. It is a story that illustrates the result of ignoring intelligence about a strong adversary. The result of Iran's intervention was not hard to predict. Iran's support of sectarian warfare and intra-Shiite conflict sapped much of the public support for the war in Iraq and also restricted the Bush administration's ability to react to the threat of Iran's development of nuclear weapons.

In order to understand how Iran gained the upper hand in Iraq, first consider Iran's goals. Iran focused on strengthening its security against the threat of two foes—the United States[2] and the possibility of a resurgence of a Sunni government in Iraq. In order to protect itself against the threat it believed the United States posed, Iran took up arms against the US military, intending to neutralize it.

Iran viewed the US military as a threat because the United States defeated Iraq's army in only a few weeks, a feat Iran was unable to achieve in eight years of war. If the United States was allowed to remain in Iraq unimpeded, the United States could develop strong ties with the new leadership of Iraq. US bases could become a permanent presence a short distance from Iran. A successful regime change in Iraq could make regime change in Iran much more tolerable to the world community.

Iran sought to rid the Persian Gulf of US forces and take away the aura of a successful war and policy. In order to achieve that goal, Iran set out to inflict casualties on US forces and make US success less likely. Iran found people who were willing to accept Iran's advice, training, and weapons. These fighters became Iran's proxy armies against the United States in Iraq.

The other major foe Iran sought to restrain was a possible Sunni government in Iraq. Sunnis had ruled Iraq since its creation following the breakup of the Ottoman Empire until the fall of Saddam Hussein's government. Under Saddam's regime, Iraq started a war with Iran that devastated the Iranian economy and, according to Iranian claims, killed 250,000 Iranians and exposed 60,000 Iranians to Iraqi chemical weapons.[3] Despite the successful US ouster of the Baathist government in Iraq, Iran was concerned that Sunni rule over the Shiite majority would somehow return to Iraq.

In addition to improving its security, Iran sought to increase its influence and power in the Persian Gulf and the Muslim world. One way to extend Iran's influence was to encourage a more conservative Islamic society in Iraq, perhaps even a society and government run by clerics similar to Iran's.

Postinvasion Iraq was not the first region to feel the effects of Iran's desire to dominate the Muslim world. Iran has been on the offensive for years, using its Revolutionary Guards and Lebanese Hezbollah, a group that was sponsored by the Revolutionary Guards. In the United States the Revolutionary Guards are known as the Islamic Revolutionary Guard Corps (IRGC) and within Iran the organization's name is the Pasdaran.

In contrast to Iran's offensive to expand its influence in the Muslim world, nearby Sunni regimes are on the defensive. Saudi Arabia, Kuwait, and Egypt all have Sunni rulers who are working diligently just to retain their power. These countries, the linchpins of the US strategy in the region, face dual threats. Within their borders are radical Sunni jihadists who believe the monarchies in Saudi Arabia and Kuwait and the repressive government in Egypt are barriers to the rise of the real Islam based on a radical view of the Koran. But these same countries also have sizable Shiite populations that have suffered economic and social discrimination for decades.

The one true democracy in the Persian Gulf is Israel, which is hated by the Islamic clerics ruling Iran. But Israel is also on the defensive. After its mediocre performance in the 2006 war with Lebanese Hezbollah, it struggles to maintain the status quo. Lebanese Hezbollah, which controls territory in southern Lebanon on Israel's border, threatens Israel from the north; Palestinian groups in the Gaza Strip and the West Bank, which receive considerable support from Iran, are sources of terrorism and rocket attacks directed at Israel.

In order to achieve its goals in Iraq, Iran has pursued a strategy of economic influence, political alliances with many different factions, and armed intervention. Iran had several connections with Iraqi groups before the US invasion of Iraq, having hosted Shiite Iraqis fleeing or kicked out of Iraq during the Iraq-Iran War. Although Iraq's population is largely Arab and Iran's population is mostly Persian, the kinship between the countries is understandable because they are the two largest countries in the Middle East with Shi'a majorities.

Iran had an ally to help it achieve its goals. One of the most influential political parties in Iraq was formed in Iran by Shiite Iraqis who fled persecution in Iraq during the 1980–1988 Iraq-Iran War. The new party formed in Iran was the Supreme Council for Islamic Revolution in Iraq and was known for many years by its abbreviation, SCIRI. In 2007, the party dropped the reference to revolution from its name and briefly became the Supreme Iraqi Islamic Council, but after recognizing the implications of the pronunciation of its new abbreviation (SIIC), the party named itself the Islamic Supreme Council of Iraq (ISCI). To avoid confusion I will use the latest abbreviation, ISCI, to refer to the party, but recognize that the name is relatively new.

In addition to the ISCI, Iran had ties to the Islamic Dawa Party, the oldest Shiite political party in Iraq. After the 2003 invasion of Iraq, Iran established contacts with Moqtada al-Sadr and his militia, the Jaysh al-Mahdi (JAM), also known as the Mahdi Militia or Mahdi Army. Although Sadr has criticized ISCI and its associated militia, Badr Corps, for having Iranian roots and allegiance,[4] he, in fact, has a close association with Iran.

Sadr is the son of Ayatollah Muhammed Sadeq al-Sadr, a Shiite religious leader of the 1990s, and a member of the family for whom Sadr City, a large Shiite section in northeast Baghdad, was named. Moqtada al-Sadr began seminary, but did not finish his religious studies, although his video game skills while in seminary earned him the nickname Mulla Atari.[5]

Iran cultivated relationships with both the leadership of ISCI and Sadr. This gave the IRGC access to the two largest Shiite militias, the Badr Corps and the Jaysh al-Mahdi. Some claim the Badr Corps, the militia associated with ISCI, was actually formed, trained, and commanded by the IRGC during the Iraq-Iran war.[6] By developing alliances with ISCI and Sadr, Iran ensured it retained influence with whichever group succeeded in controlling the Iraqi government. But because Iran gave both Sadr and ISCI funding, training, and arms, neither group has become dominant. By balancing the two largest religious Shiite groups, Iran has caused both to continue needing Iranian favors.

Sadr and ISCI represent different segments of Iraqi Shiites. ISCI draws its support from the middle class and its power base is within the religious cities of Najaf and Karbala. Sadr is supported by the urban underclass, predominantly based in Baghdad. The Hakims, the family that has led ISCI, and the Sadrs are both prominent Najaf families that have produced leading religious clerics. Both families took part in the organization of the first Shiite Islamic political party: Mohsen al-Hakim and Muhammad Baqr al-Sadr participated in the early days of the Islamic Dawa Party. Concerned about the party's activism and straying from the oversight of the *marjaeeya*, a group of the most senior Shiite clerics, Mohsen al-Hakim later distanced himself from the Dawa Party.[7] The conflict between Moqtada al-Sadr and ISCI, led by Abdul Aziz al-Hakim, is easier to understand in view of the long-standing differences between the Sadrs and Hakims.

In addition to Moqtada al-Sadr and his militia, the Jaysh al-Mahdi, and ISCI and its militia, Badr Corps, several other small Shiite political parties and militias operate in southern Iraq. Iran has formed connections with many of these to use in achieving its goals in Iraq. By encouraging many factions, Iran also encourages conflict among factions. Iran's volatile politics are dominated by personal relationships and networks, so it was natural for conservative factions of Iran to seize upon the fractious nature of the newly liberated Iraq, exploiting relationships forged in Shiite seminaries. Iranian politicians and the IRGC had much experience organizing in a crisis situation.[8] Iran benefits by maintaining a degree of "manageable" chaos in Iraq:[9] weakening the US effort, preventing the rise of a strong Iraq government independent of Iran, and, if correctly managed by Iran, preventing the total collapse of Iraq into anarchy.

Another step in preventing the resurrection of a Sunni government in Iraq that could threaten Iran was Iran's systematic dismantling of key Sunni organizations. After the fall of Saddam's regime, Sunni professors, scholars, and doctors were assassinated and kidnapped. Even more important to ensuring Sunni officers would not take up arms against Iran, army officers and Iraqi air force pilots who had participated in the Iraq-Iran War were targeted for assassination.

More than ninety air force pilots and high-ranking military officers who participated in the Iraq-Iran War were assassinated.[10]

The MNF–I's Combined Intelligence Operations Center (CIOC) noted the assassinations of Iraqi air force pilots and other military officers in intelligence summaries it published—but that's about all that the US military did. If any diplomat or general attempted to convince the Shiite politicians in charge of the interim Iraq government to use their influence with militias and Iranian forces to stop the killings, such attempts failed.

The Iranian strategy that most affected US troops was Iran's war against US forces. By killing US soldiers, Iran sought to reduce the United States' willingness to continue its role in Iraq and eliminate any temptation to attack Iran. By trapping US forces in a quagmire, Iran believed the chance of a US attack upon it was reduced.[11]

One particularly lethal tool used by Iran was the explosively formed penetrator. The EFP was first used in Iraq in 2003.[12] The trickle of explosively formed penetrator weapons accelerated in 2004 and 2005 and became a torrent in 2006 and 2007. EFPs are much more lethal than the improvised explosive device roadside bombs first used in Iraq. The use of EFPs significantly increased casualties sustained by US troops.

The EFP is a tube filled with explosives and capped with a copper plate. When fired, the plate forms a bullet-shaped semimolten copper slug that can slice through the armor of a Humvee before it shatters, creating an explosion of shrapnel inside the vehicle. An insurgent or militiaman can hide one or several tube-shaped EFPs alongside a road to attack vehicles. The firing tubes can be placed at slightly different angles, with some pointing higher or several tubes arrayed to cover a wide area, improving the chance that a target will be struck more than once. EFPs are frequently sprayed with foam and rolled in mud or concrete so they resemble rocks.[13]

When paired with a passive infrared sensor—the key component of a motion detector—the EFP is difficult to detect and defeat. With normal IED roadside bombs, a person must trigger the bomb using either a wire that leads from the IED to a detonator or a radio signal such as a garage door opener or a cell phone. This requires that the person setting off the bomb have a view of the road and be able to time the explosion to strike the target. A more sophisticated roadside bomb can be equipped with both a radio receiver and a passive infrared sensor. The infrared sensor remains off until it receives a radio signal. Then, when the activated infrared sensor detects a change in infrared light caused by the passing of a vehicle, the sensor detonates the explosive in the EFP tube, causing the projectile that sits on top of the tube to be fired.

But the use of EFPs and other sophisticated weapons in Iraq would not have been possible without the army of operatives Iran employed in Iraq. Even before the US invasion, Iranian allies were preparing to support the invasion. Based on Iraqi intelligence reports from 2001 and 2002 that were captured by US forces after the invasion, we know that ISCI asked the Badr Corps command to provide support for the US attack on Iraq by conducting reconnaissance and harassing attacks upon the Iraqi military in southern Iraq. ISCI also instructed Badr Corps to send two battalions of militia into the areas of al-Amarah and al-Nasseria to collect information and conduct attacks. These forces were supervised by General Mhamde, an Iranian intelligence officer who traveled in and out of Iraq.[14]

By 2005 my unit, the Strategic Counterintelligence Directorate, was reporting that Iran was supplying EFPs to insurgents for use against US troops. Bombs used against coalition troops were painstakingly analyzed by explosives experts stationed at Camp Victory at the Combined Explosives Exploitation Cell (CEXC). After vehicle bombings CEXC experts frequently traveled to the scene to analyze and photograph the vehicles and the blast site and prepare reports that were circulated within the MNF–I. Based on the analysis of the experts, the MNF–I knew that it was facing a weapon that was new to Iraq.

Previously EFPs had been used only in Lebanon by Lebanese Hezbollah. Because of the close connection between Iran's IRGC (especially its Qods Force unit) and Lebanese Hezbollah, it was natural to conclude there was an Iranian connection. But in addition to the logic of that connection, the SCID collected and reported human intelligence that positively linked Iran to the supply of the EFPs. Over a period of months, the SCID produced dozens of intelligence information reports that described the nature of the network that brought EFPs into Iraq from Iran, the training provided by Iran, and other details. Despite these reports, I saw no change in focus by MNF–I's senior leadership to regard the Iranian influence in Iraq as a threat to US troops.

Instead of focusing intelligence and operational assets on Iran's intervention in Iraq, our government sent Iran a diplomatic protest titled "Message from the United States to the Government of Iran." In that July 19, 2005, protest, the US State Department advised Iran that a British soldier was killed by an EFP in Maysan Province in southeastern Iraq, bordering Iran. The complaint advised that Shiite militiamen who planted the device were supplied such devices by the Islamic Revolutionary Guard Corps and Lebanese Hezbollah, which had also trained Iraqi Shiite insurgents in Iran.[15] Not surprisingly, Iran denied any involvement in the EFPs.

A month after that protest, *Time* magazine ran an extensive article by journalist Michael Ware that laid out much of what the SCID had been reporting. Abu Mustafa al-Sheibani headed a network of Shiites affiliated with Iran that imported the EFPs from

Iran into Iraq. Ware reported that Sheibani's team consisted of 280 members divided into seventeen bomb-making teams. The Sheibani network trained in Lebanon, Baghdad, and "in another country."[16]

The *Time* article also noted the reluctance to engage Iran, reporting that "top intelligence officials have sought to play down any state-sponsored role by Tehran's regime in directing violence against the coalition." Other comments in the article gave a preview of what would develop. Iran, Ware stated, had brokered a partnership between Iraqi Shiite militants and Lebanese Hezbollah and was facilitating the import of "sophisticated weapons that are killing and wounding U.S. and British troops."[17] In 2005 no US official was quoted referring to an explosively formed penetrator by name, but there is no doubt that the EFP is among the "sophisticated weapons" mentioned in the article.

The *Time* article foreshadowed the chaos that was to come in eastern and southern Iraq, areas sharing a border with Iran that were routes for importing weapons, people, and a brand of conservative Islam not common in secular Iraq. An unnamed British officer stationed in Basra described Iran's methods in the *Time* article: "They use the legal checkpoints to move personnel, and the weapons travel through the marshes and areas to our north."[18]

Given the British knowledge of Iranian forces using the area north of Basra as a smuggling route, it is odd that US forces passed on an opportunity to interdict a weapons shipment north of Basra based on human intelligence information the SCID had developed. SCID counterintelligence agents developed specific information about weapons that would be coming into Iraq from Iran in the area of Amarah, which is between the cities of Basra and Kut. While the SCID frequently identified insurgents and provided target packages to coalition units that captured the insurgents, it was rare for any unit to have specific information about importation of weapons at a particular place and time. I shook my head in amazement and disgust when I realized that despite specific information from a credible source, there was no interest in mounting an operation to capture the weapons and their smugglers. In 2005 there just wasn't that much interest in what Iran was doing. The lack of interest in acting on intelligence about the importation of more lethal weapons was symptomatic of the US reaction to Iran's 4GW attack upon us. In short, we did very little.

I have already described the disdain General DeFreitas expressed regarding collecting information about Iran's activities. Some midlevel members of the military's intelligence community, including the SCID, continued to collect intelligence about Iran's activities in Iraq. Despite DeFreitas's instructions to *not* focus on Iran, the SCID continued collecting and reporting on EFPs. And because the information we collected about EFPs linked their importation and use in Iraq to Iran and Iraqi Shiite groups operating on behalf of Iran, the SCID continued to document Iran's involvement. Intelligence reports generated by other units began to mention the Sheibani Network more frequently and efforts to locate and capture Sheibani Network members became more active.

One high-ranking government official took an interest in the SCID's intelligence regarding EFPs: Philip Zelikow held the little-known but important position of counselor to the State Department. Zelikow was an old friend of Secretary of State Condoleezza Rice, having cowritten a book with her. Zelikow has a PhD in history, is a lawyer, and previously served on the President's Foreign Intelligence Advisory Board. In his most recent position before the State Department, he had been the executive director of the 9/11 Commission.[19]

Zelikow had already made two trips to Iraq to assess the situation for Rice before he returned for a third visit in September 2005. Frequently, when high-ranking people who were interested in intelligence matters visited Iraq, the MNF–I intelligence directorate put together an agenda; the SCID often was given thirty to sixty minutes to brief someone. I had a briefing that I had used for general officers and Defense Department undersecretaries, and I expected to use that for Zelikow. Instead, he wanted to spend the time discussing very specific issues. Knowing he had an interest in EFPs and the Iranian connection, I had brought Bob Bennett, leader of the SCID team that had done most of the work on the EFPs.

Bob is extraordinarily intelligent and a real student of the craft of intelligence and international politics. Zelikow asked Bob penetrating questions that honed in on specific points. Later, Bob arranged for Zelikow to be briefed by some US Central Command intelligence officers who had studied Iran's intervention in Iraq. As was the case with the SCID, their opinions about Iran were not welcomed by the MNF–I intelligence staff.

The information Bob and his team gave to Zelikow made an impression. In his report to Rice, Zelikow described the EFP weapons and noted that by shaping the charges and directing the explosive force and projectile in a straight line, the EFP could penetrate armor. Zelikow also estimated the EFP was at least four times more lethal than IEDs that Iraqi insurgents could produce themselves.[20]

Zelikow also recognized that EFPs presented two problems. In addition to the increased lethality of the new roadside bombs, the significance of Iran's supplying the weapons was a problem. Bob Woodward described Zelikow's thinking on the issue in his book *State of Denial*:

> Some evidence indicated Iranian-backed terrorist group Hezbollah was training insurgents to build and use the shaped IEDs, at the urging of the Iranian Revolutionary Guard Corps. That kind of action was

arguably an act of war by Iran against the United States. If we start putting out every thing we know about these things, Zelikow felt, the administration might well start a fire it couldn't put out.[21]

Zelikow's assessment of the situation was accurate and may have explained the reluctance of some to confront Iran.

With the knowledge of Iran's goals of maintaining its national security while expanding its influence in the Muslim world, we can understand how Iran's strategy has worked. Iran used its IRGC Qods Force and the Shiite militias to harass and inflict casualties upon coalition forces that were not deployed in adequate numbers to combat the Sunni insurgency. The Iranian-sponsored attacks served Iran's goal of weakening US resolve and influence in Iraq and the Persian Gulf. But in addition to its armed intervention in Iraq, Iran used political connections to gain considerable influence in Iraq.

In January 2005, Iraq's citizens elected the Transitional Government, which would write the Iraq Constitution. Ibrahim al-Jaafari became the prime minister and a new era of elected government for Iraq began. Ayad Allawi, the prime minister in the Interim Government who had been appointed before the election, was a secular Shiite who had lived outside of Iraq for thirty years. Like Allawi, al-Jaafari had left Iraq, first for Iran and then London. But unlike Allawi, al-Jaafari was from the Islamic Dawa Party, a Shiite religious political party that is considerably more conservative than secular Shiites such as Allawi. One example of the Dawa Party's political position was its support of Ayatollah Khomeini's Islamic Revolution in Iran.

With the advent of the 2005 elections, religious Shiite political parties including the Islamic Dawa Party, the Islamic Supreme Council of Iraq (ISCI), Moqtada al-Sadr's party, and many smaller parties created the United Iraqi Alliance to oppose secular shiites and to ensure the shiite majority controlled the Iraq Parliament.

But even though ISCI won the most seats in the parliament, it didn't have enough control within the United Iraqi Alliance to select an ISCI candidate as the prime minister. ISCI's strongest opponent within the United Iraqi Alliance was Moqtada al-Sadr.

As a compromise, the Sadrists and ISCI agreed upon Jaafari from the Dawa Party. The Dawa Party, although it was the first Islamic Shiite party, had been weakened by its struggles against Saddam's regime and by Iran's choice to support ISCI over the Dawa Party when both were in exile during the Saddam regime. The Dawa Party was weak and had no militia, so it posed no threat to either the Sadrists or ISCI. Similiarly, Jaafari's replacement, Nouri al-Maliki, was also from the Dawa Party for the same reason.[22] Thus Iraq's prime minister lacks the power base of a majority party he controls, which makes successfully leading a government much more difficult.

But with the United Iraqi Alliance and Jaafari in control, Iraq's government institutions dramatically changed from the secular interim government run by Allawi. People and organizations with very close ties to Iran gained control of much of the government. Bayan Jabr, a Badr Corps official was appointed to head the Ministry of Interior, the ministry responsible for law enforcement and internal security. As a result, thousands of Badr Corps soldiers became police officers, but they retained their loyalty to the Badr Corps and ISCI instead of the new Iraq government.

In contrast, the Ministry of Defense was headed by a Sunni, but Kurdish and ISCI-appointed army officers exerted substantial control of the ministry.[23] Iraq's army had been disbanded and had to be rebuilt from scratch. Complicating the security issue was the overlap between the MOI and MOD. Unlike the relatively clear division between law enforcement and the military in the United States, the MOI developed paramilitary forces, including "public order brigades" that operated much like army units.

Despite the conflict among Shiites, two facts became very clear. First, religiously conservative Shiites were in control of the Iraq government. Second, nearly all of the major religious Shiite parties had a connection to Iran. Although US officials tended to characterize Abdul Aziz al-Hakim and the ISCI party he headed as the moderate alternative to the more radical Moqtada al-Sadr and his followers, even Hakim and ISCI continued close contact with elements of Iran that were engaged in planning and directing attacks against US troops. But the United States was forced to ally itself with al-Hakim and the ISCI party. After deposing Saddam Hussein, the United States discovered the secular Shiites it wanted to be aligned with, such as Ahmed Chalabi and Ayad Allawi, were irrelevant.[24] The secular Shiites had not received the votes necessary to be an effective political force.

As we look back at the situation in Iraq in 2005 after the election of the United Islamic Alliance–controlled government and the events that occurred after the 2005 elections, it is clear that when left unchecked, Iran took every advantage it could gain by supporting political leaders and those desiring to wage war against the coalition that liberated Iraq.

Although EFP attacks occurred in the Baghdad area, much of the military effort mounted by Iran and its proxies first was noticed in southern Iraq. In 2005 the main city in southern Iraq, Basra, seemed relatively peaceful compared to Baghdad, but the lower number of attacks on coalition forces was deceptive.

Although there was virtually no Sunni insurgent activity in southern Iraq, British Forces and US personnel were assaulted while traveling and their compounds were rocketed. The forces responsible for these attacks were Shiite militias, primarily the Jaysh al-Mahdi and the Badr Corps. The Badr Corps, having been formed in Iran, was a known affiliate of Iran's IRGC. But in 2005, intelligence reports—including reports developed by the SCID—indicating that Sadr's JAM militia was being backed by Iran were discounted. Over time, however, it became clear that both the Badr Corps and JAM were operating in concert with Iranian elements.

Despite their common connection to Iran, the Badr Corps and JAM were battling for control of Basra and the surrounding area. I saw indications of the battle for Basra when I visited the SCID's team in Basra in July 2005. Like most trips of any distance in Iraq, the only practical way to travel was by air. Although Basra is about a four-hour car trip from Baghdad, the security situation made travel overland dangerous and impractical because a single traveler would require several armed personnel, at least one translator, and multiple vehicles to make the trip.

When my flight on a Royal Air Force C-130 arrived, there were only a few aircraft at the Basra airport, some British C-130s and a US Air Force C-17 transport. From the flight line I could see the flames of a refinery tower in the distance. Unlike the American Southwest, the flat desert near the airport had little beauty. The area's colors were muted by the ever-present dust. The Basra airport was a large commercial airport that was deserted except for a few British military personnel operating it as a military air terminal.

Basra, the second largest city in Iraq, is contained in an arrow-head-shaped portion of Iraq that is bordered on the east by Iran and on the west by Kuwait. The Shatt al-Arab, a river that is formed about forty miles north of Basra where the Tigris and Euphrates rivers merge, runs south past Basra and empties into the Persian Gulf. A few miles southeast of Basra the Shatt al-Arab becomes the border between Iraq and Iran, a geography that emphasizes the connection Iran has with the area.

Before the invasion, Basra was predominantly Shiite but it also contained a significant Sunni population. In the secular society of

Saddam Hussein's regime, Basra, with its bars and bordellos, had a reputation as a place for fun-loving Iraqis to go.

But as the SCID's Basra team picked me up from the airport and we began our trip across the city, there was no evidence of Basra's past as a fun seeker's destination. The British Forces headquarters was at a camp near the Basra airport, but the compound that held the US Embassy's regional office, the SCID's office, and other US and British organizations was on the east side of Basra near the Shatt al-Arab—a forty-five-minute trip across the city. Shortly after leaving the airport, the lead vehicle of our small convoy of armored SUVs spotted an Iraqi police checkpoint. Even in 2005 a checkpoint manned by Iraqi police in Basra was cause for concern.

At the SCID we traveled in armored SUVs and dressed in civilian clothing. With the relaxed grooming standards resulting in beards and nonmilitary haircuts, we resembled the security teams that protected US diplomats and Western businessmen. The Basra SCID team had learned it was better to avoid checkpoints than to hope our status as US military personnel would be respected.

The uncertainty of a rapidly changing Basra was described by Steven Vincent, an art critic turned independent journalist. Two weeks before I arrived in Basra, Vincent's article in the *Christian Science Monitor* described the new Basra. No longer a city with bars, casinos, and other nightlife, Basra, according to city dwellers quoted in the article, was coming under heavy Iranian influence, both culturally and politically. Cultural changes included armed Shiite men observing women entering Basra University to ensure their dress and makeup was sufficiently modest and sending home those who violated their standards. Politically, thirty-five of the forty-one members of the Basra Province's Governing Council belonged to Shiite parties aligned with Iran, such as ISCI and the Islamic Dawa Party. Sunnis living in Basra were under attack:

Nearly one thousand people, most of them Sunni Muslims, had been killed in Basra in the past three months.[25]

Four days after my return from Basra the *New York Times* published an article by Vincent criticizing the British handling of south Iraq. Vincent described the type of people gaining control of Basra:

> Basran politics (and everyday life) is increasingly coming under the control of Shiite religious groups, from the relatively mainstream Supreme Council for the Islamic Revolution in Iraq to the bellicose followers of the rebel cleric Moktad al-Sadr. Recruited from the same population of undereducated, underemployed men who swell these organizations' ranks, many of Basra's rank-and-file police officers maintain dual loyalties to mosque and state.[26]

Vincent's description of police officers more loyal to radically anti-American Moqtada al-Sadr than to the Iraq government was accurate. Because of the infiltration of the militia into the police force, the SCID team at Basra had no faith in the Iraqi police in Basra.

Upon spotting the checkpoint, the team reversed course and began an alternate route to the embassy compound. The forty-five-minute trip turned into a ninety-minute tour of Basra. Riding through Basra I saw cars in eight lanes of traffic competing with donkey-pulled carts. At a gas station I observed a long line of cars four-abreast. "That's for legal gas," said one of the Texas National Guardsmen, part of the SCID's security element; black-market gas was available, without the lines, for a premium price. Among apartment buildings there were small cubes built of concrete block or brick that served as houses; most had a satellite dish on the roof—Iraqis had gone crazy for satellite dishes and Internet cafés, banned under Saddam's regime.

The SCID team in Basra was the only US military intelligence unit operating in the Basra area. Other than our team, the MNF–I relied on British intelligence reporting. During my visit, human intelligence sources the SCID team had recruited reported on a battle fought between JAM and the Badr Corps that lasted for hours. A couple of days later, when I returned to Baghdad, I noticed no other intelligence unit had reported the conflict between the Badr Corps and JAM. Although British Forces were probably aware of that battle and other conflicts, they found them to be unworthy of reporting. That battle was one of several confrontations between JAM, also known as the Mahdi Army, and the Badr Corps. In late March 2008, Iraqi government forces largely composed of Badr Corps personnel assaulted Basra to end the Mahdi Army's control of the city.

Similarly, the SCID's Basra team was alone in reporting on the control increasingly exerted by Sadr's JAM upon the port of Umm Qasr, near Basra. Umm Qasr, Iraq's largest port, is located about thirty miles from the Persian Gulf on a canal that extends west from the gulf.[27] Because Iraq has only a few miles of coastline, Umm Qasr is a primary avenue of foreign trade for the country. The Iraqi coastline is wedged between Kuwait and Iran. Most US supplies enter Iraq through Kuwaiti ports and are trucked north from Kuwait. Much of the supplies for Iraq's reconstruction enter through Umm Qasr, which was so neglected by Saddam's regime that coalition forces found forty wrecked ships in the port's harbor.[28] For Iraq's foreign trade to increase, an efficient port would be essential.

The commerce that flowed through the port made it an attractive target. Sadr supporters were attempting to gain control of the port, and if they succeeded it would be a large financial windfall for Sadr's forces. Contesting Sadr and his Jaysh al-Mahdi militia for control of the port was the Badr Corps, which had entered Iraq's Ministry of Interior in large numbers. The MOI controlled the Iraqi

Coast Guard,[29] giving the Badr Corps a power base in the area to resist Sadr's attempt for control.

On August 2, 2005, less than a week after Vincent's *New York Times* article was published, Vincent was killed and his female interpreter, Nouraya Itais Wadi, was wounded after both were abducted by persons in a police car. At about 6:30 p.m. on a Tuesday evening, four armed men grabbed Vincent and Wadi on a busy Basra street and spirited them away in a car. After being questioned for five hours, Vincent and Wadi were taken to a neighborhood near where they had been abducted. Told they were free to go, they took a few steps before their abductors opened fire. Vincent died but Wadi managed to survive.[30]

That was Iraq in 2005, two years after the invasion. Shiite religious parties were in charge of the Iraq government, having handily defeated secular Shiites. The sophisticated EFP roadside bomb was being deployed by Shiite militias that were supported by Iran. And in southern Iraq, there was evidence of a struggle between religious Shiites and social change accompanied by violence. Despite the evidence of Iranian intervention and the growing violence of radical Shiite militias, the Sunni insurgency in Baghdad and regions north, west, and east of Baghdad commanded the attention of military intelligence and operational units.

Years later the effects of the Iranian intervention in Iraq became substantially more lethal to American troops. The Sheibani Network continued to bring EFPs into Iraq. Casualties from EFP attacks began to climb in the last quarter of 2006.[31] During the last three months of 2006, EFPs caused 18 percent of combat deaths of US and allied troops. Emboldened by the lack of US action, Iranian-backed militias launched sixty-five EFP attacks in April 2007. By July 2007, EFP attacks reached an all-time high: EFPs were used in ninety-nine attacks in that month alone. The Sunni insurgency was no longer the most deadly force facing US troops; 73 percent of the attacks that killed or wounded US troops in Baghdad were carried out by Shiite militias according to Lt. Gen. Ray Odierno, the commander of the MNC–I.[32]

Shiite militias had expanded their use of weapons and even used EFPs against aircraft. In 2007, Shiite militias were bringing in 107-millimeter rockets and 122-millimeter mortars to be used against US forces.[33] Even more devastating to armored vehicles was the RPG-29 rocket-propelled grenade that was reported in September 2006 to be used against US forces. Previously the RPG-29 had been used by Lebanese Hezbollah in its war against Israel in the summer of 2006. The RPG-29 is particularly effective because, with its two warheads, it is capable of penetrating heavy armor: The first warhead creates a hole in the armor and the second warhead detonates deeper inside the armor.[34] On February 12, 2007, a Royal Air Force C-130 was damaged by an attack of two arrays of EFPs while landing at an airstrip in Maysan Province, east of Baghdad along the Iranian border. The aircraft, the first to be attacked with an EFP, was so badly damaged it had to be destroyed with a thousand-pound bomb.[35]

One unit that was caught in the wave of increased EFP attacks was Battery B of the 1st Battalion, 161st Field Artillery of the Kansas National Guard. Known as Bravo Battery, the artillerymen were assigned to Convoy Support Center Scania in Babil Province, about sixty miles south of Baghdad. The convoy support center supported convoys that hauled supplies along Iraq Highway 1, one of the main routes from Kuwait to Baghdad, Ramadi, and Mosul.

On the evening of February 22, 2007, two squads of Bravo Battery were assigned to patrol outside the convoy support center. The two squads, each composed of eleven soldiers and an Iraqi translator, had the radio call signs Assassin 2–2 and Assassin 2–3. While the squads were on patrol, the convoy support center started receiving mortar fire. The mortars began falling just as the squads had found an Iraqi police checkpoint manned by a single police officer, who warned them of "Ali Baba"—insurgents—hiding behind nearby trees. Ordered by the operations center at the convoy support center to locate the source of the mortars, S.Sgt. David Berry, the Assassin 2–2 squad leader, requested permission to pursue the insurgents reported by the policeman. Follow your orders, Berry was told.[36]

The Humvees headed toward the coordinates they were given for the launching point of the mortars falling on their camp. Assassin 2–3 set up an observation post to watch for any insurgents Assassin 2–2 had flushed. Berry's squad drove on, going down a curved road known by the soldiers as "Wild West."[37]

An EFP exploded on the passenger side of the vehicles. The projectile rocketed inches from the head of Spc. Sean Wing, the gunner in the turret of the second of three Humvees that made up the Assassin 2–2 squad. Spc. Johnny Jones, the driver of the third Humvee, which carried Berry, braked to a stop. Gunfire erupted from the direction of the EFP explosion.

Before the Humvees could start moving again a second EFP hit Berry's Humvee, entering through the rear driver's side door. Parts of the projectile shattered the jaw of S.Sgt. Jerrod Hays, a thirty-eight-year-old Kansas National Guardsman from Wellington, Kansas.[38] The same EFP projectile shredded the right leg of Spc. Peter Richert from ankle to knee.[39] Twenty-three-year-old Richert, who had been on the track team for Tabor College in his hometown of Hillsboro, Kansas,[40] would lose that leg.[41]

A third EFP struck Berry's Humvee, this time from the passenger side.[42] When the third EFP struck, Hays, who had worked with Berry at an iron foundry in Norwich, Kansas, realized it had killed Berry instantly. Berry was Hays's oldest friend—they had known each other since ninth grade.[43]

When explosive ordnance disposal specialists examined the scene the next day, they found four unexploded EFPs. All seven EFPs had been connected to the same controller used to manually detonate them. The EFPs had different diameters ranging from twelve inches to about four inches.[44]

Intelligence reports had warned the soldiers of the danger posed by EFPs. Sgt. Nathan Reed, an Army reservist who was in the Humvee that the first EFP had narrowly missed that night, told the *Kansas City Star*: "I'd take my chances with an IED any day over an EFP. Your chances of living are not very good. You're either going to be killed by the blast or shredded by shrapnel."[45]

The story of Bravo Battery tells of a few of the people attacked with EFPs from Iran, but there were many people on the other side of the EFP arrays that struck our troops. Those people included Iraqi Shiite militiamen, members of Iran's Islamic Revolutionary Guard Corps, and Iraqis in "secret cells" who were specially selected and trained in Iran. All were behind increased attacks upon US and allied troops.

After the US invasion of Iraq, Iranian investors and intelligence officers had spread out across the country with orders to buy as many as five thousand apartments, houses, stores, and restaurants in Baghdad, Basra, Najaf, and Karbala. These locations would be used as living quarters and command centers for Iranian agents and militias loyal to Iran.[46] The money spent on such properties was only a portion of massive spending in Iraq by Iran. General Petraeus estimated in 2007 that Iran had spent "hundreds of millions of dollars" in funding Sadr's militia, the Jaysh al-Mahdi, and other Shiite militias.[47]

Iranian funding yielded several networks of specially trained fighters who were particularly loyal to the IRGC's Qods Force. These Shiite fighters were more than willing to use their advanced training and the sophisticated weapons supplied by Iran against US forces.

By July 2007, MNF–I generals were able to specifically describe the work of the Qods Force in Iraq and the effect it had upon US efforts. The Qods Force is a special branch of the IRGC commanded by Brig. Gen. Qassem Suleimani, who reports directly to Iran's Supreme Leader, Ayatollah Ali Khamenei. The fact that the leader of the Qods Force reports directly to the Supreme Leader, bypassing the president of Iran, demonstrates the importance Iran gives the force.[48] The Qods Force recruited fighters from Shiite militias who were sent to Iran for advanced training by Qods Force and Lebanese Hezbollah instructors. These instructors trained classes of twenty to sixty Iraqis at three training camps near Tehran. Using Lebanese Hezbollah as a model, the Iraqis were organized into elements called "secret cells" and "special groups" by MNF–I officers.[49]

The smuggling of advanced weaponry by the Sheibani Network and others continued. On April 20, 2007, coalition forces captured one of the leaders of the Sheibani Network, Abu Yaser al-Sheibani, who was the deputy leader, key logistician, and financier for the Sheibani Network. Abu Yaser al-Sheibani is the brother of the leader of the network, Abu Mustafa al-Sheibani.

One incident illustrated the extent to which the Qods Force was directing operations against US forces in Iraq. On January 20, 2007, Americans awoke to news reports of a daring daytime operation that resulted in the kidnapping and death of five US soldiers at the Provincial Joint Coordination Center in Karbala, south of Baghdad. Between nine and twelve attackers dressed in uniforms and drove five suburban utility vehicles similar to those used by US forces. When they passed through checkpoints the attackers pretended to be Americans by using forged American identity cards. The attackers were carrying M-4 rifles used by US forces and threw stun grenades of a kind used in Iraq only by American forces. The attackers killed one US soldier at the center and kidnapped four others, who were found dead a short time later.[50]

Like the series of car bombs in April 2005 that caused MNF–I to switch its priority from members of Saddam's regime to al-Qaeda in Iraq, the Karbala attack on January 20 was a wake up call for US military and intelligence officials. With little pressure on them, the IRGC Qods Force and the militias they were training had become more active and were now engaged in sophisticated kidnapping operations using forged passes, fake uniforms, and stolen or captured American weapons.

For the remainder of 2007 and into 2008, US forces increased their focus on the Iranian-connected groups operating in Iraq. On March 20, 2007, Qais Khazali and his brother, Laith Khazali, were captured in the same raid in Basra. Qais Khazali's group was the group that carried out the Karbala attack. The Khazali brothers were captured with Ali Musa Daqduq, a senior member of Lebanese Hezbollah.[51]

Interrogation of the Khazali brothers and Daqduq gave insight into the extent of the Qods Force operations in Iraq. Qais Khazali had been the head of the special groups operating in Iraq since June 2006, and he interacted with the Qods Force at a high level. His main contact was Hadji Youssef, the deputy commander of the Qods Force Department of External Special Operations. According to the Khazalis, the funding of the special groups by Qods Force began in 2004. Khazali and Daqduq identified Qods Force as the supplier of EFPs, machine guns, sniper rifles, rockets, IEDs, and rocket-propelled grenades.[52]

During a press briefing Brig. Gen. Kevin Bergner, a spokesman for MNF–I, explained the Qods Force efforts to train and direct operations of the special groups in Iraq, including the attack on Karbala. When Qais Khazali was captured, a twenty-two-page document was found with him. The document detailed the planning for and the lessons learned from the Khazali Network's attack upon the Karbala Provincial Joint Coordination Center. The document showed that considerable intelligence had been collected about the activities of US soldiers, including when their shifts changed and details about fences surrounding the center.[53] But Bergner didn't mention one damning detail that illustrates the extent and sophistication of the support the Qods Force provided to its special groups operating in Iraq. The June 4, 2007, issue of *Aviation Week & Space Technology* stated that satellite imagery of a training center inside Iran revealed a mock-up of the Karbala Provincial Joint Coordination Center. The duplicate layout of the center allowed attackers to rehearse their entry into the compound and their attack.[54]

But now, in addition to the IRGC Qods Force and the special groups of Iraqi Shiite fighters they had trained to new levels, the Qods Force had introduced a new element: Lebanese Hezbollah. The capture of Daqduq was significant. He was no foot soldier. His past assignments during his twenty-four years of service in Lebanese Hezbollah included several leadership positions, including command of a Hezbollah special operations unit, the leadership of Hezbollah operations in large areas of Lebanon, and responsibility for the protection of Hezbollah secretary general Hassan Nasrallah.[55]

There had been prior reports that Lebanese Hezbollah had been training members of the Jaysh al-Mahdi in Lebanon. In November 2006, intelligence officials believed that one thousand to two thousand members of Jaysh al-Mahdi and other Shiite militias had been trained by Lebanese Hezbollah in Lebanon. There was also an indication that a few Lebanese Hezbollah personnel had come to Iraq.[56]

But the capture of Daqduq, a senior Lebanese Hezbollah commander, inside Iraq confirmed these reports and indicated the level of support Lebanese Hezbollah was providing to Shiite militias. In 2005 Daqduq began working with Qods Force to train Iraqis inside Iran. During the year prior to his capture, Daqduq made four trips into Iraq to review the training and operations of the Iraqi special groups. Qods Force directed Daqduq to organize the Iraqi special groups in a manner similar to how Hezbollah is organized in Lebanon.[57]

Following the capture of the Khazali brothers and Ali Musa Daqduq, US forces continued to unearth more Qods Force operations in Iraq. On June 18, 2007, coalition forces conducted a series of raids in Maysan province, including raids in both Amarah and Majjar al-Kabir.[58] Two years earlier, when the SCID provided actionable intelligence regarding weapons shipments and personnel entering Iraq from Iran in the area of Amarah, there was no interest in acting on it. But in June 2007, coalition forces killed at least twenty members of secret cells operating in Amarah and Majjar al-Kabir. The coalition press release stated that "intelligence reports indicate that both Amarah and Majjar al-Kabir are known safe havens and smuggling routes for Secret Cell terrorists who facilitate Iranian lethal aid. Reports further indicate that Iranian surrogates, or Iraqis that are liaisons for Iranian intelligence operatives into Iraq, use both Amarah and Majjar al-Kabir as safe haven locations."[59]

Qods Force operations were not limited to southern and central Iraq. Five Qods Force members were detained in Irbil, in the northern area of Iraq controlled by the Kurds.[60] In October 2007, coalition forces detained Mahmud Farhadi, a Qods Force officer who headed the "Zafr Command," which trains and smuggles Iranian insurgents and weapons across the border into north-central Iraq.[61]

High-ranking officials from Iran and Iraq have been involved with Qods Force operations in Iraq. In December 2006, US forces captured Brig. Gen. Mohsen Chirazi, the third highest-ranking official of the Qods Force. Even more interesting than the capture of Chirazi was where he was captured and how he was handled. Chirazi and another senior Qods Force commander were captured while inside the compound of Abdul Aziz al-Hakim, the leader of ISCI. The Iraqi government chose to recognize the Iranians' claims of diplomatic immunity even though they were operating under aliases. A few days after their capture, Chirazi and his fellow Qods Force commander were expelled from Iraq and returned to Iran.[62]

But the Qods Force presence in Iraq extended even further. According to General Petraeus, Hassan Kazemi-Qomi, Iran's ambassador to Iraq, is a member of the Qods Force.[63] The ambassador served with the IRGC throughout the Iraq-Iran War and from 1988 to 1990 was the deputy chief of the IRGC unit that trained Iraqi opposition forces in Iran.[64]

After seeing the spread of the Iranian intervention in Iraq via its Qods Force, what about the area where Iranian influence was most noticeable in 2005? By late 2007, Basra appeared to have finished its conversion from a secular city to a city shaped in the radical Shiite tradition. Posters of the late Grand Ayatollah Khomeini were plastered across Basra. Shops were prohibited from selling musical CDs. The punishment for alcohol consumption could be death. Women were pressured to wear veils in conformance with a strict interpretation of Islamic law. Moqtada al-Sadr's Jaysh al-Mahdi led the enforcement of Islamic moral practices.[65]

The Jaysh al-Mahdi had plenty of personnel to enforce its wishes. As British Forces were withdrawing from Basra, the main force that fought them, the Mahdi Army, had seventeen thousand militiamen serving in Basra. Billboards proclaimed the story of Mahdi militiamen who died fighting the British and Basra streets were named after Mahdi members.[66]

In 2005 the SCID team in Basra was reporting about JAM's attempt to gain the financial benefits from controlling the port of nearby Umm Qasr. By 2007 JAM's tentacles of control extended beyond the ports and oil terminals into several units of the Basra police force, hospitals, the education board, university, and companies that distribute oil products and electricity.[67]

The battles between JAM and the Badr Corps continue. The Badr Corps have secured positions as governors and commanders of security forces, although Sadr's JAM was suspected in the assassination of two Badr members who were governors of southern provinces of Muthana and Diwaniyah. Other Shiite factions battle for control, or at least survival, in southern Iraq. One group, the Fadhila Party, follows the teachings of the father of Moqtada al-Sadr, the late Muhammad Sadiq al-Sadr. Unlike Moqtada al-Sadr, who spent much of 2007 residing in Iran, the Fadhila Party is the rare Shiite Islamist party that opposes Iran.[68]

As the British drew down their forces in Basra, the commander of the Iraqi police force in Basra, Maj. Gen. Jalil Khalaf, noted that the British had unintentionally armed Shiite militias because they failed to recognize that the Iraqi troops they were arming were loyal to militias. Khalaf lamented that the British left the security of Basra in poor shape: "They left me militia, they left me gangsters, and they left me all the troubles in the world."[69]

In March 2008 Iraqi prime minister Nouri al-Maliki ordered the Iraqi army to push the Mahdi Army out of its control of Basra. The intense battle that ensued for several days initially appeared to have failed to weaken the Mahdi Army's grip on Basra or its influence in the area.[70] Perhaps the most disturbing aspect of the Iraq government's offensive in Basra was how it ended. A cease-fire was ordered after a meeting of representatives of the Dawa Party, the Badr Corps, and Moqtada al-Sadr that was conducted in the Iranian holy city of Qom. The representatives met with Brigadier General Suleimani, commander of the IRGC's Qods Force. As a result of the meeting, Sadr ordered the Mahdi Army to halt its resistance.[71]

The involvement of the commander of the Qods Force, the same force responsible for bringing EFPs to Iraq and causing hundreds of US casualties, in the peacemaking process between the Iraqi government and Moqtada al-Sadr speaks volumes about the direction of Iraq in the future. After the invasion of Iraq, the United States and its allies were facing an insurgency in a country adjoining Iran. We knew that Iran had many motives to oppose us and had demonstrated the willingness to attack via proxies in the past at the marine barracks in Lebanon, Khobar Towers, and in the Lebanese Hezbollah war against Israel in 2006. Yet we didn't treat Iran as a threat. We failed to take a long view of a long war.

The Qods Force succeeded in recruiting, training, and arming numerous special groups to carry out attacks against coalition forces. Despite those attacks, the coalition forces continue their initial mission to defeat the Sunni insurgency that threaten the Iraq government controlled by religious Shiite political parties. Yet those same Shiite political parties are affiliated with Shiite militias and special groups of Shiite fighters trained, financed, and advised by the Qods Force, an organization that reports directly to Iran's Supreme Leader.

Philip Zelikow, the counselor to Secretary Rice who visited Iraq and met with the SCID team chief, gave a speech after leaving his position with the State Department. Referring to the period of indecision by US leaders as to whether to address the Iranian threat, Zelikow said, "For many months American officials were torn between a desire to do something and a wish to avoid confrontation. When a government is conflicted about what to do, the usual result is inaction."[72]

Pilots have a simpler phrase for the same problem: "Honor the threat." If a pilot doesn't address a potential threat, he may get a missile up his tailpipe. In Iraq, when our military didn't honor a threat, it increased the likelihood that National Guardsmen would be ambushed with a lethal armor-piercing weapon.

The Iranian threat could have been countered earlier. The success experienced by US and Iraqi forces against the Sunni insurgency led by al-Qaeda in Iraq following General Petraeus's assuming command of forces in Iraq and the change in counterinsurgency policy was accompanied by another success. Under the leadership of Petraeus, the United States began to fight effectively the Iranian-sponsored Shiite militias and special groups while also fighting the Sunni insurgency. Unlike the lack of attention and indecision that met Iran's offensive against US forces earlier in the war, beginning in 2007, US forces struck back at the Iranian proxies.

US forces captured those behind some of the attacks, including those responsible for planning the kidnapping and killing of US soldiers in Karbala. Iran responded to this pressure with attacks that harmed more than just US forces. Iranian rockets rained down on the homes of Shiite leaders in the Green Zone.[73]

Finally, Iran's policy of balancing its support between ISCI, the Badr Corps, and the Maliki government on one hand and Sadr and his Jaysh al-Mahdi on the other tipped too far in one direction. Throughout 2007, Shiite militias supplied by Iran had terrorized southern Iraq, assassinating clerics and government officials.[74]

The Maliki government's push into Basra in March 2008 loosened Sadr's grip on the city and the financial benefits flowing from Basra and the nearby port of Umm Qasr. By June 2008, pro-Maliki graffiti covered some city walls in Basra and commerce had improved.[75] Sadr was still a strong power to be reckoned with but his domination of Basra and other parts of Iraq was effectively challenged by the Maliki government supported by Sadr's Shiite opponent, the ISCI. Because the groups that were causing most of the Shiite militia attacks upon US forces were affiliated with Sadr, the Iraq government's actions that reduced Sadr's power also reduced violence against US forces.

The progress made in less than two years following a period of nearly four years during which Iran's proxies were largely ignored was remarkable. Iran's intervention in Iraq should have been opposed in 2005 at the latest. Instead, the lack of response encouraged Iran to flood Iraq with EFPs, improved rockets, and antiarmor rocket-propelled grenades.

Regardless of Iran's eventual influence in Iraq or the relationship between the United States and Iraq that results from the overthrow of Saddam Hussein, the lesson of Iran's shadow upon Iraq should not be forgotten. Intelligence that is collected but not properly analyzed or acted upon provides no benefit.

NOTES

1. Thomas X. Hammes, "Fourth Generation Warfare Evolves, Fifth Emerges," *Military Review* (May–June 2007), p. 18.

2. "Iran in Iraq: How Much Influence?" International Crisis Group, March 21, 2005, p. 2, http://www.crisisgroup.org/home/index.cfm?l=1&id=3328 (accessed February 11, 2008).

3. Ibid., p. 8, n 46.

4. "Shiite Politics in Iraq: The Role of the Supreme Council," International Crisis Group, November 17, 2007, p. 19, n 129.

5. Vali Nasr, *The Shia Revival: How Conflicts within Islam Will Shape the Future* (New York: Norton, 2006), p. 191.

6. "Shiite Politics in Iraq," p. 4.

7. Ibid., pp. 1–2.

8. Ali M. Ansari, *Confronting Iran* (New York: Basic Books, 2006), p. 217.

9. "Iran in Iraq," p. 22.

10. Mounir Elkhamri, *Iran's Contribution to the Civil War in Iraq*, Jamestown Foundation, January 2007, p. 6.

11. "Shiite Politics in Iraq," p. 22

12. Michael R. Gordon and Scott Shane, "Behind U.S. Pressure on Iran, Long-Held Worry Over a Deadly Device in Iraq," *New York Times*, March 27, 2007, p. A11.

13. Ibid.

14. Elhamri, *Iran's Contribution to the Civil War in Iraq*, p. 4.

15. Gordon and Shane, "Behind U.S. Pressure on Iran."

16. Michael Ware, "Inside Iran's Secret War for Iraq: A *Time* Investigation Reveals the Tehran Regime's Strategy to Gain Influence in Iraq—and Why U.S. Troops May Now Face Greater Dangers as a Result," *Time*, August 22, 2005, p. 26.

17. Ibid.

18. Ibid.

19. Bob Woodward, *State of Denial* (New York: Simon & Schuster, 2006), p. 387.

20. Ibid., p. 414.

21. Ibid., pp. 414–15.

22. "Shiite Politics in Iraq," p. 15.

23. "The Next Iraqi War? Sectarianism and Civil Conflict," International Crisis Group, February 27, 2006, p. 19, http://www.crisisgroup.org/home/index.cfm?id=3980&CFID=36002396&CFTOKEN=64691213 (accessed February 11, 2008).

24. Bernard Gwertzman, "Nasr: Iraqi Prime Minister 'Irrelevant' in Shiite Power Struggle," Council on Foreign Relations, March 26, 2008, http://www.cfr.org:80/publication/15837 (accessed April 6, 2008).

25. Steven Vincent, "Shiites Bring Rigid Piety to Iraq's South," *Christian Science Monitor*, July 13, 2005, World section, p. 1.

26. Steven Vincent, "Switched Off in Basra," *New York Times*, July 31, 2005, Editorial Desk section, p. 12.

27. James Glanz, "Iraq's Big Port Has Commerce, Crime—Even Camels," *New York Times*, July 1, 2006, Foreign Desk section, p. 6.

28. Ariana Eunjung Cha, "At Iraqi Port, Progress is Matter of Perception—U.S. Role Disappoints Dockworkers," *Washington Post*, March 25, 2004, p. A1.

29. Glanz, "Iraq's Big Port Has Commerce, Crime—Even Camels."

30. Dan Murphy, "Tragic End to a War Reporter's Bracing Story—Steven Vincent, Who Contributed to the Monitor, Was Killed Tuesday in Basra," *Christian Science Monitor*, August 4, 2005, World section, p. 1; Kirk Semple, "Reporter's Death Reflects the Dread of a City Filled with Rumors and Violence," *New York Times*, October 9, 2005, Foreign Desk section, p. 14.

31. Gordon and Shane, "Behind U.S. Pressure on Iran."

32. Michael R. Gordon, "U.S. Says Iran-Supplied Bomb Is Killing More Troops in Iraq," *New York Times*, August 8, 2007, Foreign Desk section, p. 1.

33. Ibid.

34. Eric Rosenberg, "Hezbollah, Iran Linked to Attacks—U.S. Commander Thinks Tehran, Lebanese Group Are Smuggling Deadly Weapons into Iraq," *Times Union*, September 24, 2006, p. A13.

35. Gordon and Shane, "Behind U.S. Pressure on Iran."

36. David Goldstein, "Bravo Battery's Ordeal in Iraq: Night Patrol Erupts in Carnage," *Kansas City Star*, December 17, 2007, p. A1.

37. Ibid.

38. Interview with Spc. Johnny Jones, February 18, 2008.

39. Ibid.; Goldstein, "Bravo Battery's Ordeal in Iraq."

40. David Goldstein, "Retrieving the Wounded, and Families Back Home Brace for the Worst," *Kansas City Star*, December 18, 2007, p. A1.

41. Interview with Jones.

42. Ibid.

43. Goldstein, "Bravo Battery's Ordeal in Iraq."

44. Interview with Jones.

45. Ibid.

46. Elkhamri, *Iran's Contribution to the Civil War in Iraq*, p. 6.

47. Sean D. Naylor, "Iran Deeply Involved in Iraq, Petraeus Says," *Army Times*, May 25, 2007, http://www.armytimes.com/news/2007/05/military_petraeus_iran_070523w (accessed February 18, 2008).

48. Claude Salhani, "Inside Iran's Secretive Qods Force," *Middle East Times*, January 14, 2008, http://www.metimes.com/Security/2008/01/14/inside_irans_secretive_qods_force/4726/ (accessed June 29, 2008).

49. Kevin Bergner, "Press Briefing, July 2," MNF–I Combined Press Information Center, http://www.mnf-iraq.com/index.php?option=com_content&task=view&id=12641&Itemid=131 (accessed February 19, 2008).

50. James Glanz and Mark Mazzetti, "Iran May Have Trained Attackers

That Killed 5 American Soldiers, U.S. and Iraqis Say," *New York Times*, January 31, 2007, Foreign Desk section, p. 10.

51. Bergner, "Press Briefing, July 2."

52. Ibid.

53. Ibid.

54. "In Orbit," *Aviation Week & Space Technology* 166, no. 21 (June 4, 2007): p. 5–5.

55. Bergner, "Press Briefing, July 2."

56. Michael R. Gordon and Dexter Filkins, "Hezbollah Helps Iraq Shiite Army, U.S. Official Says," *New York Times*, November 28, 2006, Foreign Desk section, p. 1.

57. Ibid.

58. "Coalition Forces Disrupt Secret Cell Terrorist Network," MNF–I Combined Press Information Center, June 18, 2007, http://www.mnf-iraq.com/index.php?option=com_content&task=view&id=12378&Itemid=128 (accessed February 19, 2008).

59. Ibid.

60. "Coalition Targets Iranian Influence in Northern Iraq," MNF–I Combined Press Information Center, January 14, 2007, http://www.mnf-iraq.com/index.php?option=com_content& task=view&id=9063&Itemid=128 (accessed February 19, 2008).

61. David Mays, "More Evidence Shows Iran Directly Supports Iraq Insurgents," American Forces Press Service, October 3, 2007, http://www.global security.org/military/library/news/2007/10/mil-071003-afps02.htm (accessed February 19, 2008).

62. Joshua Partlow, "Military Ties Iran to Arms in Iraq," *Washington Post*, February 12, 2007, p. A01.

63. "Iran Diplo Furor; Ambassador Backs GIs' Killers: Petraeus," *New York Post*, October 8, 2007, p. 16.

64. Ed Blanche, "The Hidden Hand," *Middle East*, March 2007, p. 9.

65. Sam Dagher, "Shiite Taliban Rises as British Depart Basra," *Christian Science Monitor*, September 18, 2007, World section, p. 11.

66. Sam Dagher, "Basra: After the British," *Christian Science Monitor*, September 17, 2007, World section, p. 1.

67. Ibid.

68. Ibid.

69. Mona Mahmoud, Maggie O'Kane, and Ian Black, "UK Has Left Behind Murder and Chaos, Says Basra Police Chief," *Guardian*, December 17, 2007, http://www.guardian.co.uk/world/2007/dec/17/iraq.military (accessed February 19, 2008).

70. Babak Rahimi, "What Direction for the al-Mahdi Army after the Basra Offensive," *Terrorism Focus*, April 2008, p. 6, http://www.jamestown.org/terrorism/news/uploads/tf_005_013.pdf (accessed April 7, 2008).

71. Leila Fadel, "Al-Sadr Orders Militia to End Confrontation," *Kansas City Star*, March 31, 2008, p. A1.

72. Gordon and Shane, "Behind U.S. Pressure on Iran."

73. Vali Nasr, "Iran on Its Heels," *Washington Post,* June 19, 2008, p. A19.

74. Ibid.

75. Ibid.

Chapter 5

HUMINT SOURCES

D uring a meeting with a senior military intelligence officer who was nearing the end of his intelligence career, the man's eyes lit up as he told me the goal of the army's intelligence community. One day, he said, a squad leader will be carrying a small device about the size of a Palm Pilot or other personal digital assistant (PDA) while leading a patrol through hostile territory. A global positioning system (GPS) device will communicate the squad's location to its headquarters. Intelligence from intercepted cell phone calls, images from unmanned aerial vehicles (UAVs) and satellites, and information from human sources will be combined at an intelligence operations center. Like magic, the squad leader's PDA will vibrate or chirp and the squad leader will be alerted that there is an IED, ambush, or insurgent around the next corner.

I didn't realize at the time of our conversation in Iraq that the army was betting big on this kind of technology to fight future wars. Since 2003 the army has been developing its Future Combat Systems (FCS). The FCS includes a collection of fourteen weapons, drones, robots, sensors, and hybrid-electric combat vehicles. These components will all be connected by a wireless network that requires 63.8 million lines of computer code to operate. One item that has already been developed is a UAV that is a twenty-nine-pound cylinder on legs propelled by a rotary fan. Troops testing it have nicknamed it the "beer keg" because of its shape.[1]

The decision to design a new system of computer-connected weapons and battlefield tools came in part as a result of war games conducted in 1995. In the war games, Iranians had captured Riyadh and began executing the royal Saudi family on live television. When a rescue force using heavy armor became entangled in the streets of Riyadh, the army had what Maj. Gen. Robert H. Scales Jr., who ran the war games, called the "aha moment." The army needed to travel lighter and be more mobile.[2]

Four years later, in 1999, the army was embarrassed when its poorly performing logistical system prevented it from moving its Apache helicopters quickly into Albania. The Kosovo war ended before the helicopters made it into Albania. The army decided it had to develop a lighter and faster force and to do so quickly. The army estimates its lighter and faster force will cost $162 billion. The program is being built by more than 550 contractors and sub-contractors in forty-one states.[3]

TECHNO-INTELLIGENCE VERSUS HUMINT

The FCS and the whiz-bang networking of intelligence are examples of the military's fascination with technology that cause military leaders to believe technology is a silver bullet that will fix its problems. Department of Defense planning documents that analyze future warfare such as Joint Vision 2020 and the DOD's "Transformation Planning Guidance" focus on technology as the primary driver of change.[4]

But the cultural desire of the army and the Department of Defense to focus on technology as the primary source of solutions for future conflicts has also influenced their intelligence system. The preference of our intelligence leaders to develop and employ technology-based intelligence to the detriment of the capability to use human intelligence has greatly contributed to the military's difficulty in its counterinsurgency operations.

There are several reasons why leaders of military intelligence organizations favor technological intelligence. Officers who rise to become general officers within military intelligence organizations nearly all arise from backgrounds that involve technical intelligence gathering, including collecting and analyzing electronic signals such as radio communications and supervising satellites and reconnaissance aircraft and the analysis of the images they produce. Very few officers who rise to high positions of leadership spend much time in their careers recruiting persons to be sources or assets and running human intelligence (HUMINT) operations.

One reason why most senior intelligence officers come from technical intelligence disciplines is simple mathematics. The forces needed to gather and interpret signals intelligence (SIGINT) and imagery intelligence (IMINT) are much larger than those dedicated to collecting HUMINT. Consequently, many officers spend their careers as leaders in large organizations that collect radio signals and telephone calls, translate intercepted foreign language communications, and analyze intercepted communications. Other careers are focused on designing, launching, and operating satellites and UAVs that carry cameras and other sensors or interpreting photographs and other images taken by those airborne vehicles. Many other intelligence personnel are consumed in analyzing and storing terabytes of information that may or may not be useful. In contrast, relatively few officers specialize in HUMINT, a discipline that requires talents that are not possessed by every intelligence officer. Because most officers are not exposed to HUMINT, most senior military intelligence officers who are very experienced in many aspects of intelligence have little experience in HUMINT.

Although technology-based intelligence is very useful, it is not a solution for all problems. But people manage according to their strengths. By that I mean an officer who has a lot of experience solving problems using a specific discipline (infantry officer, fighter pilot, special operations officer, or technical intelligence officer) will be inclined to apply that set of skills. Because of that human tendency, the lack of practical experience in HUMINT by most senior military intelligence officers causes them to prefer technology-driven solutions for collecting and analyzing information instead of using HUMINT.

Even if an officer who comes from another intelligence discipline such as SIGINT is interested in using HUMINT, there is another problem. People new to HUMINT quickly learn that it is harder than other types of intelligence. The practice of HUMINT is full of intangibles that many intelligence officers are not prepared to address. The handler of a human source must determine the motives of the source and assess whether the source really knows the facts. The person who is supervising the HUMINT operation must ensure the source handler and the interpreter who translated between the source and his handler correctly understood the source and accurately and completely reported the information, plus any additional facts that increase or detract from the source's credibility. Finally, the analysts who receive the information must place the information in the right context. All of these actions are difficult and subjective tasks.

In contrast, intelligence from intercepted communication signals and overhead images is simpler in some respects. Although the technology and organization of effort behind the collection of SIGINT and IMINT are not simple, those intelligence disciplines deal in more tangible information. There is precision and reliability as to what was said in an intercepted conversation, how many cars were outside a remote farmhouse at midnight, and the number of times one cell phone has called another. Once a radio communication is intercepted or a UAV beams video of two trucks discharging eight people and four large boxes, those facts are not in question. We know communication was made or that boxes arrived. We may not know what the communication meant to its intended recipient or what is inside the boxes, but we know some facts with certainty.

That type of precision and reliability is often lacking when relying on a human being to observe and listen and then to report what he or she saw and heard without embellishment or leaving out important details.

THE NEED FOR HUMINT

As a result of the emphasis on technical intelligence and the lack of experience and expertise required to obtain reliable information from a human source, the collection and analysis of HUMINT is not well managed and is often not performed well. Unfortunately, technology and the intelligence disciplines based on it will not give our fighting forces the information they need to protect themselves and effectively fight an insurgency. Human intelligence is the single best type of intelligence when fighting an insurgency.

That assessment of how critical HUMINT is in counterinsurgency is not just my opinion. Men and women who served in Iraq saw the limitations of technology. Some were so concerned about the need to develop better human intelligence capabilities, they wrote about it when they returned. Interestingly, many who wrote articles in military journals that addressed the need for improvements in HUMINT were not intelligence officers. They were officers from other branches of the service such as the infantry who had learned the hard way how critical human intelligence is to fighting an insurgency.

Even as early as 2005, the second highest-ranking officer in Iraq wrote that HUMINT was needed because technology-based tools were ineffective in Iraq, a theater where developing actionable intelligence was difficult. Lt. Gen. Thomas F. Metz served as the commanding general of Multi-National Corps–Iraq. Metz and his chief intelligence officer at MNC–I came away from their duty in Iraq knowing that the US military's technological superiority was marginalized when combating an insurgency. They suggested in an article published by the school that trains US Army intelligence officers that the army needed a heavier focus on HUMINT.[5]

A field commander in the heart of Baghdad gave specific examples of intelligence collection that didn't work against insurgents. The commander of a brigade combat team responsible for operations in a large area of Baghdad found that imagery operations, electronic reconnaissance, and normal combat patrols yielded almost no intelligence on which the brigade could act. That commander concluded that in the urban environment of Baghdad, where our army faced insurgents who wore no uniforms and blended into the local population, the conventional intelligence collection methods that an army combat brigade uses are ineffective.[6]

The experience of an operations officer for a battalion that served in Baghdad, Najaf, and Fallujah also confirmed the superiority of HUMINT over other intelligence disciplines in counterinsurgency.

That battalion operations officer wrote of several lessons learned, but one key lesson was that HUMINT "is by far the most valuable intelligence source for commanders engaged in COIN [counterinsurgency] warfare."[7]

The experiences of the brigade combat team commander, the battalion operations officer, and Metz confirm what students of counterinsurgency knew long before the Iraq War: Direct human interface is the best method of gathering intelligence for counterinsurgency. In a strategy research project conducted for the Army War College, Col. David J. Clark surveyed the historical role of intelligence in fighting insurgencies. Clark found that any successful counterinsurgency effort had to have good intelligence. Without actionable intelligence, a term that refers to information specific enough that it allows a police force or army to take action such as capturing or killing insurgents, the force fighting an insurgency has no hope at all.[8]

In studying counterinsurgency campaigns from the past, Clark found that satellite and aerial photography, intercepting communications, and studying signals or radiation given off by radar, nuclear materials, and chemicals all contribute to a successful fight against an insurgency. But very few targets can be identified and successfully struck based solely on those types of intelligence without corroborating HUMINT. There have been times when technical intelligence that wasn't corroborated by HUMINT led to forces striking the wrong targets, causing "collateral damage" in which noncombatants are killed or hurt. Such collateral damage is worse than just missing the insurgents. Killing or injuring apparently innocent citizens is often publicized and used in insurgent propaganda to further turn the population toward supporting the insurgency.[9]

From the experiences described by veterans of the Iraq War and from studies of counterinsurgency, we can conclude that HUMINT is needed. HUMINT is intelligence gathered from interaction with people, including people encountered on patrol, witnesses in investigations, prisoners, and people recruited to be sources to supply information.[10]

HUMINT IN IRAQ

Using that definition, there were many organizations in Iraq that were involved in HUMINT. Any army or Marine Corps unit that interviewed witnesses to a bombing or that spoke to Iraqi residents while on patrol was conducting HUMINT operations as part of its other duties. In addition to the frontline units, there were organizations that focused on conducting HUMINT as a major part of their operations, including my unit, the Strategic Counterintelligence Directorate.

The SCID's human source operation against insurgents was one of several conducted in Iraq. There was an abundance of organizations in Iraq that conducted HUMINT, including the Central Intelligence Agency, the Defense Intelligence Agency, special operations forces, Army Tactical HUMINT Teams (THTs), and their counterparts, the US Marine Corps HUMINT Exploitation Teams (HETs.) In addition, Air Force Office of Special Investigations agents collected HUMINT near air bases and some of the Naval Criminal Investigative Service agents in Anbar Province focused on HUMINT in support of Marine Corps operations. The Iraqi government also had many intelligence operations, including the new Iraq army, several police organizations within Iraq's Ministry of Interior, and the Iraq National Intelligence Service.

In Iraq each organization that had personnel who were trained and experienced in source handling operated differently. One way in which the SCID was different from most intelligence organizations was that it had a mix of personnel from different branches of the military. We also had a combination of military personnel and civilians. Some of the civilians were employees of the government and some were employed by contractors who supplied them to us at considerable expense to the government.

At the heart of the SCID were the personnel from the army's Intelligence and Security Command, the Naval Criminal Investigative Service, and the Air Force Office of Special Investigations. Each branch of the service had different training and ways of managing their personnel, resulting in a wide variety of experiences and talents.

The army personnel were a mix of military officers, noncommissioned officers, and civilian employees of the army. The army's military intelligence personnel at the SCID had spent most of their careers focused solely on intelligence and counterintelligence.

All of the NCIS special agents at the SCID were civilian employees of the navy, except for a couple of Marine Corps NCOs who were serving four-year tours of duty with the NCIS and two navy reserve officers. Because the NCIS is responsible for investigating felony criminal cases involving navy and Marine Corps personnel as well as conducting counterintelligence that affects the navy and Marine Corps, many of the NCIS special agents had more of a background in criminal investigations than in counterintelligence.

Like the NCIS agents, the AFOSI agents at the SCID handled both criminal investigations and counterintelligence in their normal duties. The AFOSI agents included officers, NCOs, and civilian employees of the air force.

The Counterintelligence Field Activity, a DOD agency that worked for the deputy undersecretary of defense for counterintelligence and security, supplied several civilian contractors to be intelligence analysts. The analysts reviewed the source reports and other information the counterintelligence agents developed and assisted the agents in editing intelligence information reports. The most important function of the analyst was to be the subject matter expert for the targets he or she was assigned. In addition to the information the agents developed from our sources, there was a wealth of information that could be gleaned from intelligence reports from other units and combined with our information. The intelligence from other sources helped corroborate what our sources were telling our agents and often helped fill in gaps in our knowledge about insurgent cells and organizations. Sometimes it helped us realize information from our source was so different from other reports that either we were onto something very special or our source was full of hot air. Usually it was the latter.

THE LANGUAGE BARRIER

Our linguists were another crucial part of handling sources in Iraq. The military and intelligence community can supply only a small percentage of the Arabic linguists needed in Iraq. That led the military to an intensive search for linguists. Again, the government fighting a "long war" took a short war view of the situation. Instead of meeting at least part of the linguistic needs by recruiting US citizens who were Arab linguists and creating a program for them to be hired as civilian employees of the government, the government relied on contractors almost exclusively for the vast majority of its linguists.

At the SCID, our linguists were supplied by two companies, one of which was Titan Corporation. Titan's story illustrates some of the issues with the government's reliance on contract linguists. The expense of such linguists is enormous. In 2004 Titan was supplying forty-two hundred linguists to the military in Iraq.[11] That number had grown from fewer than thirty linguists supplied in 1999 by a company called BTG of Fairfax, Virginia, which Titan purchased in 2001.[12] By April 2005 Titan had almost five thousand translators working in Iraq, Afghanistan, and other locations.[13]

The company that was supplying all of these translators had problems. A foreign bribery investigation of Titan scuttled Lockheed Martin's proposed acquisition of the company in 2004.[14] An army investigation of the Abu Ghraib prison scandal found that linguists employed by Titan had participated in some of the incidents of prisoner abuse.[15] Some former Titan employees who returned from Iraq criticized the company for not supporting and protecting its employees while in a war zone. These employees complained of defective satellite telephones, unsafe vehicles, and a lack of body armor. In 2005 the army issued a "cure notice" that detailed problems with Titan's handling of its linguistics contract.[16]

But supplying linguists to the government was profitable. Titan's contract with the US Army's Intelligence and Security Command—worth $4.65 billion—was the company's single largest contract in 2005.[17] But in 2006 Titan lost the army's linguistic services contract.[18]

There were larger problems with contract linguists than poor management and the expense of such services. Linguists who were contractors posed operational and security issues. Fortunately, at the SCID and other intelligence units, all of our contract linguists were US citizens. Because of a shortage of US citizen translators, however, many field units were forced to use Iraqi citizens who spoke English as their translators. Several Iraqi translators turned out to be part of the insurgency; these translators supplied information about operations of our soldiers to insurgents.

The translators at the SCID and other intelligence units were naturalized US citizens who had immigrated to the United States from Iraq or other Arab nations. Many had immigrated at a young age and had lived in the United States for twenty years or more. The US citizen translators performed a noble service that only a few could perform for their country. But even those who were naturalized citizens could pose problems.

Some translators spoke neither Arabic nor English particularly well. They could make themselves understood in both languages, but for some, their limited education in both worlds detracted from their grammar and vocabulary. Many of the translators came from the US middle class. They had been shop owners, store clerks, and laborers. The salary they received, which was in the low six-figure range, was a lot of money for most people. But for many, that salary was something they could never achieve back home. As one translator told me, "I get paid like a basketball player." As a result of their limited linguistic abilities and extended absences from the Middle East, many of the translators often overlooked nuances or even main points in both Arabic and English. Some translators worked diligently to improve their vocabularies, referring frequently to Arabic-English dictionaries while translating written documents, but others were content to guess.

Because many Iraqis had learned English, it was possible to have a disconcerting moment when a source—who apparently needed his conversation interpreted—suddenly interrupted the translator to correct the English word or phrase the translator had just used. I told our agents to never assume an Iraqi could not understand English. Many could understand written and spoken English quite well. If necessary, many Iraqis we encountered could carry on a rudimentary conversation in English, but, embarrassed by their pronunciation of English, they preferred a translator.

The other difficulty with using translators who were not experienced in intelligence operations is that they soon figured out they were the vital link in the communication between source and source handler. Nothing happened without the translator. Frequently sources would call the translator and carry on entire conversations out of the hearing of the agent because the agent and translator usually were together only when translation was needed. As a result, the source's information was filtered by the translator. Details the translator considered irrelevant or unimportant were not passed on to the agent.

Some agents deferred to the translator because of the translator's heritage in Arabic culture and because the translators stayed in Iraq for a year or more. Although the translators could be the source of much cultural knowledge and advice, as a result of that deference an agent, without realizing what was happening, could easily become the number two agent on the case. Some translators, if not managed carefully, would substitute their judgment for the agent's judgment on matters of intelligence tradecraft and operational security.

Despite those difficulties, it was impossible to operate without our translators. Agents compensated by developing rapport with the translators and by agreeing with the interpreters about procedures to use for personal source meetings and telephone calls.

OPERATING IN THE RED ZONE

In addition to the language barrier, another issue we faced in working with Iraqi sources was the danger and difficulty involved in moving anywhere outside of a base. Because of the threat to Westerners everywhere in Iraq except in the Kurdish-controlled areas, Iraqi sources were hard to meet in person. Movement in

Baghdad nearly always required two or more vehicles. Although the primary threat was roadside bombs, our small convoys also faced suicide bombers. Many IED attacks were accompanied by small-arms fire.

Interviewing a witness and meeting a source were tasks that needed only one or two agents, but when an interview or source meet required travel outside a base, the mission could consume an entire team because of the number of people needed for self-protection. Less than two months before I arrived, a platoon of Texas National Guardsmen were detailed to the SCID to serve as our security element. Their addition was a tremendous benefit and allowed us to increase our operations because while one or two agents on a team were meeting a source or going to Camp Victory to meet with interrogators regarding insurgents we had helped capture, the other agents on the team could be conducting other source meetings or writing reports about intelligence they had previously collected.

The security element soon became the experts on travel in the red zone (the area outside of the guarded perimeter of a base). By employing their training and experience at route and mission planning and small unit tactics, the security element made our travel in the red zone as safe and as efficient as it could be.

But "safe" and "efficient" are relative terms in a place like Iraq. A few months after I left the SCID and less than two months after the Texas National Guard contingent had been replaced by members of the Kansas National Guard, tragedy struck. On President's Day of 2006, an SCID team was traveling within Baghdad to complete an intelligence mission when an explosion knocked the first light armored vehicle off the road. Sadly, the source was an explosively formed penetrator. The EFP killed AFOSI Special Agent Daniel J. Kuhlmeier and Army Spc. Jessie Davila. The explosion severely wounded another AFOSI agent and less seriously injured two other soldiers in the vehicle.

Kuhlmeier and Davila were the second and third members of the SCID to die in Baghdad. In September 2005 S.Sgt. Shawn A. Graham was leading an SCID convoy from Camp Victory to the Green Zone when an Iraqi vehicle that had pulled over to allow the convoy to pass suddenly swerved back into traffic and tapped the rear of the LAV. The impact caused the LAV's tires to lose traction. As the driver fought to control the heavy LAV, which was traveling at high speed down Route Irish, the vehicle left the roadway and rolled over several times. Graham died en route from the Baghdad hospital to the medical facility at Balad Air Base.

OPERATIONAL SECURITY

Another danger that was as real as traveling in the red zone was the security of the operation and the source. Insurgents or criminal gangs in Iraq would kill someone they merely suspected to be an informant. The Iraqis who provided information had their own lives complete with wives, girlfriends, or, in some cases, both. Many had kids and employers. A wife or child who meant no harm could inadvertently say something that would reveal their husband or father was associated with US intelligence. A source invited death into his house if he told a friend, no matter how close, or an employer, regardless of the reason, of his work for us.

Just working in the Green Zone, regardless of the type of work, was dangerous for many Iraqis. An experience of Gary Rodriguez, an NCIS special agent who replaced Tom Reid as the SCID operations officer, was an example. Having worked undercover for NCIS for several years before being promoted into supervisory ranks, Gary was a natural at undercover and source work and frequently evaluated Iraqis he encountered as potential sources. One young Iraqi who worked in the Green Zone told Gary of the pressure he felt from just working in the Green Zone.

Leaving his apartment each day, the Iraqi would take a cab to a busy area of town and then walk a block or two before hailing a second cab to take him to another busy area. There he would find a third taxi that would take him to an entrance of the Green Zone. His neighbors and friends thought he was working elsewhere in Baghdad at a clothing store. When one neighbor said he wanted to come to the Iraqi's shop, he was horrified. Telling his neighbor the area surrounding his shop was too dangerous, he took the man's measurements and then bought clothing to take to him.

One day when Gary met with the man, he was very upset. That morning, he told Gary, he had walked out of his apartment past a man dead in the street. A handprinted sign proclaimed the man was killed for working for the Americans. People who passed by the body kept walking, not wanting to be affiliated with the dead man. Under those circumstances, it was surprising that anybody was willing to work with us.

HUMINT SOURCES

Despite such potential danger for Iraqis who cooperated with us, the SCID handled many sources. In my experience, sources can be generally classified in three categories. At the first stage there is the person who provides information to soldiers or marines on patrol. This kind of casual source may be motivated by a desire to get rid of undesirables in his neighborhood or may want to cash in on a reward. US forces that patrol the same neighborhoods frequently encounter the same shopkeepers, residents, and police officers. Through that interaction, the Iraqis begin to trust the US forces, and a person who wants to provide information can supply it.

Another method for the casual source to begin providing information is through a "tips hotline," a telephone number set up for Iraq citizens to safely report on insurgents. In Iraq, both the Iraqi government and the coalition forces operated tips hotlines. The MNF–I hotline was operated by British police officers.

Whether encountered on a patrol or through a tips hotline, a casual source is usually concerned with a single situation and doesn't want to have a continuing relationship. But rarely does the person who is calling a tips hotline or who gives information to a soldier provide information that is sufficient for action. More information is usually needed.

Sometimes people who make a report can be encouraged to provide additional information on the topic they have reported. Often the possibility of a reward motivates the person making the initial contact with a patrol or the initial telephone call to continue reporting information.

Although much of the information supplied by a casual source is not specific enough to act on or doesn't address the insurgents US forces are hunting, some tips lead to big captures. One example of such a source was the person who provided information that led the SCID to locate a member of Saddam Hussein's regime who was one of the highest-ranking persons on the list of high-value targets, the people most actively hunted by US forces.

Fadhil Ibrahim Mahmud al-Mashadani had been the chief of the military bureau in Baghdad and was believed to be a critical link between the senior Baathist leaders hiding in Syria and insurgents within Iraq. Mashadani had kept a low profile, but apparently someone had recognized him. Despite this recognition, he might still be a free man but for the work of agents and analysts of the SCID.

Some of the SCID agents had become friendly with British police officers who operated the MNF–I tips hotline that was publicized in the Iraqi media as a way to report suspected insurgents and former regime members. British policemen supervised Iraqi employees who answered the telephone and took down the information that the policemen then analyzed. During one visit by a couple of SCID agents, a British officer lamented the difficulty he had in getting anyone in the MNF–I intelligence empire to pay attention to the many leads the tips hotline generated. Out of the several hundred personnel assigned to MNF–I intelligence, none paid a visit to the tips line operation or followed up on the tips generated by the British police operation.

Our agents sympathized with the British officer and promised to follow up when the next good lead came in. A few days later their empathy was rewarded when the British officer provided information about the possible whereabouts of Mashadani. Because Mashadani is a popular tribal name in Iraq, tracking down a Mashadani in Baghdad was a bit like looking for Mr. Smith in New York City.

Working with the British police officers, our agents began communicating with the informant who stood to receive the $200,000 reward publicly offered for Mashadani's capture. The agents working the case were helped in large part by Bill Cooper, an Army Special Forces noncommissioned officer who had fought in Afghanistan and northern Iraq during the initial invasion. Bill had retired from the army and immediately came to the SCID as an intelligence analyst. Bill studied prior reports by other intelligence units about Mashadani. Using the information Bill developed, the agents were able to ask the informant about certain details that led them to believe they might have the right person. The SCID agents developed a target package that was a summary of the information they had about Mashadani and his whereabouts and shared it with a coalition special operations element in Baghdad, Task Force–Black. Tina Taylor, an NCIS agent working on the investigation, went with soldiers from Task Force–Black to reconnoiter the area via helicopter.

Task Force–Black struck a farm northeast of Baghdad in a late-night raid. The next day, April 12, 2005, the MNF–I press office announced the capture of Mashadani. The announcement of the capture came on the same day as a surprise visit to Iraq by Secretary of Defense Donald Rumsfeld. I chuckled when I saw the capture of Mashadani included in the same CNN story as Rumsfeld's visit because I knew there would be conspiracy theorists who believed the US military had been sitting on Mashadani for a while and pulled him out to have good news when Rumsfeld visited. But as was always the case when high-ranking administration officials visited, I was surprised by Rumsfeld's arrival.

There were no more easy pickings from the British police tips hotline. After the success we had with Mashadani's capture, the MNF–I intelligence directorate assigned an army intelligence NCO full time to the tips hotline. There would be no more surprise successes by the SCID using information ignored by others.

Despite the limited time a casual source spends providing information for a limited time, such a source still exposes himself to danger. In one case, a person who provided information to a tips hotline that led to the capture of an insurgent was given a reward and cautioned to be careful and not display any new wealth. Two weeks later that informant was found shot to death. His death could have been for other reasons, but the timing of his death suggested he may have revealed his work for the coalition.

Keeping a source safe usually means keeping a source safe from himself. Any source, from the casual source to the more complex sources discussed below, is the greatest threat to his own safety. It is human nature to brag and to share secrets. Neither activity is good for a source.

Recruited Sources

A second type of source is one who is willing to maintain a longer relationship with his or her handler. This type of source may have previously provided information or may be approached by an intelligence officer who believes the person has access to the information the officer wants. When he or she is recruited, this type of source agrees to take direction from the source handler, to meet and communicate over an extended period of time, and often is asked to seek information on a variety of topics.

The recruited source serves as the eyes and ears for an intelligence organization. The goal is for the source to reliably report what he or she sees and hears. A recruited source can serve for weeks, months, or years. A recruited source, especially one reporting against an insurgency, is usually paid. In a place like Iraq, where the economy is sputtering and well-paying jobs are scarce, being a paid source can support the source and his or her family.

One purpose of a recruited source is to have a local person who is willing to be sent into areas to observe and report. The dangerous environment in Iraq, especially in areas prone to sectarian violence, imposed limits on where a source could go. Shiite sources didn't want to enter some of the Sunni neighborhoods that were insurgent strongholds because any stranger to such a neighborhood risked death. Another use of a recruited source was to corroborate information provided by another source. Often the source didn't know he was acting on another source's information, but if he did we did not provide enough details to identify the original source.

As you can see, a recruited source is asked to do a lot more than a casual source. Recruited sources are best handled by an experienced source handler. Recruited sources are trained about how to communicate with us and might be given a telephone, a GPS device, or other aids for collecting information, such as money for a car or for other expenses.

A source's loyalty can never be presumed. Agents and intelligence officers have to be careful the sources are not working against them. An intelligence agency or insurgent organization could have sent an Iraqi to be recruited by a US organization and to report back to an intelligence officer on the other side. In Iraq we had information that suggested US forces were bombarded with people controlled by Iranian intelligence or insurgent organizations that instructed the volunteers to offer to supply misinformation in order to tie up and mislead our intelligence organizations.

Assets

The third type of source is the most advanced. He or she is focused on major threats such as the highest level of the insurgency or on an issue that affects national level issues. I'll call this type of source an "asset." An asset requires skillful and deliberate selection and training. An asset receives more training than a recruited source and is often trained for a longer period of time before being directed against the intelligence officer's main target. As part of his training, the asset may be sent to perform a meeting or to collect information in contrived situations using US intelligence officers as role players in a situation the asset doesn't know is a test. By testing the asset in this way, the intelligence officers handling the asset can assess how well he or she follows instructions and whether he or she is noticeably nervous or gives clues to his association with US intelligence. Another way to test an asset or a recruited source is to have him or her submit to a polygraph examination.

In talking about sources and assets, the terminology varies among source handlers depending on their training and organization. AFOSI and NCIS personnel have the title "special agent" and are routinely referred to as agents. The army has a career field for "counterintelligence agents," and many of the army personnel assigned to the SCID were counterintelligence agents. Because "agent" was the most common term for source handler at the SCID, I have used this term to refer to the source handler and the terms "source" and "asset" to refer to the person who is collecting the information on behalf of the agent. But in many intelligence organizations, the source is frequently called an agent and the person handling or directing his activities is called an officer, intelligence officer, or case officer.

Despite the differences in terminology, the basic methods for handling sources or intelligence agents are essentially the same. But agents with a criminal investigation background and intelligence officers have different types of experience handling sources before being deployed to a war zone. Despite those differences in training and experience, both are able to succeed in HUMINT operations in an insurgency.

But before we leave this summary of different types of sources, keep in mind that sources are not bolts that can be easily categorized by length, diameter, and type. Sources can move up or down on the continuum of source handling that I have outlined above. Sources encountered through a tips hotline or by a patrol may have great access and provide excellent information even though they have very little training or testing. On the other hand, well-trained sources who have poor access to relevant information or targets waste the time of those handling them. One solution for better HUMINT is to move more sources up the scale, making them recruited sources or assets handled by experienced source handlers.

HANDLING A SOURCE

As a practical matter, a casual source can be handled by an infantryman. But the army has set up a substantial bureaucracy full of rules and prohibitions that make handling even a casual source difficult. Lt. Col. Douglas A. Ollivant is the battalion operations officer in Baghdad I mentioned earlier who noted limitations in the way Tactical HUMINT Teams were employed. Ollivant complained that if an Iraqi came to a US checkpoint and told soldiers that his neighbor was an insurgent attacking US forces, nobody in the entire battalion—including the battalion intelligence officer—was allowed to task the Iraqi with providing actionable intelligence.[19]

The issue of tasking is an example of the army's bureaucracy at work. Tasking a source means telling the source what information to gather and how to gather it, that is, giving the source a task to accomplish. As Ollivant recounted, under the army's system, neither the soldiers confronted with the walk-in source nor their superiors could ask the informant to obtain the specific location of the insurgent's house or to gather information that would allow US forces to continue to detain the insurgent if captured. Doing so would possibly result in disciplinary action against the soldiers who asked the informant to gather information. Instead, the army required that the battalion soldiers and their intelligence officer defer to a THT.[20]

THTs were manned by soldiers with a variety of backgrounds

and training. Many were young, with relatively few years of intelligence experience. Further, THTs were given many duties including interrogating detainees, recruiting and handling sources, and conducting investigations. Before their first combat tour, the experience of most army intelligence personnel handling sources was based on role playing done in school and during exercises. Even Lieutenant General Metz, the former commander of Multi-National Corps–Iraq, noted the lack of training by THTs in advanced source-handling techniques.[21] Training is a great equalizer in many areas of endeavor, and more training in handling sources would have benefited most THTs. But training goes only so far in intelligence operations and is a poor substitute for actual experience.

In contrast to the limited experience in source handling of many personnel in THTs (and among intelligence personnel assigned to other units), I encountered several National Guardsmen and reservists deployed to Iraq whose civilian careers were in law enforcement. These folks had much more experience evaluating, recruiting, and handling sources than the young troops frequently found in a THT. Sadly, most of these citizen soldiers with source-handling experience were not in the intelligence field so they were not handling sources.

Another problem with THTs noted by Ollivant was that local Iraqi officials want to deal with someone of importance. In the words of Ollivant, "[I]t is folly to believe that a prominent sheik, imam [Muslim religious leader], or businessman would want to speak with a sergeant."[22] I'm sure Ollivant meant no disrespect to the NCO corps, the backbone of the US military, but it is human nature to want to deal with the person in charge. Iraqis—and any local national in a country saddled with an insurgency—understand the US military rank structure and know that except for very small units, there is usually an officer leading the unit.

This is another area where wearing civilian clothing assisted the agents in the SCID. Although there were many Westerners who wore civilian clothing in Iraq, there weren't that many who showed up driving SUVs instead of Humvees, packing rifles, grenades, and radios, and equipped with their own translators. Detainees and sources picked up on the differences in dress and attitude. Because our best source handlers had experience or a natural talent at handling sources, they approached discussions with Iraqis with confidence and clarity. Sources and witnesses noticed the difference.

The confidence that comes from experience helped the SCID agents with another problem that perpetually faces source handlers. People are people, despite the culture or languages spoken. Many motivations and behaviors are the same. Lying, fabricating information, and providing information with the intent to settle a past wrong are stock in trade for sources around the world.

An agent or intelligence officer working with any source benefits from any prior experience dealing with people, but especially from time spent handling sources. An experienced agent knows how to describe to a source what to find and what details are crucial to remember. Training a source how to communicate with his or her handler in a way that doesn't disclose his affiliation with an intelligence agency is important. The best source handlers are good communicators, adjusting their words and manner to the source. Another skill that experienced agents bring to source handling is dealing with a cocky young man who thinks he is much smoother than he really is. Young, outgoing, and, often, overconfident men frequently are the most willing in any population to volunteer their services as a source. The allure of money or the thrill of being a "spy" motivates many. A firm, experienced source handler can cajole or intimidate a source, as required, to get the source to focus on the task at hand or to understand the measures the agent employs to prevent compromise of the source's affiliation with the government.

It's easier to deal with a source who has a healthy respect for what might happen to him or his family. But people with that attitude rarely become sources. Teaching an inexperienced but overconfident source is a situation a law enforcement officer who handled sources in the United States has previously encountered. For that reason, it was possible to convert an investigator who had handled criminal sources into an insurgent hunter conducting HUMINT with Iraqi sources.

Handling an asset, the highest-level source, requires the best intelligence and counterintelligence officers the military and the intelligence community has. An asset may be sent on trips with the people he is watching, even across borders. Some assets provide information that affects national policy. Normally an asset isn't recruited, or at least not used operationally, without an extensive background investigation, psychological evaluation, polygraph examination, and training. Those are pretty hard to pull off in Iraq or anywhere the United States will face an insurgency.

Background investigations can be done discreetly in the United States, Europe, and other parts of the world. Trying to develop independent information about an asset in Iraq was extraordinarily difficult. Even confirming residences, employment, military service, or family connections was difficult. Yet there are opportunities to use assets that are difficult to resist. Lengthy debriefings of what the asset claims to know that are backed up by a polygraph examination are sometimes the only course available for the intelligence officer handling an asset in an insurgency.

Using sources can be a real hit-or-miss proposition. Even among organizations like the SCID, with agents drawn from the ranks of army counterintelligence officers, the Air Force Office of Special

Investigations, and the Naval Criminal Investigative Service, not every intelligence officer could recruit or run a source.

Even before I went to Iraq, I knew from supervising investigators that fewer than half of the investigators I had supervised were good at handling sources. Even fewer were good at spotting, approaching, and recruiting a source. One example of a good source handler was Brad Upshaw. After college Brad had become a police officer in Florida, but a couple of years later was recruited into the AFOSI as a civilian investigator. With less than two years' experience as a federal investigator, Brad came to the SCID, where he took over a source from a departing agent.

The source had provided occasional information, but his information was not sufficient to identify or capture insurgents. Brad began by tasking the source and holding him responsible to report on those taskings at the next meeting. As odd as it seems, some source handlers fail because they don't remember what they asked the source to look for or don't ask follow-up questions. After a few meetings, Brad realized the source was on the periphery of some young Iraqi men claiming to be tough guys who were striking US forces. By tough guys, I mean they bragged in front of the source about killing another Iraqi. The propensity for violence suggested by their claim to have killed an Iraqi made me believe Brad's source was involved with men who were likely to be insurgents. Violence-prone criminals were drawn to the insurgency as a way to make money and an opportunity to engage in violence. Contrary to the propaganda of some Islamic terrorists, many insurgents were motivated by money and an innate evil, not by their religion.

ANALYSIS AND SOURCES

Brad's handling the source more efficiently was good, but it was only the first step. Remember the basic steps of intelligence: Collect information, understand information, and act on information. To help Brad understand the information, we assigned an intelligence analyst to work on the operation with him. When he wasn't busy with other duties, Brad had been trying to organize the information the source was providing into a link diagram. But the time he spent working with the source and on other matters left little time for exploiting the information—and exploiting information is what a good analyst can do.

Many analysts never get past the stage of being organizers and synthesizers of information. Most can draw some conclusions that are essentially summaries. But to be effective in counterinsurgency, an analyst must use the information from the source as a springboard. By comparing the source's reporting with the thousands of other intelligence reports generated in Iraq, the analyst can begin to put the information from the source into context.

Kathy Hecht was the analyst assigned to work with Brad against the cells of al-Qaeda in Iraq he was uncovering. Kathy was part of a wave of new analysts that hit the SCID in June 2005. Like many of the analysts, Kathy had gained her experience in the army by serving as an intelligence analyst for several years. But as a young woman with a pierced tongue, she stood apart from the mostly middle-aged male analysts who were being replaced by the group of analysts that included Kathy.

Although he liked Kathy, Brad was a bit hesitant about working with any analyst. Things had been going well the way they were. But Kathy soon proved her value to the operation by uncovering a lot of information that fleshed out the source reports and gave us a better idea of who we were working against. As time went on, Brad and Kathy developed respect for each other and worked together very well until Brad's departure in August.

ACTIONABLE INTELLIGENCE

For the third step in the intelligence sequence, acting on the information, Brad had to develop contact with someone who would be an action arm and conduct raids to capture insurgents. Brad had worked on the Mashadani case and had established a working relationship with several members of the special operations unit Task Force–Black. Coordinating with another group of warriors was natural for Brad because law enforcement officers frequently have to work with investigators and officers from other agencies. There is no central law enforcement agency that controls all police agencies. In law enforcement, things get done because of relationships and the friendships, trust, and respect that flows from those relationships.

Brad prepared a target package, which is a summary of the information he had developed. Task Force-Black operators had a lot of experience from working in other parts of the world. With their special training and experience, they were able to operate in the red zone and observe some of the locations Brad's source had reported. After corroborating the information, they struck in the middle of the night.

Brad's reporting indicated the insurgents Task Force–Black had captured were members of Abu Musab al-Zarqawi's organization, Tawhid wa'l-Jihad. As I mentioned in chapter 2, TWJ was also known by another set of initials, QJBR, which were the first letters of the Arabic words for "Organization of Jihad's Base in the Country of the Two Rivers." This organization was eventually known as al-

Qaeda in Iraq. Brad had started some excellent work that would continue. Brad and Kathy started supplying information to Task Force–Black that resulted in the capture of AQI insurgents.

FOCUS AND MOTIVATION

The series of AQI insurgents captured because of the information supplied by Brad's source were a good example of another issue that develops in HUMINT. Even units that have a decent source program often are not in control of exactly who they are hunting. The intelligence officers are just accepting targets of opportunity. Much of the action taken today by many units results from who walked up to a checkpoint yesterday or last week. That type of HUMINT is valuable and useful, but it only goes so far. Ralph Peters, a retired army officer who writes extensively about military issues, saw the same problem when he served as an intelligence officer in Washington: "Intelligence products were tailored to the available information, when we should have been demanding information to support our genuine intelligence needs."[23]

Early in my time at the SCID I concluded that we were in the position of working against the targets of opportunity that our sources were giving us. At one meeting of some of the SCID staff, I challenged them to identify targets and then drive our sourcing in the direction of those targets. An analyst I respect a great deal was the only one willing to speak up as most of the people at the meeting suddenly had an urge to intensely study their notes. It doesn't work that way, the analyst said.

The analyst was half right. For many agents and organizations, it doesn't work that way. But as Brad Upshaw was able to prove, insurgent cells can be successfully targeted. By keeping the source motivated and focused on the AQI cells that we were targeting, Brad began a campaign of pulling insurgents away from their bomb making and killing and putting them in Abu Ghraib.

I have noted that Brad kept his source motivated. That is harder than it may seem. Sources have different motivations. Of course money is often number one in the hearts of many sources. But you would be surprised how many sources, even in Iraq, were motivated to a certain extent by the excitement of undercover work. When I mentioned the difficulty of dealing with an over-confident source, this is the type of source I had in mind. Whether in the United States or in Iraq, there are some sources who seek the rush of walking into a room hoping to find something to report, but also knowing that if the other people in the room knew a source was in their group, his life span would be measured in hours or minutes.

Other motivations for some sources included the desire to gain favor with the United States for future benefit. Unfortunately, the rigid State Department rules for visas and our country's immigration laws make it impossible for most Iraqis to even visit the United States, let alone immigrate. Even sources who provide considerable information that saves American lives can't be promised a chance to immigrate to the United States.

The agents and analysts at the SCID had to sort through these varying motivations and what the sources reported in order to determine whether we were paying money for made-up information and whether our source was working for us or for insurgents or Iranian intelligence.

Part of the source's motivation was his or her family, but families and friends were also a big operational concern. We expected sources to keep their association with us secret from their parents, spouses, and children, as well their employers, coworkers, friends, and neighbors. Other parts of the source's life, especially family and job, controlled how much time and interest a source had to devote to his work for us. Our sources were bombarded with the same problems all Iraqis had. They had to make a living in a devastated economy, cope with limited electricity and other infrastructure problems, and avoid sectarian violence and criminal gangs making money from kidnapping or robbery. Because of these other concerns, sources weren't exactly standing by the phone waiting to hear what we wanted them to do.

SELF-INFLICTED HUMINT PROBLEMS

If you haven't worked with sources, you can't believe how temperamental and hardheaded they can be. This is one example of why source-handling experience is vital to a senior intelligence officer's understanding of the total intelligence picture. The army has a field manual for everything, and some in the army are inclined to believe that HUMINT can be managed like any other activity. Some think it is just a matter of hiring enough people and supervising them according to some manual.

A senior NCO, colonel, or general is used to barking orders and having them followed. It doesn't work that way with HUMINT. Recruiting and working with sources is an extension of human interaction. People who are not comfortable meeting new people and working with people don't adapt to HUMINT very well. One of the agents at the SCID was an excellent investigator, but didn't take to source recruitment. Gary Rodriguez, the SCID operations officer, told me of his efforts to help the agent to recruit a source. Later in the day, Gary told me he had encouraged the same agent to overcome his shyness and to talk to a woman he had been admiring from a distance. I told Gary the two were related. If you can't talk to a pretty woman while looking her in the eye, you can't recruit a source. Both require interpersonal skills that some of us lack. People who have not recruited a source don't understand that most people can't recruit sources.

Another example of the need to understand the human part of HUMINT involved information from Iraq government officials. We received much information from Iraqi police and army personnel. Although we met such officials openly, they told us things their superiors may not have wanted us to know. Most often it was the very information that their superiors wanted kept quiet that was the most valuable to coax from them.

Some of these government officials enjoyed a drink after work despite Islam's prohibition on alcohol. General Order 1 prohibited US military personnel and civilian personnel assigned to the Department of Defense from possessing or consuming alcohol in Iraq. Although DOD personnel could easily obtain alcohol from several stores or restaurants in the Green Zone, people who drank took the risk of being disciplined if caught. About a month after I arrived at the SCID, an incident involving a couple of our personnel caught drinking gave me reason to remind our troops that General Order 1 applied to us even though we wore civilian clothing and performed a unique mission.

One of my team leaders asked about drinking with Iraqis when invited to a function where alcohol was served and the Iraqis were drinking. Well, that's different, I said—after all, it's part of our intelligence gathering. Not accepting an invitation for a drink could be considered insulting or curious. But I wanted to comply with the rules, so I went to an army lawyer on the MNF–I staff. He assured me that getting an exception to the order would not be a problem. After all, units would get exceptions to allow troops to have two (not three or four) beers for special occasions. The lawyer instructed me on the paperwork I needed to submit.

The approval had to come from General DeFreitas, the chief of intelligence for MNF–I and the first general officer in my chain of command. Of course, you don't just walk into the general's office with a sheet of paper and point to where he should sign. All paperwork had to be submitted through the staff. About a week or two after I submitted the request, I received a call from a colonel who worked for DeFreitas and supervised logistics and administrative matters for the intelligence directorate. The colonel told me that the general didn't want us drinking with Iraqis. The tone of her voice conveyed the message that I was nuts for asking. Here was another example of an intelligence officer who doesn't understand where the best information comes from—actually, there were two intelligence officers who didn't understand: the colonel and the general.

Neither the CIA nor the State Department had to worry because General Order 1 didn't apply to them. In fact, both organizations had bars on their premises. At the US Embassy, controlled by the State Department, there was a large swimming pool next to the palace used to house the embassy. At the swimming pool there was a bar that was open in the afternoon and evening. Military personnel walked by the bar knowing their State Department counterparts were enjoying a cocktail at the end of the day. Apparently the idea of honoring our Muslim hosts and their religious taboos—which was one of the reasons for General Order 1—didn't apply to the State Department.

The CIA had developed a better use of its bar. Instead of making it available to just anybody, like the State Department bar, it was in the heart of the CIA compound in the Green Zone. Special passes were required to get into the compound, even for a guest who was escorted. It didn't surprise me to learn that attractive women were supplied with passes allowing them to visit the bar, while others were left at the gate. It wasn't quite as bad as the attractive people being invited into the hot club in Manhattan, but the same principle applied.

Playing "Gotcha"

Although the disparity in policies about alcohol consumption is amusing, it's important to note that my experience attempting to get an exception to General Order 1 was an example of how army and Department of Defense rules work against the use of HUMINT. There was a lot of infrastructure built to monitor and control a limited number of source handlers and intelligence gatherers. In addition to the roughly 132 US Army THTs, several Marine Corps HETs, and an untold number of intelligence officers and NCOs assigned to battalions, brigades, and divisions, the MNF–I intelligence staff at Camp Victory numbered in the hundreds. Many MNF–I intelligence staff were under the Combined Intelligence Operations Center, which analyzed and coordinated intelligence in Iraq. Within the CIOC was an office of people devoted to reading the information reported in intelligence information reports and assessing the credibility of the source and the reliability of the information.

Sadly, the assessment activity had been reduced to a game of "gotcha," with reviewers quick to criticize the handling of a source and the quality of the information provided by him or her. The report reviewed by the analyst who was grading intelligence reports was the culmination of much field activity. In the SCID, a source meet required scheduling the meeting over the telephone via a translator. Then our security element and the agent handling the source planned a mission to the location of the meeting and traveled through the red zone, exposing everyone in the mission to EFPs, IEDs, small-arms fire, and traffic accidents. If the source provided information that was worth reporting, the SCID agent would have to write an intelligence information report, which is a very structured report in a format established by the DIA.

The agent's team chief, the team analyst, the SCID reports officer, and the SCID operations officer all reviewed the report before it was e-mailed to Camp Victory to be officially released as an intelligence information report. But at Camp Victory our reports were reviewed and graded by people assigned to the CIOC. Because of a shortage of military personnel, much of the grading was done by contractors.

Most of the contractors doing this review work had no experience handling sources in the Iraq theater. In fact, most analysts have never handled a source anywhere. But these analysts didn't hesitate to critique the reports, sometimes with comments like "This doesn't tell me anything I don't know." Reviewers who wrote comments like that failed to recognize that we were duty bound to report information that answered the priority intelligence requirements that others on the MNF–I staff had written, regardless of whether some other unit had already reported similar information.

Such criticisms also failed to recognize that considerable intelligence could be gained by culling bits of information from several intelligence reports from different units. We realized the information often wasn't new, but we reported it in order to corroborate other intelligence reports and because we were continuing to task the source to provide further information.

Rules for Tasking a Source

The tasking of sources could be an Alice in Wonderland experience in the army bureaucracy. I've already mentioned Lieutenant Colonel Ollivant's dismay at not being able to task a walk-in source to go back and get the address of an insurgent. Under the army's intelligence rules, a person who had not been formally recruited in an exacting process could not be tasked. In other words, a person who had supplied information to an army unit and appeared willing to take direction could not be told what to look for, who to seek out, or what information to report, unless a THT did it.

In one discussion, some very experienced army intelligence officers left Tom Reid, the SCID operations officer before Gary Rodriguez's arrival, and me dumbfounded when they argued vehemently that before formal recruitment, a potential source or volunteer couldn't be tasked. But, according to the intelligence officers, the source could be "sensitized" by telling him what the handler is interested in. "Sensitizing the source" required the conversation to be worded in a way that it both satisfied a "legal requirement" that the handler not tell the source what to do, but also gave the source an idea of what information to provide. It was a ridiculous exercise in semantics.

The concept of "legal requirement" and the idea that it is illegal to task a person who isn't formally recruited as a source is a self-inflicted wound upon the army's intelligence system. It apparently dates back to 1970, when a former army intelligence officer exposed the army's covert Civil Disturbance Collection Program, which involved hundreds of counterintelligence agents collecting information on antiwar demonstrators. An investigation of the army's activities was summarized in a US Senate report. The Senate investigating committee found that up to fifteen hundred army intelligence agents were involved in monitoring civilian protests against the Vietnam War and that agents had covertly joined and participated in the activities of several antiwar groups, including fifty-eight army intelligence agents who were inserted into the demonstrations that took place in Chicago during the Democratic National Convention of 1968.[24]

As a result of the army's activities, the Defense Investigative Review Council was created to oversee all military investigative activity. Later a series of presidential executive orders created the concept of "intelligence oversight" and another government office that administered intelligence oversight replaced the Defense Investigative Review Council. The latest executive order, EO 12333, is applied to the Department of Defense in a regulation that prohibits a variety of activities directed at US citizens and residents.[25]

But all the intelligence oversight prohibitions were directed at protecting US citizens, not Iraqi insurgents. The army's desire to never again be embarrassed and investigated like it was following the dismantling of its Civil Disturbance Collection Program caused it to establish rules that go far beyond what are needed. These rules were based on army policy created by overly cautious lawyers and intelligence leaders and are not based on federal law. These rules made it difficult to operate, unless, as the brigade combat team commander described below, one chose to go it alone.

The lack of effective sharing of information resulted from the army's rigid intelligence organization that was designed for firm control of subordinate units by intelligence leaders, not for operations against a decentralized enemy. It did not encourage the sharing of information. The organization of the army intelligence system may have worked well in a conventional war, but it was not well suited for attacking an insurgency. Counterinsurgency work demanded HUMINT, and in order to be effective, HUMINT and other intelligence had to be shared and coordinated. The army had created an organization to coordinate HUMINT: the HUMINT Operations Cell (HOC), which in Iraq was part of the intelligence structure of the Multi-National Corps–Iraq.

Although the HOC should have been a beehive of coordination between units that were operating human sources, it was ineffective in large part because it didn't encourage sharing of information. The HOC was intended to supervise the activities of the many THTs under the control of the corps. Because the SCID, the DIA, and the intelligence apparatus of the special operations forces in Iraq were not under the control of the MNC–I, the HOC didn't attempt to coordinate our operations with those of the THTs that reported up to the HOC. This lack of coordination was a big breakdown in the intelligence system.

I encountered the HOC's lack of cooperation after I suggested that some of our operations in Baghdad be coordinated with the Baghdad-area THTs so that we could take advantage of any sources who might be working targets aligned with what we were doing. Our agents who approached the local THTs were told they couldn't make the decision to share information. It seemed that one cause for the reluctance was fear of sharing a source. One tenet of source handling I learned early in my career is that a source belongs to the United States, not to a particular source handler or unit. I understood the strong resistance to sharing a source or turning it over to another unit—recruiting sources was difficult and intelligence personnel were evaluated on how many sources they recruited and the information produced. But turf battles prevented sources from being used as effectively as they could have been.

When SCID agents ran into resistance by THT personnel who said they couldn't share information without the permission of their supervisors, we met with the next level of supervision for THTs, the operational management team (OMT). An OMT is composed of an officer and a small staff who supervise several THTs. We brought personnel from the local OMT to the SCID office and I presented a briefing on the SCID operations and explained why we were seeking to exchange information. I told them our agents and analysts were standing by to exchange information and after the briefing the soldiers from OMT left us with the impression that information would soon be exchanged. I later learned that the OMT leader decided he didn't have the authority to share the information.

Continuing my pursuit to exchange information and improve source operations, I next spoke to the intelligence officer for the MNC–I, an army colonel who had spent his career in intelligence. He directed me to the HOC chief to provide the specifics of what I desired. Meetings with the HOC went nowhere. The entire experience with the THT, the OMT, the corps intelligence officer, and the HOC reminded me of my days in Korea dealing with the Korean National Police and the Korean Agency for National Security Planning (the Korean CIA). The Koreans I met were very polite and hospitable; when I made a request, I was almost always told it would be granted. But for some of my requests, the information never came. I came to learn that in many Asian cultures, it is impolite to refuse a visitor's request. Instead of having an argument, it is simpler to agree and then not comply.

The response of the THTs, the OMT, the HOC, and the corps intelligence officer was a similar process of appearing to cooperate while intending to ignore or actively prevent cooperation. Instead of telling us the THTs wouldn't share source information or coordinate source operations, everyone deferred to someone else or simply put coordination with the SCID on the back burner.

Such decisions damaged the battle against the insurgency. The SCID and the DIA had the most experienced military source handlers in the Iraq theater because those source handlers were constantly working with sources and assets in their duties before being deployed. By contrast, many THT troops didn't have an opportunity to handle sources except when they were in a combat theater. As a result, inexperienced source handlers at the THT level were being led by an HOC composed of personnel with no more experience in HUMINT than the THT.

The system of the HOC, the OMT, and the THTs was designed for a very centralized collection of information about a single enemy. It doesn't work well against a decentralized networked set of insurgent groups that have conflicting goals and strategies. By retaining strong centralized control of sourcing, the army prevents a miscue similar to what happened with its intelligence personnel at Abu Ghraib, but it sacrifices effectiveness. Unfortunately, it is soldiers and marines on patrol and at forward operating bases who make those sacrifices.

Intelligence units with theaterwide responsibility, such as the SCID or the DIA, should be able to obtain information from other units, including information about the source, and have the ability to task the source. A theater-level intelligence organization doesn't have to take over the source. It only needs to be able to task and more directly handle the source. If such a process was implemented, the original source handler would remain in contact with the source, but another agent or intelligence officer might accompany the original source handler or review the specific taskings to provide to the source. By working with more-experienced source handlers, the NCOs and warrant officers in the THTs would learn more about their intelligence craft and become more effective for their own operations.

THE MILITARY INTELLIGENCE BUREAUCRACY IS THREATENED

But that's not the way the military intelligence system worked in Iraq. And when the intelligence system doesn't work, infantrymen and others responsible for frontline operations take matters into their own hands. The experiences of a brigade combat team commander illustrate how far they will go. Col. Ralph O. Baker was the commander of the 2nd Brigade Combat Team of the army's 1st Armored Division, which was posted in Baghdad. After exposing his troops to considerable danger by searching hundreds of residences in an area near Haifa Street, which was one of the most dangerous areas in Baghdad, Baker realized there had to be a better way. The neighborhood sweep conducted during the night caused great upset to the Iraqi citizens the United States was hoping to win over, but found only a few weapons and a handful of suspects.[26]

The intelligence system Baker's brigade combat team brought to Iraq was designed to identify conventional enemy formations, and his intelligence personnel were trained to analyze and predict what the enemy would do based on understanding the enemy's equipment and doctrine. Confronted by an insurgency, the intelligence system Baker was given simply didn't work.[27]

Recognizing that HUMINT was the only intelligence that would allow his unit to be effective in its mission, Baker led his soldiers in the development of an extensive network of human sources. So important was HUMINT that Baker wrote, "[S]uch human sources of intelligence represent a critical capability that no ISR [intelligence, surveillance, and reconnaissance] technology, no matter how sophisticated or advanced, can match."[28]

Because HUMINT operations require much manpower to collect and analyze information, Baker moved personnel from other careers, such as infantry and armor soldiers, cooks, communication specialists, and mechanics, into intelligence operations. In particular, Baker noted, National Guard and reserve soldiers have unique skills and experiences, including law enforcement and computers, that make such soldiers excellent choices to augment intelligence operations.[29]

Remember Lieutenant Colonel Ollivant, the battalion operations officer who complained about not being able to task a source? Baker solved that problem by operating independently and developing informants among members of political parties, government officials, prostitutes, police officers, retired Iraqi army officers, and businessmen. Sources were given GPS devices, digital cameras, and cell phones. In addition to using telephones, Baker's team took advantage of the growing number of Internet cafes to communicate with informants by e-mail.[30]

Baker wrote in a *Military Review* article that HUMINT operations were not just a supporting effort, but were decisive components of US strategy. To conclude the article, he wrote, "No longer can we allow our greater comfort with conventional combat operations to minimize these decisive components of a winning COIN [counterinsurgency] strategy."[31]

Contrast the flexibility of this brigade combat team that adapted to fighting an insurgency with the intelligence system that continues to favor technology and poorly manages HUMINT. United States soldiers and marines are the finest ground troops in the world. But they are not supported by an intelligence system that is willing to grasp the lessons learned by those on the front lines in the battle against insurgencies. Snared in a web of bureaucracy and a culture that doesn't encourage decentralized operations or sharing of information, the military intelligence system flounders when it faces an insurgency.

By not focusing on producing HUMINT that can assist frontline units, the military's intelligence system is in danger of becoming irrelevant. As more commanders adopt the lead of commanders like Colonel Baker, the military intelligence system loses control over the activity that it claims as its core competency, the collection and analysis of intelligence. This is richly ironic considering that much of the bureaucracy was created by the army's intelligence organizations in order to maintain control over their own intelligence personnel. But by overcontrolling intelligence personnel and not properly employing the most effective intelligence discipline available to fight an insurgency, the military intelligence community cedes control of HUMINT to the untrained and the inexperienced.

Human intelligence can be done by almost anyone. But doing it well requires training and experience. Field units that are in the best position to recruit sources could benefit immensely from the experience and training that might be gained from an organization with experienced source handlers and trained intelligence officers. But instead, the rigid intelligence apparatus and the military's poor management of HUMINT have forced operational units to create their own HUMINT capability. Central to this problem is a cultural inability to share information. We will look at the issue in chapter 7.

NOTES

1. Alec Klein, "The Army's $200 Billion Makeover—March to Modernize Proves Ambitious and Controversial," *Washington Post*, December 7, 2007, p. A1.

2. Ibid.

3. Ibid.

4. Thomas X. Hammes, *The Sling and the Stone: On War in the 21st Century* (St. Paul, MN: Zenith Press, 2004), p. 6.

5. Thomas F. Metz, Jerry Tait, and J. Michael McNealy, "OIF II: Intelligence Leads Successful Counterinsurgency Operations," *Military Intelligence Professional Bulletin*, July–September 2005, http://www.universityofmilitaryintelligence.us/mipb/article.asp?articleID=172&issueID=12 (accessed December 8, 2007).

6. Ralph O. Baker, "HUMINT-Centric Operations: Developing Actionable Intelligence in the Urban Counterinsurgency Environment," *Military Review*, March–April 2007, p. 13.

7. Douglas A. Ollivant and Eric D. Chewning, "Producing Victory: Rethinking Conventional Forces in COIN Operations," *Military Review*, July–August 2006, p. 57.

8. David J. Clark, "The Vital Role of Intelligence in Counterinsurgency Operations," March 15, 2006, p. 2, http://www.strategicstudiesinstitute.army.mil/pdf files/ksil309.pdf (accessed February 23, 2008).

9. Ibid., p. 17.

10. Ibid.

11. Bruce V. Bigelow, "Titan's Next Move—Troubled San Diego Defense Contractor Aims to Restore Shaken Investors' Faith," *San Diego Union-Tribune*, July 18, 2004, p. H-1.

12. David Washburn, "L-3 Protests Loss of Contract—Company Provided Translators to Military," *San Diego Union-Tribune*, December 29, 2006, p. C-1.

13. Bruce V. Bigelow, "Titan Corp. Reports Turnaround 1st Quarter—San Diego Company Logs 23% Revenue Surge," *San Diego Union-Tribune*, April 29, 2005, p. C-1.

14. Ibid.

15. P. W. Singer, "Outsourcing War," *Foreign Affairs* 84, no. 2 (April 2005).

16. Washburn, "L-3 Protests Loss of Contract."

17. Bigelow, "Titan Corp. Reports Turnaround 1st Quarter."

18. Washburn, "L-3 Protests Loss of Contract."

19. Ollivant and Chewning, "Producing Victory," pp. 57–58.

20. Ibid., p. 58.

21. Metz, Tait, and McNealy, "OIF II: Intelligence Leads Successful Counterinsurgency Operations."

22. Ollivant, "Producing Victory," p. 58.

23. Ralph Peters, *Beyond Terror: Strategy in a Changing World* (Mechanicsburg, PA: Stackpole Books, 2002), p. 196.

24. United States Senate, Final Report of the Select Committee to Study

Governmental Operations with Respect to Intelligence Activities, book 3, http://www.icdc.com/~paulwolf/cointelpro/churchfinalreportIIIk.htm (accessed March 2, 2008).

25. DoD Directive 5240.1R, http://www.defenselink.mil/atsdio/documents/5240.html (accessed March 2, 2008).

26. Baker, "HUMINT-Centric Operations," p. 12.

27. Ibid., p. 13.

28. Ibid., p. 14.

29. Ibid., p. 16.

30. Ibid., p. 18.

31. Ibid., p. 21.

Chapter 6

MORE HUMINT

Human sources provide much information to intelligence officers and the troops who depend on good intelligence. But HUMINT is more than covert human sources. Any activity that involves people telling us what they have seen or heard is a form of HUMINT. HUMINT also comes from prisoners, through investigations, and from liaison with other coalition forces, especially Iraqi organizations.

Baghdad was a great spot for meeting important people. Iraq drew many officials who had reasons to visit a war zone, or at least thought they did. Visitors included senators, representatives, congressional staff, military officials who represented organizations that supplied people or equipment to the war effort, and senior members of the administration. The secretaries of defense and state visited Iraq periodically, but more often visitors were a step or two below the cabinet secretary level.

Visitors whose primary interest was intelligence operations were hosted by the MNF–I deputy chief of staff for intelligence and his staff. The intelligence staff would develop an agenda of meetings and visits for the visitors, depending on their particular interests. Intelligence operations also attracted the attention of visitors who were hosted by the US ambassador or other officials and they sometimes asked for briefings or meetings regarding aspects of intelligence.

Frequently, the SCID was on the schedule for such visitors. I briefed many of them, including three deputy directors of national intelligence, the undersecretary of defense for intelligence, the director of intelligence for the Joint Chiefs of Staff, the commander of the army's Intelligence and Security Command, and, as I mentioned in a previous chapter, Philip Zelikow, the counselor to the secretary of state. In order to save time on the schedule, visitors would sometimes spend several hours in a conference room in the Republican Palace, where the US Embassy was housed, and a series of people would come to brief them.

HUMINT FROM PRISONERS

At one such briefing where the commander of a DIA intelligence unit was present because he was briefing the same visitor, I mentioned that SCID analysts and agents were frequently in touch with the analysts and interrogators at the 3rd Infantry Division's interrogation facility to compare the information obtained from interrogations with information from our sources. We sought the information from interrogation of prisoners in order to know where to direct the attention of our sources. The person being briefed asked the DIA commander if his unit did something similar. It did not. After the subject of their sourcing was captured, the DIA unit moved on to other targets using information developed from their sources.

I was a bit surprised at that answer and mentioned it to Kathy

Hecht, the civilian analyst who was doing much of the analysis for the SCID's work against al-Qaeda in Iraq cells. Like other SCID analysts, Kathy had established a good working relationship with the interrogators and analysts at the division interrogation facility (DIF). Kathy and Brad Upshaw, the agent whose source had been the start of our work against AQI, worked closely with the DIF to ensure that when a prisoner was captured as a result of the work of the SCID, the interrogators had a copy of our target package and any information we had about the activities and associates of the prisoner.

Kathy had learned from a DIF analyst that the SCID's coordination and sharing of information with the DIF was not a common practice. Many times the interrogators and analysts at the DIF had the barest of facts to work with when beginning their interrogation of the prisoners. Having interrogated criminal suspects, I knew that increasing the amount of information the interrogator had about the suspect increased the odds that the interrogation would produce information.

If a prisoner was captured by a line army unit, the prisoner normally went to a brigade interrogation facility for several days to a few weeks. Some prisoners might be released after initial questioning. Prisoners who continued in the system were then passed to the next highest level, the DIF. After interrogation at the DIF, prisoners that were to remain in detention were sent to Abu Ghraib, near the Baghdad International Airport, or Camp Bucca in far southern Iraq. The army had interrogators and translators at each of the three levels. Intelligence analysts assisted the interrogators. Because the army did not have sufficient numbers of interrogators to supply all of its needs, many of the interrogators and analysts were civilian contractors.

Many of the prisoners captured as a result of the SCID's work skipped the stop at a brigade interrogation facility. Prisoners captured by Task Force–Black, which was a special operations unit to which the SCID provided intelligence, were sent directly to the DIF. Task Force–Black was part of Task Force 145, which was composed of special-operations forces and CIA operatives who pursued high-value targets such as Saddam Hussein and Abu Musab al-Zarqawi. Many prisoners taken by Task Force 145 were interrogated at the task force's own interrogation facility. But after the task force had extracted what it wanted, they took the prisoners to the DIF at Camp Victory near the BIAP, which was operated by the 3rd Infantry Division. A 3rd ID intelligence officer mentioned to me that sometimes the task force would fly their prisoners to the 3rd ID's interrogation facility and drop them off with not much more information than the name of the prisoner. With no idea who the prisoners were, why they had been detained, or what they should be questioned about, the DIF was in a difficult position. The task force's habit of dropping off such prisoners had increased to the point that the intelligence officer had threatened to refuse to accept any more prisoners from the task force if it didn't provide more information about the circumstances of the prisoners' capture.

The protocols of prisoner handling violated by the task force were part of a large set of rules and practices the army had developed for handling detainees. A supercharged bureaucracy for prisons had resulted from the investigations and news reports that followed the disclosure of the abuse of prisoners by prison guards and military intelligence personnel at Abu Ghraib in 2004. The army's official investigation determined that "numerous incidents of sadistic, blatant, and wanton criminal abuses were inflicted on several detainees" by several members of the military police guard force and recommended that a single commander be responsible for detainee operations throughout the Iraq Theater of Operations.[1] Task Force 134 became the organization in charge of all detainee operations in Iraq. In response to recommendations of the officer who investigated the Abu Ghraib prisoner abuses, Task Force 134 created stringent standard operating procedures for detainee operations.

Another army investigation uncovered prisoner abuse by members of Task Force 145, the organization that had caused the 3d ID problems when it dropped off prisoners. Retired army colonel Stuart A. Herrington, former commander of the army's Foreign Counterintelligence Activity, conducted an investigation and found that the task force had abused detainees throughout Iraq. At the time of Herrington's report the task force was known as Task Force 121, but it later changed its designation to Task Force 145. In a comment that anticipated the new counterinsurgency manual that would be published years later, Herrington warned in his report to the army that such abuse of prisoners inflamed the insurgency instead of quelling it.[2]

Leadership failures that allowed the prisoner abuse at Abu Ghraib led to strict rules that stifled effective exploitation of the prisoners who had information that could have been used to counter the insurgency. It was another self-inflicted wound. One particular SCID investigation is a good example of rules that enveloped the prison and interrogation operations. The SCID investigated simultaneous bombings of a café and market in the Green Zone on October 14, 2004, that killed at least five people, including four Americans.[3] The investigation had resulted in the detention of some insurgents, but the SCID was still investigating others believed to be involved in the bombings. After the capture and initial interrogation of some of the people involved in the bombings, those prisoners had been moved to Camp Bucca, south of Basra.

From studying intelligence reports and the results of the SCID investigation, the SCID's analyst who had worked with the investigators on the case uncovered information that indicated the prisoner had more information than he had disclosed during initial interrogation. Because of the complexity of the investigation, the analyst thought interrogation by the SCID agents would be more productive than submitting questions to interrogators at the prison.

The prisoner was at Camp Bucca, in far southern Iraq, and in order to make the prisoner available for more questioning, the analyst submitted a request through several layers of bureaucracy to get him transferred to Abu Ghraib, which is on the outskirts of Baghdad. Weeks of working with the detainee bureaucracy succeeded in having the prisoner moved to Abu Ghraib. But the SCID agents were not able to interrogate the prisoner. Although the agents were trained in interviewing witnesses and interrogating suspects in criminal and counterintelligence matters, army rules mandated that only interrogators who had gone through the army's prisoner interrogation training, which lasts several months, could interrogate prisoners at facilities under the control of Task Force 134.

But the SCID analyst found a gray area in the rules: The Task Force 134 rules didn't apply at the 3d ID's interrogation facility. By checking the prisoner out of Abu Ghraib and transporting him to the DIF at Camp Victory, the SCID agents could interrogate the prisoner. Finally, after all of the analyst's work, SCID agents interrogated the prisoner. But despite all the effort to move the prisoner, little usable information resulted from the interrogation.

That experience with the Task Force 134 bureaucracy and our attempt to interrogate a prisoner already detained for several months confirmed my theory about getting information from prisoners. Prisoners suspected of participating in the insurgency are most likely to disclose information during the early stages of capture. The shock and disorientation of capture is powerful, but it begins wearing off within hours and almost completely dissipates in a matter of weeks or months. Continued interrogation of prisoners captured during counterinsurgency efforts over a long period rarely yields more than the information obtained in the first few months of captivity.

In addition to becoming more accustomed to their status as prisoners, detainees who enter the general population of large prisons at Abu Ghraib and Camp Bucca are exposed to more hardened fighters. In the large prisons the detainees are often interrogated less frequently than in the DIF, where a detainee may be interrogated several times a week. When transferred to a large prison the new detainees are able to talk with more experienced prisoners in an environment that is less restrictive than the DIF. As a result of these changes, the spirits of the detainees rally in many cases and they become more resistant to interrogation. The detainee begins to have the advantage in interrogations because he has assimilated to the experience of captivity, is less likely to be interrogated, and, when he is interrogated, faces an interrogator who frequently is a young soldier who may have little knowledge of the detainee's background.

The problem of how to extract information from large numbers of prisoners without making the prisoners more of a threat was not unique to prisons in Iraq that were operated by the United States. Saddam Hussein's regime encountered similar issues in its efforts to imprison Shiite resisters and other dissidents.

Many of those captured by Saddam's regime entered prison largely uneducated as to how to effectively oppose the government. Many of the Shiites sent to prison had been raised in a secular society and were only nominally religious. In prison, they encountered fervently religious Shiites who followed the fundamental Islamic teachings of Iran's Grand Ayatollah Khomeini and his successors. The nominally religious prisoners were sometimes indoctrinated into radical Islamic beliefs by prisoners who were dedicated to the overthrow of Saddam's regime. The new prisoners received instruction in religion and were exposed to people who knew much about bomb making and other tactics to resist the regime. On occasion, relationships forged in prison continued upon a prisoner's release, and a prisoner who had entered with not much more than hard feelings about the regime exited prison as an effective and hardened opponent to the regime.

Similarly, many imprisoned Sunni insurgents whose opposition to the United States and the new Shitte-dominated Iraq government was grounded in economics or pride were exposed to Sunni jihadists who occupied the same cells and prison grounds. This is particularly important because many of the Iraqi prisoners once held by the United States have been released. As Elaine Grossman reported in *Inside the Pentagon*, as of July 2007, US and Iraqi government officials had released approximately forty-four thousand of sixty-five thousand suspected Iraqi insurgents or sectarian killers who were detained at the theater level since March 2003.[4]

The problem of the Islamic radicalization of prisoners has spread to the Western world. An influx of Islamic terrorists into the British prison system has caused concern that such prisoners may indoctrinate susceptible young prisoners in radical beliefs. Richard Reid, the "shoe bomber," was radicalized while serving a sentence for a petty crime. Similarly, Muktar Said Ibrahim, the leader of the group responsible for the attempted bombings of the London Underground on July 21, 2005, was radicalized in a British prison. Other European countries have reported similar problems.[5]

HUMINT FROM INVESTIGATIONS

Some of the prisoners detained by US forces were detained because of investigations of insurgent attacks. Another form of HUMINT is information that is developed during investigations. As mentioned in chapter 3, restoring law and order as a means to protect the population is the highest priority of the new counterinsurgency policy adopted by the United States. The ability to effectively conduct investigations is the police skill that is most necessary for counterinsurgency warfare. As Colonel Clark noted in his study of intelligence in counterinsurgency actions, the police work needed to fight an insurgency "is complex detective work involving surveillance, the recruitment and management of informants, informal questioning and solicitation, detainee operations, and the formal interrogation of suspected insurgents and their associates. This is not routine law enforcement. The police commander must be more police detective than anything else."[6]

But as important as investigations are, they were difficult to effectively conduct in an unsettled environment like Iraq.

Jeffrey Ake

A kidnapping of an American in April 2005 was an example of how difficult investigating in the red zone could be. On April 11, 2005, Jeffrey Ake was kidnapped from a water treatment plant in Taji, a city about twelve miles north of Baghdad. Ake owned a company in LaPorte, Indiana, that made water-bottling equipment. At least for Westerners, bottled water was a necessity, not a luxury, in Iraq. The tap water delivered by the water system was not safe to drink. Insurgents appeared at a water plant where Ake was working to repair the equipment and took him, according to several Iraqis who witnessed the abduction.

The SCID was asked by the US Embassy's hostage working group to provide investigators to interview the Iraqi witnesses at the water plant as soon as possible. The hostage working group coordinated the response to kidnappings of nonmilitary personnel. Like so many government functions in Iraq, the hostage working group was manned by two very competent contract employees who worked for the embassy. They collected information and advocated for the recovery of hostages, but I came to realize that civilians—even US citizens—who were kidnapped in Iraq were in a precarious position.

The hostage working group came to the SCID because we had experienced investigators and, more importantly, the ability to operate in the red zone. The FBI had dozens of special agents stationed in the Green Zone but had no armored vehicles to take them into the red zone, a circumstance that limited them to staying in the Green Zone or catching flights to Camp Victory and BIAP. Additionally, the FBI understandably had placed significant restrictions for travel by its special agents in the red zone.

The best chance to gather credible information about Ake's kidnappers was through interviews of witnesses conducted by trained investigators and nobody else was willing or able to take on the mission. SCID operations officer Tom Reid and the SCID's security element began planning the mission. Ground travel in our LAVs was not safe because of the water plant's distance from the Green Zone. The hostage working group coordinator promised he could obtain two helicopters to transport our team. Late in the evening on the day before we were to launch investigators, translators, and some of our security element, we were told to stand down. The FBI would take the mission.

Because there was no military connection to Ake's kidnapping, I was relieved to hear the FBI would take over. My relief turned to dismay in the next few days as I learned there was no immediate trip to the water plant. The FBI never traveled to the site of the kidnapping. Instead, questions were provided to the army unit responsible for securing the area where the kidnapping occurred and an army patrol made contact with some of the witnesses according to a report I saw several days later. Ake was seen in a video on Al-Jazeera television soon after his kidnapping, but as of this writing he is still missing.

I don't know if a quicker and more thorough response to the site of the kidnapping would have yielded any clues that would have led to Ake's release. Most kidnap victims are recovered by paying ransom, so information developed from interviews probably wouldn't have helped. Ake's kidnappers contacted Ake's wife soon after the abduction and demanded a ransom. Mysteriously, Ake's captors ceased contact with Ake's family on May 1, 2005.[7]

Ake's kidnapping was my introduction to the danger to which Westerners who are not operating with the military are exposed in Iraq. Many Iraqis were being kidnapped and held for ransom in cases that never were publicized. As a result, there were many experienced kidnappers operating in Baghdad and other cities. Once someone was kidnapped, it was not hard to keep him or her hidden. Iraqi homes frequently had walls surrounding the perimeter of the property, forming a walled compound that deterred inquisitive eyes. Also, the attitude of most Iraqis was to mind their own business. Some of the kidnappings were political, but most of them were for money. Either way, an Iraqi citizen who told the police about a house suspected of holding hostages might well discover he was talking to a confederate of the kidnappers.

The hostage working group had an opportunity to debrief some hostages who were released, and those debriefings revealed groups of kidnappers who were often more interested in money than in politics. One debriefing told of several hostages held in a cellar below a house where each hostage had just enough room to lie down. The only opening was sealed with bricks and mortar when the captors were not present. Water and food were scarce, lights were turned on only when captors were present, and fans were the only escape from the brutal summer heat.

Security Investigations

Fortunately, the SCID had better results in some of its other investigations. In one case the SCID investigated an Iraqi employee who worked in the US Embassy and was sharing information with insurgents. The SCID investigators traced a leak of information about the trials of Saddam Hussein and other regime officials to a particular employee. Once the investigation linked the employee to known insurgents, the employee was arrested.

In another investigation the SCID received information from some US Air Force Security Forces airmen who provided law enforcement services in the Green Zone. The information indicated there was the possibility that a US citizen employed as a contractor was supplying identification badges that allowed Iraqis to enter the Green Zone. Because the information concerned a US citizen who was not affiliated with the military, we turned the case over to the FBI.

About a month later, the SCID agent who had received the original tip obtained more specific information about Thomas N. Barnes III, an employee of DynCorp International, the contractor that controlled the identification badge process for the Green Zone. Barnes had supplied badges that allowed several Iraqis access to the Green Zone. Among the Iraqis who received badges from Barnes was an Iraqi woman he had been dating.[8] When the SCID agent obtained the information, she also learned the FBI was not actively investigating the prior allegation.

With the more specific information, the SCID and the FBI conducted a joint investigation that resulted in Barnes's arrest by federal agents when he arrived at Dulles International Airport upon his return from Iraq. He was the first American charged by the US Attorney in Alexandria, Virginia, who had begun a crackdown on fraud in government programs.[9] Barnes pled guilty to charges connected with his activities in Iraq.

Al-Dulaymi

Another example of how thorough and persistent investigation yields significant HUMINT is the case of an insurgent known as al-Dulaymi. On January 7, 2007, three US Air Force explosive ordnance disposal (EOD) specialists were killed while examining a truck containing artillery shells in preparation to disarm the explosives. Air Force Office of Special Investigations agents stationed at BIAP investigated the killings of the three airmen, which had apparently occurred when an insurgent watching the EOD team work used a command wire triggering device to set off the IED.[10]

Because the explosion occurred a distance away from BIAP, the AFOSI's source network was not very productive. This case highlights the value of investigations in HUMINT operations. Despite the lack of source coverage, AFOSI was able to use forensic evidence collected at the bomb scene by the army's Combined Explosive Exploitation Cell and intelligence previously reported by other agencies to identify Iraqis who might have been involved in the attack on the three airmen. [11]

Then AFOSI used its relationship with the local Iraqi police to identify potential suspects. Nearly two months after the attack, the

Iraqi police arrested al-Dulaymi, who confessed to taking part in the fatal bombing of the three airmen. Al-Dulaymi had helped plant the truck with the bomb, but the AFOSI investigation suggested that others were involved in the IED attack. During interrogation by AFOSI agents, al-Dulaymi provided physical descriptions and names of others involved in the attack. The names and descriptions of the others involved in the attack on the three airmen were provided to US units. The dangerous conditions in Iraq make locating and capturing the other insurgents more difficult, so as of this writing, they have not been captured. But without the investigation by AFOSI, al-Dulaymi wouldn't have been captured and the other insurgents would have never been identified.[12]

HUMINT FROM LIAISON

As part of the investigation of the IED that killed the three airmen, the AFOSI agents worked closely with Iraqi police officers. This is an example of another type of HUMINT that is useful but underutilized in Iraq. Some intelligence officers use the term "liaison" to describe this type of HUMINT. "Liaison" describes meeting with police or intelligence officials or local leaders on a peer-to-peer basis, instead of as an intelligence officer handling a covert source. In Iraq, liaison could be conducted with police officers or others in the Iraqi Ministry of Interior or Kurdish police or intelligence officials in northern Iraq. Other source of liaison information are village chiefs, tribal leaders, and other civic leaders with whom US personnel meet regularly. Effective liaison relies on regular meetings, many of which don't produce any startling new intelligence. It also helps to be able to supply something the local official wants, whether it's equipment, money, or training.

Liaison is underutilized in some intelligence organizations. Army and Marine Corps officers serving in frontline units have probably practiced liaison more effectively in Iraq than most intelligence organizations. Commanders of companies, battalions, and brigades who meet with Sunni tribal leaders and mayors of small towns pave the way to developing an exchange of information.

Ministry of Interior

Most opportunities for the SCID to develop liaison relationships were with Iraq police and army units. But even in 2005, two years after the invasion, establishing relationships with such organizations while the new Iraqi government was still in its infancy was difficult. In the case of the Ministry of Interior, we faced a dilemma. The ministry had many resources that would be useful in identifying and capturing Sunni insurgents, including AQI affiliates and Sunni insurgents not affiliated with al-Qaeda. On the other hand, the Ministry of Interior was being taken over by Shiites who were more than sympathetic with Iran. Thousands of members of the Badr Corps joined the MOI. Badr Corps was the militia arm of the Islamic Supreme Council of Iraq that was formed in Iran during the Iraq-Iran War.

In order to work with Iraqi police officers who would have some of the best intelligence about the Sunni insurgency, we would have to work with Iraqis who were affiliated with Shiite militias that were increasingly taking up arms against US troops. It wasn't a hard decision to make. For better or worse, the US position in Iraq was tied to the new government that had been formed by the coalition controlled by the Shiite fundamentalist elements, especially ISCI and Moqtada al-Sadr. ISCI's militia, the Badr Corps, was formed in Iran. Many in Sadr's militia, the Jaysh al-Mahdi, splintered off into secret cells of militiamen who emplaced EFP weapons against US forces. Despite the duplicitous nature of some in the new government, in order to have any influence or cooperation with the Iraq government, US intelligence and security organizations had to maintain a relationship with the Iraqi police and army.

The United States had established a considerable effort to recruit, organize, equip, and train the Iraq police. This training program was undertaken by the Multi-National Security Transition Command–Iraq. In 2005 MNSTC–I was run by David Petraeus, then a lieutenant general, who later returned as a four-star general to command MNF–I. His MNSTC–I headquarters were in the Green Zone.

In support of the MNSTC–I effort to train police and army officers, my boss, the MNF–I deputy chief of staff for intelligence, had the responsibility of training the Iraqi army and police to do intelligence work. Intelligence training for the Iraqi Ministry of Interior and Ministry of Defense was supervised by a group of army and Marine Corps intelligence officers and NCOs who were headquartered in the embassy building in the Green Zone. These intelligence officers were assigned to the MNF–I intelligence directorate but worked in support of MNSTC–I.

The group responsible for intelligence training was headed up by a marine colonel. He was a sharp fellow who had extended his service in Iraq several months past the original one-year tour because he was so dedicated to making the training program as effective as possible.

One day, when the colonel learned I was an AFOSI agent, he mentioned that AFOSI owed him a couple of special agents who would be trainers for one of his operations at the MOI. Five or six weeks after that conversation, I learned that two AFOSI agents were arriving in the Green Zone for assignment in the intelligence training operation.

One day two young AFOSI special agents showed up at the SCID office in the embassy. One was a lieutenant with a little over a year of AFOSI experience; the other was an NCO with several years' experience as an AFOSI agent. I told them about their assignment, some of which was new to them. Because AFOSI had not supplied any trainers before, they had not been told much before leaving the United States.

I told them to expect a change from being deployed as AFOSI agents in support of an air force base: "You are working with the army and it's a much different environment." AFOSI agents traditionally wear civilian clothing and use the term "special agent" instead of their rank. The two newly arrived agents were in civilian clothing and I surprised and disappointed them when I told them they should report to their new assignment in uniforms with their ranks displayed.

AFOSI agents wear civilian clothes to assist them in their role as criminal investigators and counterintelligence officers. The army's Criminal Investigations Division (CID) has a similar policy for the same reason. But in Iraq the CID agents wore uniforms. The agents' new assignment didn't require they wear civilian clothing, and doing so would make them stand out. I didn't want them to stand out as anything more than a first lieutenant and a staff sergeant. That was their best protection from harm and the best way for them to learn about the MOI.

The two agents would be assigned to the MOI headquarters building at a small forward operating base in the heart of Baghdad, two or three miles east of the Green Zone. They would be able to visit the Green Zone periodically, but the bulk of their time would be at the FOB. The SCID was familiar with the FOB where the agents would be working. In order to develop a working relationship with the MOI, one of the SCID agents visited MOI headquarters frequently.

Visit to the MOI

On one of those trips I tagged along and took Bob Jeffries, a civilian intelligence analyst, with me. Bob was from the Kansas City area, where I resided, and was only a few years younger, so we had something in common. He had come to the SCID in the same wave of new analysts that brought us Kathy Hecht.

The security team dropped Bob and me at the MOI headquarters building after a trip to the FOB in some LAVs. One of the AFOSI agents assigned to the FOB met us and led us to the eighth-floor office where his unit worked.

As we walked into the lobby of the building, we passed a dozen angry-looking dark-haired men who were armed with AK-47 rifles and handguns. We walked past the elevators and started up eight flights of stairs. "Can't trust the elevators in this building," the agent said.

As we walked up the stairs, we continued to be the focus of angry stares. I recalled talking to an army lieutenant colonel who was the number two officer in the group we were visiting that day. He told me that the members of his team were always armed and made a point of going to the bathroom in pairs. The same officer also told me that different floors and sections of MOI headquarters were the province of different factions—Shiite, Kurd, and Sunni. These were the allies they were training.

Arriving on the eighth floor, I met the army colonel in charge of the intelligence training team at MOI headquarters. The colonel gave us a briefing using a power point slide show and we received a tour of the MOI office his unit was training.

The building was a target of Sunni insurgent attacks. Someone had died at the front entrance to the building in a recent mortar attack. The colonel and his team showed me a set of photographs that depicted a truck that had been discovered across the street from the FOB. It was a panel truck that had been modified to hold a launcher for about twenty rockets.

When discovered, the truck was in place and pointed at the MOI building. A photograph taken from inside the truck showed the rocket launchers aligned with the MOI building, which was in the background of the photograph. Viewing the photo while sitting in the building that had been the target of those rockets, I wondered if there was an insurgent in a similar truck lining up the sights of a rocket launcher on the eighth floor.

The colonel's team was assigned to advise the MOI's Criminal Intelligence Service (CIS.) But the MOI and the CIS were still getting organized. Even the name of the CIS was being debated. The word "intelligence" had bad connotations from the Saddam Hussein era. The CIS had more than a thousand members in Iraq but was slated to expand to three or four times that size. The AFOSI agents were teaching investigative techniques to Iraqis who would be investigators and intelligence agents at the highest level of the MOI. The CIS was supposed to be the Iraqi version of the United States' FBI.

The colonel described how frustrating it was to deal with Iraqis who had not been part of government before the invasion but now were responsible for running it. The colonel's counterpart, the head of the CIS, had not been available to work with the colonel for three days because he was personally conducting the interrogation of a suspect. Shaking his head, the colonel wondered aloud how he was supposed to help build a professional organization when its leader would not focus on the difficult issues of planning and organizing instead of personally handling work that others could do.

I had a chance to talk to the two AFOSI agents. Since I had last seen the two agents, word of my instructions to the agents to wear uniforms with their rank displayed had reached AFOSI headquarters. Of course, the explanation of why the agents were using their military ranks had not been briefed. When a colonel from AFOSI headquarters told me that my decision had not been well received, I tried to explain, but my arguments about safety of the agents fell on deaf ears.

My contemporaries back at AFOSI headquarters at Andrews Air Force Base near Washington, DC, didn't appreciate that the agents were two air force members in a desert full of army personnel. The air force had tried to avoid problems caused by the differences between air force and army cultures by having an "airmen working for airmen" policy. For instance, the air force lieutenant colonel in charge of the Air Force Security Forces element in the Green Zone worked for an air force commander at Balad Air Base, about fifty miles north of Baghdad, instead of the army colonel who was in charge of force protection in the Green Zone. This arrangement antagonized the army colonel in no small way.

But the "airmen working for airmen" policy didn't reach us airmen who were embedded in joint organizations like MNF–I. While I was in Iraq I didn't work for the commander of AFOSI. Neither did the two agents working on the Iraqi MOI base. All three of us were assigned to CENTCOM. But on the issue of wearing a uniform with the rank displayed, I realized I had to go home in a few months, where I would once again be working for someone who didn't agree with my decision.

I explained to the two agents that the vice commander of AFOSI had relayed the very specific instruction of my boss at home, the commander of AFOSI, that they were to not use their rank. I figured the two agents would be overjoyed at having my decision reversed. So I was surprised when they explained they were both more comfortable with the way things were. They were accepted as experts by their army bosses and didn't receive special attention from any of those angry-looking MOI officers I had passed on the trip up the stairs.

I left them with these instructions: "Do what you think is best." I briefly thought about calling AFOSI headquarters and trying to explain the situation, but then I realized it was just going to be an argument I would lose. There were a lot more important things I should be spending my time on.

Working with the Iraqis

But the trip to MOI headquarters reinforced one lesson: If the SCID and other intelligence organizations were going to be effective in Iraq, we would have to pair up with our Iraqi counterparts. For the SCID, that meant learning as much as we could about the MOI and how it operated while making ourselves known to them. We realized that the ministry that ran the police force in Iraq was aligned with Shiite militias that were already inflicting casualties on US troops. Despite their affiliation with Shiite militias and Iran's IRGC, which was backing the militias, some within the MOI were not colored by the pro-Iran, anti–United States stance taken by some in their organization. If we didn't work with the MOI, we would lose a valuable source of information. It was up to us to evaluate the veracity and motives behind the information we could gain from the MOI.

The United States had something the MOI personnel wanted: We could provide training, advice, and equipment. The AFOSI agents and the others on the colonel's team working with the CIS were one example of how a relationship could be built. The SCID continued to visit the MOI frequently in order to cultivate a working relationship with its personnel.

To avoid dealing with a security and intelligence agency that had the Iranian bias of the MOI, the CIA helped create its counterpart agency within the Iraq government, the Iraq National Intelligence Service. The INIS was created in February 2004 and was intended to be an agency that wasn't motivated by sectarian concerns. Unlike the MOI, the INIS was not aligned with the fundamentalist Shiite parties that were in control of the government. The INIS recruited officers and agents from all of Iraq's major religious groups. The leader of the INIS, Mohammed Abdullah Shahwani, was a Sunni and his deputy was a Kurd.[13] The INIS didn't depend on the Shiite-led government of Iraq to fund it because the CIA completely funded its operations.[14]

One reason the CIA created the INIS was to deter Iranian meddling in Iraq. In order to focus on Iranian efforts within Iraq, Shahwani recruited into the INIS the former chief of the Iranian section of the Iraqi intelligence service under Saddam Hussein. Shahwani's concerns about Iran's intentions were well founded. In 2004, INIS officers discovered that Iranians had a hit list that contained names and home addresses of senior officers from the former regime, including Shahwani. About 140 INIS officers had been killed as of June 2007.[15]

Iran's activities in Iraq continued to interest Shahwani. In February 2008, shortly before Mahmoud Ahmadinejad, the president of Iran, visited Iraq, Shahwani told the press that Iranian "secret services" had sent agents to sabotage the Sunni groups fighting al-Qaeda in Iraq in concert with the US military.[16]

In a move that illustrates the sectarian divide in Iraq and the battle between the United States and Iran for influence with the Iraq government, the Shiite-controlled Iraqi government created a second intelligence agency that, like the MOI, is aligned with Iran. The Ministry of Security was created in 2006 and has about 5,000 officers, about the same size as the INIS. The Ministry of Security is led by Sheerwan al-Waeli, who has received training in Iran and who maintains liaison with Iranian and Syrian intelligence officers in Baghdad.[17]

Behind the Green Line—Kurdistan

A trip to the Kurdish-controlled part of Iraq was a contrast to my visit to the MOI. In Kurdistan, there was no sectarian tension such as the battle between the INIS and the Ministry of Security. Instead of the uneasy relationship that US forces had with the MOI, liaison with our Kurdish counterparts was much more cordial. But as I learned in my trip to the SCID team in Kurdistan, there were strong undercurrents from past alliances and conflicts between the Kurds and their Iraqi neighbors that affected what HUMINT we developed and the extent to which we could trust it.

"We call it Mordor." Bill Hanson, a young AFOSI special agent with a crew cut, was explaining the haze hanging over Kirkuk as S.Sgt. Phil Reeves drove us through Kirkuk in a LAV as quickly as he could. Bill was the team chief of the SCID team at Irbil, a city in Kurdish territory in northern Iraq. He and some of his team had driven down to Kirkuk Air Base to pick up Lt. Ron Kellogg and me to take us to Irbil.

As I looked at shadows cast by the haze and took in the petro-chemical smell of the refinery we were passing, I had to admit that Mordor—the evil land described in the *Lord of the Rings* books and movies—was a fitting name. For the first time in more than a month I was unable to see the daytime sun that beat down on Iraq from skies that were cloudless from May through October. An SCID security element convoy had dropped Kellogg and me at the BIAP military passenger terminal, where we waited about three hours for our C-130 flight to Kirkuk Air Base. I was surprised at the miserable conditions at the passenger terminal, considering that Baghdad was a big air passenger hub for military and civilian personnel coming into and departing Iraq. One or two Quonset hut–shaped structures were air-conditioned and had cots, but troops who had been stuck at the airfield for hours or days had claimed that space.

Ron was the platoon leader of the Texas National Guard platoon of reconnaissance troops that served as the SCID's security element. They drove and manned the LAVs transporting agents, analysts, and visitors to the SCID and performed a variety of other security related tasks. Ron had found a fellow lieutenant from his Texas National Guard brigade who was going to Kirkuk Air Base on our flight, and they had drifted away. I camped out under some camouflage netting that provided a limited amount of shade while sitting on a sandbag that had slightly more give to it than the concrete below.

The flight to Kirkuk was crowded and hot, but mercifully short. When we landed, the C-130 pulled close to the passenger terminal and dropped its rear ramp, and, with the engines still running, those of us getting off at Kirkuk quickly exited. A forklift speared the pallet with our bags and the C-130 pulled away with a few new passengers who boarded as we were exiting. Bill Hanson told me the quick drop off was necessary because mortar and rocket attacks were a frequent occurrence and insurgents often waited for airplanes to land before striking. Because our flight was late, Bill was in a hurry to get going. He didn't want us traveling at night any longer than necessary.

As Reeves brought the LAV up to speed on a highway leaving Kirkuk and we headed north toward Irbil, I sensed the tension in the LAV start to bleed off. Bill and Maria White, who was in the backseat with me, were both AFOSI agents. Reeves was the team leader of the security element that was part of Bill's team at Irbil. The three of them told me that Kirkuk was the most dangerous part of the run.

Since the fall of Saddam's regime, Kirkuk had been a contested city. The Kurds claimed it as theirs, but after they were displaced by Saddam's regime, Sunni Arabs had become the majority of the Kirkuk population. With the change of fortune, Kurdish forces were taking back homes and property that had been taken away by Saddam's regime. Both the Kurds and the Sunnis wanted to control the oil fields and refineries in and around Kirkuk and the wealth they generated. As a result of the forced relocation of both Kurds and Sunnis and the battle over oil wealth that could finance Kurdish independence, attacks between Kurds and Sunnis had become common. Even more frequent were attacks by Sunni insurgents on US forces traveling in and around Kirkuk. Tikrit, Saddam's hometown and a Sunni stronghold, was only about seventy-five miles southwest of Kirkuk, so insurgents had no shortage of people or weapons.

This was my first trip in a LAV that took more than fifteen minutes, and after leaving Kirkuk I was able to watch the countryside. Combines that were harvesting wheat reminded me of the Kansas farm on which I was raised. We passed a huge concrete structure that was an abandoned prison. Saddam had imprisoned so many of his citizens that massive facilities had been constructed to warehouse those who offended him or his cronies. After the prison we came upon shepherds tending their sheep near the highway, something their ancestors may have done in the same area centuries before. Unlike in the Baghdad area, more men dressed in the traditional Arab dishdasha, a garment that many US troops called a "man dress."

About twenty miles before reaching Irbil we came to a place that looked like a turnpike tollbooth. It was a checkpoint where we crossed the Green Line, the demarcation between Kurdish-controlled territory and the rest of Iraq. Kurdish milita and police manned the checkpoint and examined every vehicle. Arabs and other non-Kurdish people, although citizens of Iraq, had to explain why they were traveling into Kurdish territory. It was the first sign of many I saw on this short trip of a very independent Kurdish state within Iraq.

Coalition forces were safer in Kurdish territory than in other parts of Iraq. The SCID team posted in Irbil moved with greater freedom over much longer distances than the teams in Baghdad and Basra. The Kurds were proud of their record for safety from insurgent attacks. But the Kurds' confidence had been shaken a couple of weeks before my visit when a suicide bomber slipped into a line at a police recruiting station and detonated explosives he carried under his loose clothing. More than sixty people died in that terrorist attack in Irbil, reminding Kurds that they too could be touched by terrorist attacks. Despite that attack, however, the Kurdish areas were by far the safest parts of Iraq. The tight controls the Kurds had placed on entering Kurdistan helped protect the area from insurgent violence and preserved Kurdistan as a home for Kurds and the handful of coalition forces and nongovernmental organizations (NGOs) that were in the area.

The separation between the Iraqi Kurds and the Arabs, Turkomens, and other groups that made up Iraq is a historical division. Ethnically, the Kurds have more in common with the Persians of Iran than the Arabs with whom they share Iraq. Kurds primarily live in Iraq, Iran, and Turkey but also are present in Syria, Armenia, and Azerbaijan. They constitute the world's largest ethnic group that has no nation-state of its own and that fact gives rise to tension between Kurds and the governments of Turkey and Iran, which have fought Kurdish insurgents seeking independence in those countries. The Kurds speak their own language and began operating a semiautonomous region within Iraq after the United States and the United Kingdom established the no-fly zones following the Gulf War in 1991. Without the use of helicopters and airplanes to move military forces, conduct reconnaissance, and attack Kurdish forces, the Saddam regime had limited control in the area.

In Iraq the Kurds live primarily in the northeast section of the country, where the cities of Irbil and Sulaymaniyah serve as the centers of Kurdish government and trade. The provinces around those two cities share the same names as their principal cities and, with the third province of Dahuk, they form the majority of Kurdistan. The name Kurdistan refers to both a Kurdish homeland and the regional government authority established by the Kurds.

Crossing the Green Line into Kurdistan was like entering another country in several respects. The topography is different than the rest of Iraq. Unlike the flat terrain found in the rest of Iraq, the Kurdish areas have rolling hills in the south that give way to small mountains in the northern and eastern parts of Kurdistan.

As we entered the city of Irbil, traffic was heavy, but, unlike in Baghdad, I saw no Americans or other Westerners. There was a visible presence of Kurdish police and militia that patrolled Irbil and surrounding areas. The Kurdish police and militia operated independently from Iraq's Ministry of Interior and Ministry of Defense. Men and most women in Irbil wore Western-style clothing. I didn't see any women wearing the hijab, the loose, ankle-length cloak many women wore in Baghdad.

As we approached the compound where the SCID team lived, I saw evidence of other differences. There were many signs advertising beer for sale, primarily Tuborg. I don't recall ever having a Tuborg beer, but since it had been about two months since I had become subject to General Order 1 and its prohibition on consuming alcohol, I was developing a powerful thirst for a Tuborg. The Tuborg route salesman had been a busy guy. As the LAV navigated through side streets to the compound where the SCID team stayed, it seemed every other building had a Tuborg sign lit up.

Operating in Kurdistan

The SCID team lived in a predominantly Christian area near the Irbil airport in a Kurdish neighborhood that was partially walled off from neighboring areas. Western relief agencies and other NGOs, along with a few US government organizations, including the State Department's Agency for International Development (AID), had settled in the neighborhood. By erecting additional barriers and hiring some guards, the Westerners had created a guarded compound. Within the compound were several blocks of houses, small stores, and a couple of restaurants. Many of the houses were rented by the NGOs, the US government, and security contractors hired to provide security for the NGO and AID representatives who ventured out of the compound to work on various humanitarian and economic development missions. Like the Green Zone, the compound was not a government installation. Many Kurdish families who were not affiliated with the United States or the relief agencies continued to live in the neighborhood after it became a guarded compound.

Reliable electrical power was a problem across Iraq. In a country rich in oil, the aging infrastructure that pumped the oil out of the ground, refined it, and used it to generate electricity had deteriorated, especially after the Gulf War. In the Baghdad area, most neighborhoods received only about eight or ten hours of power per day. Power to Baghdad was frequently interrupted by insurgent attacks on power lines and transformers, events that added to the normal difficulty of keeping an aging and poorly maintained power grid up and running.

Even in Irbil, where attacks on power lines were not a factor, the power grid was not reliable. Outages and power fluctuations made running air conditioners and computers, the hallmarks of a Western presence, difficult. As a result, the compound generated its own power using several generators the size of semitrailers operated on behalf of an ad hoc group of Western organizations that had offices and homes in the compound. But that solution had its own set of problems. The generators were outside the compound, and the line from the generators to the compound was tapped by neighbors outside of the compound who were seeking free power. Additionally, the electric lines inside the compound were frequently tapped by Kurdish residents to obtain electricity that was free and more reliable than the electricity supplied by the Iraqi power system.

The SCID team lived in comfortable quarters in houses adjacent to one another in the compound. The US government paid a contractor a large fee to hire a small staff of local residents to buy and prepare food for the team and to maintain the building. Unlike most US military organizations in Iraq, the SCID team and a handful of other military personnel in the area didn't benefit from trucks escorted by the army that delivered large quantities of food to be prepared by a contractor-operated dining facility. Instead, the Kurdish staff purchased food locally and prepared it. Those rations were augmented by whatever food the SCID team could scrounge from the dining facility (known as a DFAC) on one of their visits to Kirkuk Air Base. The supervisor of the DFAC had taken pity on the SCID team and given them cereal and dry goods that were due to expire soon.

Between the use of local meat and produce that didn't undergo the same quality control as the food sent to the DFACs and hygiene problems that came from three Kurdish women working in a hot kitchen that was home to a squadron of flies, some of the team at Irbil had experienced health problems. The only NCIS agent at Irbil was a pleasant young man named Dick Engel. When I met Dick I immediately noticed bruising on his arms that ran from his biceps to just above his wrists. The bruising had faded but was still notice-able. Dick explained that he had become ill soon after arriving and, because of the lack of US medical facilities in Irbil, was treated by some members of the SCID security element who had attended the army's Combat Lifesaver course. The course focused on battlefield injuries but included instruction on inserting an intravenous line to administer fluids. Because Engel had become so dehydrated, the security element troops had given him fluids intravenously. Unfor-tunately, their initial attempts to get the IV lines started were a bit off the mark, causing severe bruising.

Engel's experience pointed out how far away from the main-stream the team operated. Medical care was more than ninety min-utes away, and an emergency would require much of the team to stop other activity to get two LAVs on the road to Kirkuk. Air evac-uation was a possibility, but that could take longer by the time the team requested assistance, gave a location, and a helicopter found its way to a landing zone. Even worse was an emergency that arose when the team was traveling around Kurdistan. The nearest US Army quick-reaction force was far away. The primary MNF–I unit in Irbil was a South Korean army unit that stayed close to the Irbil airport where it was stationed.

Waking up in Irbil was like being on vacation from my regular schedule in Baghdad. Instead of awakening to the noise and vibra-tion of helicopters passing over the house where I lived, I heard a man in the street calling in Kurdish. After a pause, he continued calling out, but seemed to walk farther away until I could hear him no more. At breakfast I found fresh bread baked in small rounds, about the size of a large hamburger bun, but with a coarser texture. The man in the street was a bread merchant, and our cooks pur-chased bread for the day from him. For breakfast I had some cereal and noticed the milk container was like the containers I saw stacked in the hallway. The milk was specially treated by heating it to an ultrahigh temperature that allowed it to sit unrefrigerated for long periods of time. The team would toss milk in the refrigerator to chill it before using it, but there wasn't enough cold storage to keep large quantities of cold drinks.

I noticed Bill Hanson and others using the bread as a staple, eating it with peanut butter and honey. Bill told me later that he ate a lot of peanut butter because his system still had trouble with the food even after being in Iraq for three months. He and the others had to purchase the peanut butter in the Kirkuk Base Exchange or have relatives mail it to them. After a few days of meals at Irbil, I understood the references by some of the team members about "chicken, again." The cooks relied heavily on chicken, and the only local vegetables that were plentiful seemed to be cucumbers and tomatoes, which found their way into many dishes or were chopped together as a salad.

Liaison with Kurdish Security

Bill and the other agents had continued a relationship with local Kurdish police and intelligence officials that had been going on since the invasion in 2003. Before I stepped foot in Iraq, I knew of the friendliness and cooperation extended by the Kurds to US forces. Kevin Harris, a friend and fellow AFOSI agent, had been in Irbil within weeks after the invasion in 2003. Kevin was a sergeant with a northern California police department and also a major in the air force reserve. Kevin had told me of a friend from his days in Irbil, a man named Ahmed, and I was hoping to track him down if he was still in Irbil.

Some of the Kurdish police and intelligence officials came by the SCID house to allow me to meet them. The Kurdish security organization is known as the Assayish, but there are really two different organizations called the Assayish. Two political parties vie for control of Kurdish territory, the Kurdistan Democratic Party (KDP) and the Patriotic Union of Kurdistan (PUK). Both have a security arm known as the Assayish. The KDP is stronger in Irbil and the PUK is stronger in Sulaymaniyah. Because we were in Irbil, I was meeting officials from the KDP's Assayish.

The SCID team used a room of one of their houses to host local guests when they visited. All quarters and offices where US military personnel work and live worldwide have the same rule. There is no smoking. As a nonsmoker, I appreciate the rule and remember what it was like in the old "smoke 'em if you got 'em" days. But the ban on smoking goes out the window when you're hosting someone from another culture. Our team chief, Bill Hanson, understood the need to honor the customs of our host nation and made the Assayish officers comfortable, bringing water and other drinks and smiling as they lit up. Once our guests fired up their smokes, the SCID agents and the interpreter who smoked took advantage of the opportunity to smoke without having to go outside, and soon a blue haze hung over the room.

Using one of the SCID's interpreters to translate, the senior Assayish officer went past the pleasantries that often fill conversations in liaison visits. He steered the conversation toward Iran and asked my opinion about the country whose border was only sixty miles from where we sat. I told him I thought Iran posed a potential danger. I was interested in his reaction because Iran has many allies among the Kurds. The officer leaned toward me. He was a large man, accustomed to being an imposing presence, whether with his own officers or people who found themselves in an interrogation cell.

"Dangerous!" One day the Iranians would have to be faced.

The Kurdish Struggle for Self-Rule

I was interested in this man's opinion because I knew a little about the difficult time the Kurds had faced in this region, trapped between Saddam's regime and the Shiite Islamic Republic government of Iran. Iran had been the enemy of Saddam during the Iraq-Iran War in the 1980s, at the same time Saddam's regime was victimizing the Kurds. At times under Saddam, Kurds had fled Iraq into Iran, similar to the experience of many Shiites in southern Iraq. Kurdish leaders had struck alternating alliances with Iran and Saddam on behalf of the KDP and PUK over the years. With the fall of the Saddam Hussein regime, the KDP and PUK were working together to govern Kurdistan, but that cooperation was a fragile armistice and didn't prevent each party from seeking a leading role over the other.

The dispute between the KDP and the PUK goes back to the early days of the KDP. The KDP was founded in 1946 by Mustafa Barzani with the goal of achieving autonomy for Kurds in Iraq. Barzani's son, Massoud Barzani, had assumed leadership of the KDP in 1979. After the Baath Party seized control of Iraq in 1968, the KDP negotiated with officials of the new government, including Saddam Hussein, hoping to have Kurdish autonomy recognized by the new government or to at least achieve better treatment of Kurds from the new government. The KDP's hopes for a new style of government from Baghdad were dashed when Saddam masterminded an unsuccessful attempt to assassinate Mustafa Barzani by wiring a cleric with explosive and detonating it as the religious leader sat across a table from him. Apparently the cleric had been told the device was an audio recorder. One of the KDP officials present believed it was detonated by security personnel accompanying the cleric.[18]

After the Gulf War the United States and the United Kingdom created a no-fly zone in Northern Iraq, which allowed the Kurds to live a mostly autonomous life, with limited interference from Saddam's regime. This new freedom also allowed the dislike among Kurdish leaders to grow into more intense hostility. Jalal Talabani, the leader of the PUK, had once been a member of the KDP, but now he and Massoud Barzani were bitter rivals. In 1996 the PUK succeeded in kicking the KDP out of Irbil, capturing the city for the PUK. Viewing the turn of events from his stronghold in Salahuddin, a town in the foothills about twenty miles northwest of Irbil, Massoud Barzani chose to ally himself with the man who had attempted to kill his father: He called on Saddam Hussein to intervene in Irbil. Hussein granted that wish, sent thirty thousand troops into Kurdish territory, and returned Irbil to KDP control.

When the Iraq transitional government was elected, Jalal Talabani became president of Iraq, the country's second-highest position. Massoud Barzani became the president of the Kurdistan Regional Government (KRG.) Some thought that Barzani wanted the KRG job instead of the position of Iraqi president because he believed the Iraqi president's role would be minor. If that was so, he may have been disappointed. Talabani became a very visible face of Iraq to the world and retained that role even when Ibrahim al-Jaafari stepped down as prime minister and Nouri al-Maliki replaced him.

Security and intelligence agencies are critical for Talabani and Barzani to maintain security within their respective portions of Kurdistan and to prevent threats to their power. In addition to the Kurdish police, the Assayish, the KDP also has an intelligence agency, the Parastin. Some of the people I met at the SCID office may have actually been members of the Parastin. Both the Parastin and Assayish reported to Masrour Barzani, the chief of KDP intelligence and the son of Massoud Barzani. Government of the Kurds is a family profession for the Barzanis. Nechervan Idris Barzani, the grandson of Mustafa Barzani and nephew of Massoud Barzani, is the prime minister of the KRG.

Meeting with Masrour Barzani

On the fourth day of my visit to Irbil, I went to pay my respects to Masrour Barzani. Leaving the high plains of Irbil, we traveled along a two-lane highway approaching the town of Salahaddin, perched near the crest of a small mountain. As we drove through the quiet countryside, I saw sheep and other signs of agriculture. We passed tents and small shacks along the roads that were large enough for two or three men. Some had a single man outside, in the shade if he could find some. Others had a couple of men standing or sitting. Some appeared unmanned.

"Peshmerga." Bill Hanson noticed me looking at the men and he told me who they were. The Peshmerga were the Kurdish militia. These Peshmerga soldiers were standing guard on the approaches into Barzani-controlled territory, equipped with a rifle and a radio or a cell phone. There would be no surprises for KDP officials who favored the slightly cooler climate and safety of Salahaddin over the traffic and crowds of Irbil. I remembered my friend Kevin Harris telling me of Peshmerga soldiers providing security for his counterintelligence operations when he was in the Irbil area soon after the invasion.

Not only would I be meeting Masrour Barzani, but I would also be meeting Kevin's friend Ahmed. He was to meet our two LAVs and take us to a house to meet Barzani. The KDP had not disclosed the meeting site to us. Agreeing to such an arrangement was a sign of our trust of the KDP. Being led on a trip to an unknown destination was tantamount to giving ourselves up to an ambush.

Kevin's vouching for Ahmed and our office's two years in Irbil working with the KDP eased my concerns about the meeting arrangements. Realistically, Barzani was much more of a target than we were.

We waited for only a few minutes before Ahmed and another man pulled up in a car, waved at Bill Hanson, and pulled away. We followed for a few minutes along a main street that ran along the crest of the hill the city sat upon. Then we turned and drove down a long approach to a house. But this house was unlike any house in my neighborhood. It sat on the edge of the mountain with a beautiful view of the valley below. Stepping out of the LAV, I looked at the massive house with two story columns framing the entrance. If this was to impress a visitor, it was working.

Walking up the steps, Bill introduced me to Ahmed and I told Ahmed I brought greetings from Kevin Harris. "How is my brother, Kevin?" asked Ahmed with a large smile on his face. Moving at a quick pace, Ahmed led us into the building. The first floor had the feeling of a museum: quiet with a wide hallway and tall ceilings. We walked up a wide marble staircase to the second floor and were ushered into a room with Barzani. On that day in May, I wore a tie and sport coat. It was the only time I would wear a tie in Iraq, but I was still underdressed for the occasion.

Masrour Barzani, as well as Ahmed and his silent partner, were all wearing suits. Nice suits. Barzani, a graduate of American University in Washington, DC,[19] spoke flawless English. We could have done without our translator. Barzani is a sophisticated man whose birth into the Barzani family selected his career.

Although I could tell Barzani was experienced in dealing with American officials, I didn't realize the extent of his expertise in diplomatic affairs. A story recounted by Peter W. Galbraith in his book *The End of Iraq*, published a year after my visit with Barzani, would have been helpful to know beforehand. According to Galbraith, Ambassador Paul Bremer, the head of the Coalition Provisional Authority, had appointed a consultant from the RAND Corporation to negotiate the dissolution of the Peshmerga with Masrour Barzani. According to the book, the consultant reached a deal with Barzani that would dissolve the Peshmerga, but the Kurdistan Region Government would establish three new forces: mountain rangers, a rapid reaction force, and a counterterrorism strike force. As the consultant was waiting for the helicopter that would take him back to Baghdad, he asked for the Kurdish translation of mountain rangers. He was told, "Peshmerga."[20]

Unlike that consultant, I was merely paying my respects to the head of the security and intelligence organization that controlled much of northern Iraq with the hope that his organization would more freely share information that we wanted in order to better protect US forces in Iraq. We discussed the recent attack at the police recruiting station that was attributed to Ansar al-Sunna, an Islamic fundamentalist group composed of Sunni Arabs and Kurds with ties to both al-Qaeda and Ansar al-Islam, another terrorist group the KDP had battled.

The Barzani family and the Kurdish people were accustomed to seeing people like me come and go. People at my level are just trying to accomplish a mission. We seek to catch or neutralize terrorists before they can kill US service members. But my mission was made more difficult because US officials at levels far above mine had not treated the Kurds well for many years.

The treaty struck among the allies following World War I called for the establishment of an independent Kurdish nation. That promise wasn't kept. Decades later the US government worked with the Kurds and with the shah of Iran in the 1970s against the new Baath government of Iraq. The Shah provided assistance to the

Kurds with the knowledge of the United States. In 1975 Iraq and Iran reached the Algiers Accord, which settled several issues between the two countries. As part of the bargain struck with the Baathists, the shah agreed to withdraw support for the Kurds, and the United States soon followed suit.

Years later, in 1992, the postwar remarks of President George H. W. Bush and other US officials were interpreted by the Kurds in northern Iraq and Shiites in southern Iraq to mean their revolt would be supported by the United States. But the United States and the coalition that removed Iraq from Kuwait sat on its hands when the Kurds and Shiites revolted. The Kurds paid a heavy price for expecting the United States to assist them.

So when a visit by a lowly colonel didn't move the Kurdistan Regional Government to change its ways to accommodate my mission, I understood. The best I could do was ask and attempt to demonstrate the areas where our interests were aligned. Security officials at some levels share a desire to cooperate. International politics, however, interfere with what seems a straightforward task. For that reason, I wasn't surprised when I learned from other sources that the KDP had a lot more information than they shared with us that day. If I were a Kurd, I'm not so sure I would be too eager to tell all I knew to an American intelligence officer.

But at the same time, I had to make sure the SCID team in Irbil kept their eyes open and didn't go native. It is easy for Americans who are helpful and trusting by nature to assume that people in other cultures who are friendly and welcoming share all of our goals. Sometimes an inexperienced US military or intelligence officer is overmatched, like a fraternity boy playing poker with serious gamblers. We would work well with the Kurds, but we always had to remember that they might not be telling us everything they knew.

Liaison Requires Caution

This is the nature of HUMINT gathered through liaison. The people providing us information are usually more professional than covert human sources. They are people who have pursued careers that are similar to the careers of our own intelligence officers and military personnel. Frequently, liaison contacts are friendly or even charming. Information is often shared over coffee or a meal, and the experience can be pleasant. But what is lost on many people, including some intelligence officers who have not developed HUMINT through liaison, is that the liaison contacts who meet with US intelligence officers have some discretion in what they tell us. Our Iraqi counterparts don't have to tell us anything, and their willingness to provide information is not always based on the cold logic of a decision tree. They are more inclined to share information, even information their superiors would prefer not be disclosed, if they perceive the US official they are meeting is professional, sincere, and able to deliver what is promised.

All of the Iraqi officials (or local officials in other countries) that US forces encounter have an agenda. But valuable and accurate intelligence can come from such liaison. Our intelligence officers have to identify the other party's agenda and always remember that even our allies place their interests ahead of our interests.

One place where few people shared our interests was in Mosul, only about fifty miles west of Irbil. The difference between Mosul and Irbil highlighted the contrast between the safety of Kurdistan and the danger of Mosul, which was a hotbed of Sunni insurgents, especially al-Qaeda in Iraq.

One night while I was in Irbil, we shared dinner with a couple of Army Special Forces soldiers living in a nearby compound. They were from the 1st Special Forces Group and were augmenting the

10th Special Forces Group that was pulling the special forces duty in Iraq at the time. On their tour of duty to Iraq, these two soldiers had been in Humvees hit by IEDs seven times, which, they proudly noted, was a record for their outfit. Every attack upon them occurred when they were in Mosul.

The 101st Airborne Division under the command of then Major General Petraeus had been stationed in Mosul in 2003 and had succeeded in pacifying the area. Since then the security of the area had deteriorated. In 2003 and 2004 our Irbil office would travel to Mosul in LAVs as part of their liaison and intelligence gathering. Trips to Mosul by the SCID stopped after an SCID team came under small-arms fire that managed to stop one LAV. Later, after the LAV was recovered and examined, the team learned a bullet had found its way under the LAV and severed a small length of fuel line that wasn't protected by armor. The interrupted flow of fuel caused the LAV engine to stop, but it coasted far enough out of the kill zone to allow the team to bail out, secure the damaged LAV, and escape in the remaining LAV. That experience was one of several events while I was in Iraq that reinforced how important it was to travel with more than one vehicle. The special forces troops told our team to not travel to Mosul in a LAV. Even armored Humvees had more than they could handle some days.

The day after I met Masrour Barzani, the Irbil team took Ron Kellogg and me back to Kirkuk Air Base to catch a C-130 back to Baghdad. We arrived in Kirkuk in time to visit the AFOSI office before our flight. Special Agent Rick Ulbright, a polygraph examiner with AFOSI, had been killed by a rocket attack less than a year before, on August 8, 2004. When I saw the area where he was struck, I was reminded how random death can be. Ulbright was standing outside the office, about twenty feet from the front door, when the rocket landed within feet of him. Shrapnel gouges still marked the exterior of the building as I stood there ten months later. People inside the building were unhurt. Because the rocket that struck Ulbright was the first incoming rocket, there was no warning. Ulbright became another warrior lost to explosives in the form of rockets, mortars, IEDs, EFPs, and car bombs that caused the majority of US casualties in the Iraq War.

Such attacks not only preserve the small insurgent force bringing the attacks, but also make it more difficult to conduct intelligence operations, especially HUMINT collection. When a mortar drops on your unit or your Humvee gets hit by an IED or EFP, there is usually no opportunity to return fire. Frustration builds among US troops because they are targets in a fight that frequently doesn't allow them to strike back. Daily exposure to the danger of such attacks, whether or not they occur, causes stress to build up. The stress of being exposed to anonymous attacks with no chance to counterattack is cumulative and added to the difficulty of performing HUMINT operations, whether they were source meetings, investigations, or liaison with coalition forces.

There were other impediments to HUMINT operations in Iraq. These problems were internal to US forces and interfered with developing good intelligence against the insurgency almost as much as the difficulties caused by travel in the red zone and the danger and stress from attacks upon our intelligence forces. The next chapters describe the other enemies of good intelligence including stovepipes and a war among intelligence officers.

NOTES

1. Major General Antonio M. Taguba, "Article 15–6 Investigation of the 800th Military Police Brigade," http://news.findlaw.com/hdocs/docs/iraq/tagubarpt.html (accessed March 9, 2008).

2. Josh White, "U.S. Generals in Iraq Were Told of Abuse Early, Inquiry Finds," *Washington Post*, December 1, 2004, p. A1.

3. Steve Fainaru, "Blasts Inside Green Zone Kill at Least 5—Fortified Area in Baghdad Hit by Likely Suicide Attacks," *Washington Post*, October 15, 2004, p. A1.

4. Elaine M. Grossman, "U.S., Iraq Freed Roughly 44,000 Suspected Insurgents Since March 2003," *Inside the Pentagon*, July 12, 2007, http://www.d-n-i.net/grossman/iraq_freed.htm (accessed March 9, 2008).

5. Raffaello Pantucci, "Britain's Prison Dilemma: Issues and Concerns in Islamic Radicalization," *Terrorism Monitor*, March 4, 2008, p. 6, http://www.jamestown.org/terrorism/news/uploads/TM_006_006.pdf (accessed April 4, 2008).

6. David J. Clark, "The Vital Role of Intelligence in Counterinsurgency Operations," US Army War College, March 15, 2006, p. 15, http://www.strategicstudiesinstitute.army.mil/pdffiles/ksil309.pdf (accessed March 9, 2008).

7. Peter Slevin, "'We Have Your Husband'—Anguish Continues for Family of Man Kidnapped in Iraq," *Washington Post*, June 7, 2006, p. A1.

8. Jerry Markon and Josh White, "Contractor Charged in Baghdad Badge Scam," *Washington Post*, September 21, 2005, p. A19.

9. Ibid.

10. Erik Holmes, "How OSI Agents Are Catching Killers in Iraq," *Air Force Times*, March 8, 2008, http://www.airforcetimes.com/news/2008/03/airforce_osi_030708/ (accessed March 14, 2008).

11. Ibid.

12. Ibid.

13. David Ignatius, "A Sectarian Spy Duel in Baghdad," *Washington Post*, June 14, 2007, p. A27.

14. Michael Ware, "Pro-Iran Agency May Take Over Iraq's Intelligence," CNN.com, March 7, 2007, http://www.cnn.com/2007/WORLD/meast/03/07/iraq.intelligence/index.html (accessed January 31, 2008).

15. Ibid.

16. "Iran Agents 'Sabotaging' Anti-al-Qaeda Groups," *Australian*, February 28, 2008, http://www.theaustralian.news.com.au/story/0,25197,23289273-12335,00.html (accessed March 15, 2008).

17. Ibid.

18. "An Interview with Dr Mahmoud Ali Othman," *Frontline*, PBS, http://www.pbs.org/wgbh/pages/frontline/shows/saddam/interviews/othman.ht ml (accessed March 23,2008).

19. "Iraqi Kurdish Leader Honored," *American Weekly*, American University, November 1, 2005, http://veracity.univpubs.american.edu/weeklypast/110105/ 110105_iraqikurdish.html (accessed April 4, 2008).

20. Peter W. Galbraith, *The End of Iraq: How American Incompetence Created a War without End* (New York: Simon & Schuster, 2006), pp. 135–36.

Chapter 7

STOVEPIPES

T he last two chapters discussed how intelligence officers use HUMINT sources, gather information from prisoners and investigations, and conduct liaison with Iraqi officials as part of the first of three steps of intelligence (collect intelligence, understand intelligence, and act on intelligence). Most intelligence that is collected must be compared with other information to be fully understood and to determine if the information is credible. If the accuracy of the intelligence can't be determined, US forces can't act on the intelligence. Similarly, if a military unit doesn't have all of the intelligence about a target, the unit can't act on the target or, because it doesn't have all the facts, may expose troops to unnecessary risk.

THE FAILURE TO SHARE

The single largest hindrance to effectively understanding and acting on intelligence is the intelligence community's collective failure to share information. This chapter addresses how the failure to share information reduces the quantity and quality of intelligence we collect and detracts from our ability to understand and act on intelligence that we do manage to collect.

The failure to share information also affects what information intelligence officers target for collection. All of the methods used to collect HUMINT can be directed. This is a powerful capability that is often not used. Covert human sources can be targeted against specific insurgent cells or threats. Investigations can be focused on specific issues that are relevant to the threats posed by insurgents, militias, or criminal gangs. The interrogation of prisoners can be conducted in a way to extract information about specific people, neighborhoods, or insurgent operations. And—perhaps the most powerful tool in countering an insurgency—relationships with members of the local police and army can be cultivated to make our intelligence collection much more productive.

But in order to direct HUMINT efforts, intelligence officers must know where to look. Collecting intelligence, especially HUMINT, becomes more focused when intelligence officers have a clear understanding of what is important. The initial intelligence efforts of any military force that first enters a foreign area resemble a vacuum cleaner sucking up everything in its path. As troops become more familiar with an area, as they did in Iraq, they develop knowledge of the leaders, criminals, and insurgents in their area of responsibility (AOR). As they become more familiar with their AOR and its people, our soldiers and marines develop a better sense of who and what threatens them. From that understanding, they then know what information to collect to counter those threats.

In deciding what information to collect, one priority of every military commander is intelligence that will protect his unit from attack. In addition to directing intelligence for purposes of force protection, intelligence collection is also focused by the priorities of the officers leading the military campaign. In the language of the US military, these intelligence demands are known as priority intelligence requirements (PIRs). By developing a list of information that the commander believes is necessary to carry out his mission, the commander's intelligence officers can focus on collecting information that will assist the commander in completing his mission. Commanders at all levels, from Multi-National Force–Iraq down to the battalion, issue PIRs as a way to let intelligence personnel and troops in the field know what information is important to report.

But the use of PIRs to direct intelligence collection has its limits. To be useful, the PIRs have to communicate on a broad level and can't be specific to every insurgent cell or group that has splintered off from a Shiite militia. To be effective, an intelligence officer must select his or her targets, decide what information is needed, and develop a plan to collect the information. This process is necessary whether the intelligence officer is a battalion S-2 focused on threats and insurgents in his battalion's AOR or a DIA HUMINT officer pursuing targets across the entire theater.

In order to select the right targets and effectively collect intelligence about those targets, the intelligence officer must have access to all of the information the intelligence community has about the targets. By knowing of other military and intelligence organizations with an interest in the same targets, the intelligence officer can coordinate his or her efforts to avoid duplication or interference with another operation.

This is where the US intelligence system breaks down. Frequently information that is uncovered by one part of the US military or intelligence community is not made available to others. Military and intelligence units may be working on the same or overlapping targets and not realize it.

THE SPECIAL OPERATIONS STOVEPIPE

There are several reasons why information is collected by many but shared by few. In Iraq the lack of a well-coordinated intelligence effort dates back to operations soon after the invasion in 2003 that created specialized units that operated separately from MNF–I. After the fall of Baghdad, the US intelligence community had two priorities for collecting information. One priority was intelligence regarding the location and activities of Saddam Hussein and leaders of his regime. The other priority for intelligence collection was information relating to weapons of mass destruction (WMD), including nuclear, chemical, and biological weapons.

The searches for WMD and Saddam Hussein and members of his regime were led by specially formed units. In 2003 the Department of Defense set up the Iraq Survey Group, commanded by Maj. Gen. Keith W. Dayton, commander of the Defense Intelligence Agency's Defense HUMINT Service, to direct the search for evidence of WMD and efforts to develop such weapons. The search for information about Iraq's WMD program required the Iraq Survey Group to find, capture, and interrogate former members of Saddam's regime who were most likely to know whether Iraq possessed any such weapons and, if so, where they were hidden.[1]

To search for Saddam Hussein, the US Joint Special Operations Command created a task force composed of US special operation forces from the army, navy, and air force[2] and paramilitary operatives of the CIA.[3] This task force was initially known as Task Force 121. The new task force was intended to act rapidly on intelligence in a hunt for Saddam Hussein and other former Iraqi government officials.

By 2005 Saddam Hussein and many of his regime's leaders had been captured, and the Iraq Survey Group had been disbanded after finding no WMD. But, as described in chapter 2, there were new threats facing US forces in Iraq. Abu Musab al-Zarqawi's group, which eventually became known as al-Qaeda in Iraq, had increased its violence to the point that General Casey, the commanding general of MNF–I, changed the focus of conventional forces in Iraq from searching for members of Saddam's regime to fighting AQI.

Special operations forces and the CIA continued their collaboration as they turned their focus to the hunt for Zarqawi and the leadership of AQI. Task Force 121 evolved into Task Force 626, with a mission to kill or capture Zarqawi and other AQI leaders. Later the task force was renamed Task Force 145. An *Army Times* article describes how the task force is composed of Delta Force personnel, Army Rangers, Navy SEALS, and the British Special Air Service. According to the *Army Times* article, Task Force 145 is divided into four subunits—Task Force–West, Task Force–Central, Task Force–North, and Task Force–Black—each commanded by an army lieutenant colonel or equivalent-ranking navy or British officer. Each of the subunits operates independently, that is, they are able to conduct missions without having to request permission from Task Force 145 headquarters.[4]

The people in Task Force 145 are a very small percentage of the US troops stationed in Iraq. In many ways the task force is self-contained with its own intelligence personnel, air support, and detainee and interrogation center. The task force has the best-trained and, after years of war in Afghanistan and Iraq, the most-experienced combat troops in the world. The results achieved by the men and women of the task force have been stellar. But the task force, with its associated CIA personnel, also represents the largest stovepipe in Iraq.

The term "stovepipe" refers to the lack of sharing among intelligence organizations. In a stovepipe, intelligence is collected by an organization, analyzed by the same organization, and passed up the chain to that organization's higher headquarters—but not shared outside of the organization. Much of the information developed by the task force travels only as far as it serves the purpose of the task force. The task force operates throughout Iraq and has the authority to conduct raids wherever its intelligence leads it. Every raid conducted by the task force is in an area that is assigned to a conventional unit of the Multi-National Corps–Iraq. The intelligence officers in the divisions, brigades, and battalions and the Tactical HUMINT Teams and Marine Corps HUMINT Exploitation Teams in areas in which Task Force 145 conducts operations are all collecting and analyzing intelligence in the same areas. But frequently the intelligence relating to insurgents captured by the task force is not shared with those units or the military intelligence community in general.

The stovepipe was so rigid that important information developed by the task force could leave Iraq and be communicated around the United States without the military's highest-ranking intelligence officer in Iraq even being aware of the information. I learned this one day when I received a telephone call from another colonel on the MNF–I intelligence staff. He was the C2X, which is the name of the staff officer responsible for supervising human intelligence and counterintelligence operations for MNF–I. (Intelligence officers at the division and corps levels are known by the designation G-2; on a coalition staff, such as MNF–I, the intelligence officer is the C-2.)

The C2X explained that during a raid on an insurgent's house, Task Force 145 had found a computer that contained some classified US military information. But the raid had occurred about a month before and the computer with the classified information had been analyzed by the CIA and by computer specialists in the United

States. I was about to tell the C2X that the lengthy delay in reporting the capture of the computer would prevent a thorough investigation and I was going to decline the case because the SCID was busy conducting other investigations and operations that had more potential to be successful.

Then the C2X said, "I need to know right now if you will run an investigation because this is going in the PDB." He paused. "You know what the PDB is?"

I knew. It was the Presidential Daily Brief, a classified document produced each morning for the president.

"Yes," I said. "The SCID will run an investigation."

The classified information had been discovered by the task force and the computer had been analyzed by the CIA office in Baghdad and sent to the United States without anyone on the MNF–I staff knowing about the discovery of the computer. The MNF–I deputy chief of staff for intelligence learned about the insurgent's possession of classified information when he was asked by an intelligence official based in the United States for more information about the incident. That's a pretty big stovepipe.

THE INEFFICIENT HIERARCHY OF MILITARY INTELLIGENCE

The existence of stovepipes has been criticized for years as one of the biggest impediments to effective intelligence. Stovepipes exist for many reasons. One reason is that there are a lot of people involved in the collection and analysis of intelligence who work for several different organizations that have different missions.

The organizations collecting intelligence in Iraq begin at field level. Patrols reported their observations and any information received during the patrol to their platoon and company to be forwarded to the battalion intelligence staff. Tactical HUMINT teams also operated in the same areas as the frontline units responsible for security in an area, but THTs reported their information separately.

Battalion and brigade intelligence officers and their staffs reviewed the information from patrols and the THTs. At the next level, division intelligence officers and the intelligence staff of MNC–I analyzed information from the brigades and THTs and gave direction to lower level intelligence officers and the people handling sources. The HUMINT Operations Cell described in chapter 5 supervised the THTs but worked on the staff of the intelligence officer for the MNC–I.

Within the Iraq intelligence hierarchy, the intelligence officer for the MNC–I worked for the commanding general of the MNC–I but also served on the staff of the intelligence officer for the MNF–I. In addition to the MNC–I's intelligence staff, the MNF-I intelligence staff numbered several hundred personnel, many of whom were assigned to the Combined Intelligence Operations Center. The CIOC supervised the work of hundreds of intelligence specialists who handled myriad tasks such as managing the human source program, reviewing and publishing intelligence information reports written by intelligence collectors across Iraq, analyzing the information produced by HUMINT sources, and writing in-depth analyses of insurgent groups and intelligence trends.

Understanding the names and relationships of the various levels of the army structure (platoon, company, battalion, brigade, division, MNC–I, and MNF–I) isn't necessary to recognize part of the problem. There were many layers of a rigid but confusing hierarchy through which intelligence flowed. The people handling sources and meeting with Iraqis were far away from the leaders of the intelligence apparatus.

But in addition to the pyramid of intelligence staffs just described, there were other elements in the intelligence maze. MNF–I had intelligence organizations that reported directly to it, including a DIA HUMINT unit and the SCID. Both of those units operated throughout Iraq. Also operating independently throughout the country was Task Force 145, which had its own intelligence-gathering and analysis section. In addition to the task force, there were other special operations personnel conducting intelligence operations in Iraq. Army Special Forces units served as advisors to Iraqi army units. Some of the Iraqi army organizations had significant intelligence operations that collected very useful information. In addition to all of these personnel operating under the direction of the commanding general of MNF–I, US Central Command intelligence officers were also in Iraq. They reported directly to CENTCOM headquarters in the United States.

The military intelligence organizations were not alone. Baghdad was home to the world's largest CIA station and several smaller CIA offices were in several cities around Iraq. But the CIA worked for the newly created director of national intelligence. Neither the CIA nor the Defense Department was in charge of all intelligence for the Iraq counterinsurgency effort. The lack of a senior intelligence officer in Iraq furthered the creation of stovepipes. The senior military intelligence officer in Iraq had no control over the CIA's activities and the CIA's chief of station could only influence, but not direct, military intelligence operations.

Another factor that led to stovepipes was the wide variety of missions of the many different organizations that collected intelligence. Battalions and their supporting THTs, which were responsible for the security of their area of operations, had only a limited interest in collecting intelligence that didn't focus directly on their area. Collecting information about insurgents fifty miles away from a battalion's AOR, while useful for the overall effort, did not support its mission, which was to secure the part of Iraq for which they were responsible.

THE RELUCTANCE TO SHARE INFORMATION

Unlike army and Marine Corps units responsible for securing a specific sector, Task Force 145 and the CIA were assigned tasks that took them across the country in search of Saddam Hussein, WMD, Abu Musab al-Zarqawi, and members of AQI. In its hunt for AQI members, Task Force 145 would raid the house of a suspected insurgent based on intelligence such as intercepted cell phone calls or reports from sources. Soldiers raiding houses would sometimes discover a cell phone, satellite telephone, or computer with connections to other possible insurgents. When interrogated, insurgents captured by the task force also provided leads about other insurgents that resulted in more raids.

But some of the intelligence gathered by Task Force 145 and the CIA wasn't shared with other military units that were also pursuing members of the insurgency. If Task Force 145 developed information about Iraqis who didn't appear to be connected to significant AQI members, that information might not make it into an intelligence report that was shared with other units. Similarly, information developed about high-level AQI members might not be shared because the task force was closing in on a target and didn't want another unit to interfere with the task force operation.

The reluctance to share information for fear that another unit might prematurely act on the information was common among intelligence personnel and was another reason for stovepipes. A military unit that developed HUMINT that was reportable under a priority information requirement was supposed to write an intelligence information report. By writing an IIR, a military unit could report HUMINT information to the intelligence community as a whole. The IIRs were placed in classified databases that were searchable by intelligence officers and analysts. To preserve operational security, the IIRs didn't identify the source by name and were not supposed to report information that would identify a source. The reports summarized the source's information, but didn't provide every detail reported by the source. The CIA had a similar type of report that allowed it to provide HUMINT to consumers of intelligence.

Once an IIR was released, the reporter of the intelligence had no ability to restrict what was done with the information. Any military unit could act on the intelligence. There was no requirement for a military unit that received an IIR to coordinate action it planned to take based on the intelligence. At the SCID, we experienced occasions when we reported information in IIRs and later learned that a frontline unit had acted on it while we were still attempting to gather more definitive intelligence.

On one occasion, one of the brigades in the Baghdad area received one of the SCID's IIRs that reported an insurgent was living in a certain area. The SCID agent who prepared the IIR was actively working to get more information to allow a local US brigade or Task Force–Black to strike with precision and detain the insurgent we believed to be responsible for armed action against US troops. Before we could gather more detailed information, the brigade responsible for the area used the information to set up a cordon and search operation in the insurgent's neighborhood. Our source told the SCID handling agent that the insurgent was returning to the neighborhood, saw the cordon that had been set up, and turned away instead of returning home. Once spooked, the insurgent stayed away from the neighborhood for weeks.

Despite the problems of units acting on our intelligence in a way that made our mission more difficult, the SCID reported a lot of intelligence in IIRs. If the information was specific and we were concerned some unit might act on it prematurely, before reporting the information in an IIR we would brief it to an action element such as Task Force–Black or the battalion responsible for the area. Units that knew they would be able to conduct a raid based on our information were willing to wait until our source had identified specific insurgents to capture and specific buildings to be searched.

But if the information wasn't specific enough to allow such action or we knew we would probably obtain no further information, we would report it in an IIR. By reporting the information, another intelligence officer could use the information to corroborate a report from his source or to cause a source handler or patrol to further investigate the information. The SCID agents were both intelligence officers and investigators. As investigators, we knew that a fact that seemed insignificant at first glance could make or break an investigation. The same is true for tracking insurgents.

THE BALANCE BETWEEN INVESTIGATION AND ACTION

That investigative mindset was missing from many who collected and handled HUMINT. For instance, special operations forces and conventional infantry soldiers conducted source operations in Iraq, but for many, recruiting and handling a source and following up on the source's information was not their primary specialty. The soldiers and sailors who are members of Task Force 145 and Army Special Forces are among the best warriors this nation produces. They are trained to act quickly and decisively. That is a different mindset and culture from that of an intelligence officer or investigator, who is trained to look for missing pieces of the puzzle and to infiltrate the enemy's military or intelligence operation in a long-term operation.

This difference in cultures was another reason why stovepipes were so pervasive and corrosive to the US effort in Iraq. Soldiers are trained to go on the offensive and to strike the enemy hard and often. Doing so keeps the enemy off balance and prevents it from mounting offensive operations.

The intelligence officer and investigator who are fighting an insurgency, however, see the value in a different approach for some situations. Capturing insurgents and their supporters helps reduce violence and protects the population, which are critical steps to a successful counterinsurgency operation. But some effort must be directed at longer-term operations. By accepting fewer results in the beginning, an intelligence officer can insert a source deeper into an insurgent organization. By inserting a source deeper into the organization, more valuable information can be gathered.

The strategy of raiding an insurgent's residence and collecting intelligence from a computer or from interrogating an insurgent and then using that information to capture more insurgents in a process that keeps repeating can be effective especially at the rapid pace practiced by Task Force 145. In the *Army Times* article cited above, one of the task force members states that the task force was "going balls to the wall, doing hits all over the place."[5] But this strategy risks becoming activity oriented (hit more houses faster) instead of results oriented (capture the insurgents doing the most damage). A complementary strategy pursued at the same time using an investigative approach that focuses on the insurgents who are most dangerous would enhance the US counterinsurgency effort.

Joseph Juran, an expert in quality management who died in

2008, set forth the 80–20 Rule, which states that 80 percent of consequences flow from 20 percent of causes.[6] This same rule applies to an insurgency. Although the insurgency we face in Iraq is a loose network of various groups, only a minority of the insurgents are ultimately responsible for the majority of the violence and instability that continues the insurgency.

There is no empirical evidence that proves 20 percent of insurgents are causing 80 percent of the bombings or deaths. But the 80–20 Rule seems to apply when you consider how the insurgency would be impacted if key members of the insurgency were killed or captured. Insurgents who emplace and detonate IEDs, EFPs, and car bombs cause most of the casualties in Iraq. The critical insurgents to identify and neutralize, however, are those who build IEDs, import EFPs from Iran, operate car bomb factories, recruit and pay those who detonate the explosives, and publicize the results of their evil on Web sites and in the news media. Killing or capturing such people does far more damage to the insurgency and the 4GW activities of Iran than merely capturing those who use the weapons they supply.

One example of the differences between these two cultures occurred during an operation that the SCID worked on with an Army Special Forces unit. The unit was advising an Iraqi army unit that had developed an excellent intelligence gathering capability. Using that intelligence to identify insurgents, the Iraqi unit, supported by its US advisers, would strike the insurgents. Some of the information from the Iraqi intelligence operation, however, was appropriate for a longer-term intelligence operation the SCID was working.

During the operation, the special forces soldiers were briefing two SCID agents about some of the intelligence gathered by the Iraqis. During the briefing, one of the SCID agents noticed several references to Iran's Ministry of Intelligence and Security (MOIS).

The MOIS and the Islamic Revolutionary Guard Corps both operated in Iraq, but our information had indicated the IRGC was much more active than the MOIS in the Baghdad area, so she asked about the increase in MOIS operations.

The special forces soldier told her that if his unit learned about the activities of "Iranian intelligence," it reported the activity as MOIS activity. To a special forces soldier who is an expert in small-unit infantry operations, training soldiers from other countries, and a host of other skills, the difference between the MOIS and IRGC is not important. But to a counterintelligence officer or investigator, misreporting such information can lead to the wrong conclusions being drawn.

In contrast to using intelligence to drive a process of rapid and continuous engagement of the enemy, consider the example of a SCID agent who patiently turned an insurgent and sent him back as a source. You may recall from chapter 5 the work of Brad Upshaw in working a covert HUMINT source against AQI insurgents. By the time Brad's tour of duty at the SCID was over, he and Kathy Hecht, the analyst who worked with him, were responsible for the capture of several AQI insurgents.

The 80–20 Rule seemed to apply to our side of the equation also. Not everyone was as adept as Brad at handling sources. Because of the importance of the operation, I diverted Jim Logan from an assignment elsewhere in the SCID to become Brad's replacement. It was one of the best decisions I made at the SCID. Jim was more than an experienced source handler. In his assignment as an AFOSI agent back in the United States, Jim trained AFOSI agents in source handling and other operational tradecraft. After being introduced to the source and studying the information that Kathy and Brad had developed, Jim realized more sources were necessary.

Most sources handled by military intelligence officers in Iraq were volunteers. The intelligence officers handling those sources were limited to accepting the information to which the sources had access. Effective management of those sources could produce valuable intelligence. But rarely would a second individual offer his services against a target that was already being worked by another source.

Jim began searching for another source to use against the same group of insurgents. Jim and Kathy discussed their desire for another source with an analyst at the division interrogation facility, where most of the insurgents captured with the SCID's information were taken for initial interrogation. As a result of army rules governing detainees, SCID agents could not approach a captured insurgent in the DIF. But the personnel at the DIF were sympathetic to our need and helped identify a recently captured insurgent as one who might be recruited. John and Kathy planned their recruitment pitch to the insurgent using information from the original source (who didn't know of the planned recruitment) and the insurgent's interrogation. The insurgent was released from the DIF but was instantly picked up by an SCID team and taken to a safe house.

At the safe house, Jim didn't threaten the insurgent. Instead, he used his mastery of information about the insurgent he had gleaned from our source's reporting and from interrogations of the insurgent and other insurgents to create the impression that Jim knew all there was to know about him. Jim convinced the insurgent that his best option was to work with us.

Recruiting the insurgent was not going to provide immediate results. Jim knew that the newly recruited source probably didn't have any actionable intelligence to provide that he hadn't already disclosed during interrogation at the DIF. Jim also recognized that the source would not be immediately productive because it would take time for him to be accepted back into his neighborhood and among his fellow AQI members.

But as an experienced investigator and source handler, Jim was willing to accept that delay and the risk that the source might later refuse to cooperate. Because Jim had chosen a person who had not adjusted well to captivity and who was noticeably struck by the depth of knowledge Jim exhibited, the chances for success were improved. Jim also recognized that the source might produce only minimally useful information for months or even years as he became more accepted into the AQI network, but he knew that having an informant who penetrated deeper into the organization would more likely than not provide information eventually. Recruiting a source was difficult and it remained to be seen whether the source would follow instructions and accept his new role as informant. But the more insurgents Jim turned and sent back into the community as sources, the more effective the SCID's work against AQI would be.

Unfortunately, the different backgrounds, skill sets, and willingness to accept delayed results possessed by special operations forces and military intelligence officers encourage a tendency to not work with each other. This tendency must be overcome, because special operations forces have unique opportunities to develop intelligence that could be exploited far better if it was shared. Special operations forces have access to information from human sources they handle and from intelligence gleaned from raiding insurgents' residences. Some of that HUMINT could best be developed with the longer-term approach used by intelligence organizations.

The failure to share information created by special operations forces and military intelligence personnel not working together across the Iraq theater also wastes one of the best opportunities for intelligence gathering against the insurgency. The ability to develop bilateral HUMINT operations with Iraqi forces that are advised by special forces and other military or civilian trainers is a tremendous opportunity that is not used as well as it should be. Many Iraqi soldiers and policemen are eager to receive training, equipment, and funding that comes from the United States. Because Iraqis have the language skills, cultural knowledge, and experience to spot and recruit sources among other Iraqis, US forces that advise and train police officers and soldiers are in an ideal position to receive and direct that intelligence. If the intelligence received from Iraqi police and military units was shared with US intelligence personnel, the intelligence efforts of those Iraqi units could be much better directed. Some of the intelligence could be used to satisfy the strategy of frequently raiding houses used by insurgents. But some of the intelligence is better suited for longer-term operations.

THE CIA STOVEPIPE

So far, I've described factors that cause stovepipes that are internal to the military and that could be corrected by the military on its own. But there are two intelligence operations in Iraq. One is the military intelligence apparatus I've outlined. The other is the CIA. Because neither works for the other, there is a division of effort that takes away from the US battle against the insurgency.

The CIA has the potential to be a large asset in a war against an insurgency. CIA officers are provided excellent training and have experience at operations that exceeds that of most military intelligence officers. In addition to their large talent pool, the equipment and funding provided to the CIA is amazing—especially to someone accustomed to mounting operations on the military's budget. For example, in Iraq most military personnel and equipment were hauled on regularly scheduled flights between several bases. In contrast, the CIA had its own fleet of aircraft to deliver people, supplies, and vehicles to various locations. But mixed in with the CIA officers who were clearly competent and experienced were some young officers who were carried away with their status and the incompetent who had been parked in an office away from Baghdad with little supervision.

Although the CIA and the military intelligence system don't work for the other, the CIA has some advantages in the relationship. Prior to the creation of the director of national intelligence, the CIA director also served as the director of central intelligence, a position that gave the CIA director the ability to issue rules that affected all agencies in the US intelligence community, including military intelligence agencies. Those rules gave the CIA ultimate authority in most intelligence operations, even to the point of being able to shut down operations proposed or conducted by the military. Such rules have a purpose in peacetime, but they don't function well during a war. In recent years the military intelligence community has sought independence from the directives set forth by the CIA director acting as the director of central intelligence. Along those lines, the military took the position that military intelligence operations in a war theater didn't require the CIA's approval.

Despite the efforts of many military intelligence officers to operate independently of the CIA, the agency still retained much of its status as the leader of the intelligence pack. But that status as top dog sometimes generated arrogance. One example of the difficulty some military intelligence officers perceive in working with the CIA occurred when one of the SCID teams attempted to coordinate an operation with a CIA office outside of Baghdad. The SCID team at Irbil had a matter that required a personal meeting with a CIA officer in northern Iraq.

The SCID team mounted a special mission that required most of a day for travel and to conduct the meeting, which had been arranged by secure e-mail. When the SCID team arrived at the CIA compound, the SCID agent was turned away by the guards. The CIA officer who had agreed to the meeting was at the office, but he wouldn't come to the compound entrance to explain what was happening. The SCID agent went to a nearby office and borrowed a secure e-mail terminal. In an exchange of e-mails, the CIA officer finally explained that she had chosen not to meet. She also explained that no appointment she made was considered "firm" unless she confirmed it twenty-four hours in advance.

The CIA officer was a relatively young woman who had only a few years' experience. The army intelligence officer from the SCID was a veteran of deep-cover HUMINT operations in Europe against the Soviet and Eastern European intelligence services. By any measure, the army intelligence officer had superior experience, but she was forced to appease a CIA officer impressed with her status. Instead of a meeting to pass information and coordinate a source operation that should have been of interest to the CIA, the team went back to Irbil. Much of a workday had been wasted for the agent and the six others from the team required to safely make the trip.

Considering the experience of the senior military intelligence officer in Iraq, the young CIA officer's behavior toward the military is understandable. The CIA assigned a very senior officer to the Baghdad station to be the CIA's representative to the commanding general of MNF–I, which at the time was General Casey. The CIA officer excluded Major General DeFreitas, who was Casey's deputy chief of staff for intelligence, from some of the briefings to Casey. The actions of that CIA official implied that the senior military intelligence officer couldn't be trusted. Yet the decisions of DeFreitas and his successors were probably more critical to the effort to defeat the insurgency than any actions of the CIA's personal envoy to the commander of MNF–I.

OUR COLLECTIVE CHARACTER FLAW

The war against the insurgency is complicated and degraded by the intelligence community's failure to share information. There are several reasons for not sharing information but most arise out of hubris, an exaggerated and arrogant self-confidence. This hubris is revealed in decisions to not share information because the collector of the intelligence believes he or she can do more with the information alone than by letting others know. The belief that one person or organization possesses all of the skills or has the best method for handling all intelligence issues helps create and maintain stovepipes. Worse yet, some intelligence officers may withhold information based on the belief that sharing intelligence reduces the credit he or she may be accorded.

Operational concerns about others acting prematurely on intelligence that is shared can be addressed by coordination with other agencies. That process is made much more difficult by the awkward hierarchal system the military uses for distributing intelligence. Chapter 9 contains some suggestions to alleviate that problem. But the fear of having a source compromised or an operation wrecked is significantly overblown compared to the actual risk in most cases.

Stovepipes are not the result of rational thought. They are the product of emotion. Our troops and the American public are paying the price for such selfish sentiments.

NOTES

1. Stephen A. Cambone, Undersecretary of Defense for Intelligence, Press Briefing, May 30, 2003, http://www.defenselink.mil/transcripts/transcript .aspx?transcriptid=2685 (accessed March 18, 2008).

2. Thom Shanker and Eric Schmitt, "Pentagon Says a Covert Force Hunts Hussein," *New York Times*, November 7, 2003, Foreign Desk section, p. 1.

3. Seymour Hersh, "Moving Targets," *New Yorker*, December 15, 2003, http://www.newyorker.com/archive/2003/12/15/031215fa_fact (accessed March 18, 2008).

4. Sean D. Naylor, "SpecOps Unit Nearly Nabs Zarqawi," *Army Times*, April 28, 2006, http://www.armytimes.com/legacy/new/1–292925–1739387.php (accessed March 18, 2008).

5. Ibid.

6. Nick Bunkley, "Joseph Juran, 103, Pioneer in Quality Control, Dies," *New York Times*, March 3, 2008, Obituary Section, p. 23.

Chapter 8

WAR AMONG THE INTELLIGENCE OFFICERS

Iraq, like other counterinsurgency conflicts, is an intelligence war. In Iraq our intelligence officers are engaged in several wars. The most obvious war facing an intelligence officer is the battle against the Sunni insurgency, especially the jihadists of al-Qaeda in Iraq. In addition to the intelligence war against the various Sunni factions, intelligence officers in Iraq also face Shiite militias and Iran's intelligence and special operations forces. In addition to those wars, there is a war among intelligence officers that causes stovepipes and red tape and hinders our efforts to defeat the insurgent groups we face.

To illustrate the nature and effect of these intelligence wars, consider the tale of two hypothetical combatants in Iraq. Although the two warriors are fictional, they represent what has occurred in Iraq. The first is Capt. Mike Simpson. He is the deputy intelligence officer for an army brigade stationed in Baghdad. He works for a major who is the intelligence officer, or S-2, for the brigade. Simpson's brigade has been in Iraq for about three months. He joined the brigade about a year before it deployed to Iraq. In his previous assignment, Simpson was the platoon leader of a ground surveillance radar platoon.

Much of Simpson's day is spent in an office inside a building on a forward operating base in the middle of a neighborhood that was historically a mix of Shiites and Sunnis. But many of the Sunnis have been driven from the area by the Jaysh al-Mahdi, the militia of Moqtada al-Sadr. Much of Simpson's duties involve reviewing reports and sending reports and e-mails down the chain to the NCOs in the intelligence section that he supervises and up the chain to his boss and people on the intelligence staff at the division, which has its headquarters at Camp Victory near the Baghdad International Airport.

The mission of the brigade is to keep the peace in the section of Baghdad it has been assigned. That requires identifying and capturing the bad guys. It is Simpson's job to identify the bad guys and figure out where to find them.

Sgt. Charles Phillips, one of the NCOs who works in the brigade's S-2 section, has been collecting a great deal of intelligence and has been advocating for some action against a Jaysh al-Mahdi cell he has identified. Last week, however, Simpson realized from one of Phillips's reports that most of the militiamen live a few blocks outside of their brigade's area of responsibility. Phillips was a bit upset when Simpson told him the brigade needed to delay action on the information until they could catch the militiamen inside the brigade's area of responsibility. After all, an officer's effectiveness report is much more impressive if it gives the officer credit for running the operation that catches bad guys instead of passing the ball to someone else to make the score.

Simpson's boss, Maj. Dale Smith, has been foul tempered for the last couple of weeks because of a dry spell in intelligence about Sunni insurgents and Shiite militias in the brigade's AOR. The previous brigade that held the AOR had taken advantage of the change of tactics that came with the "surge." Most of the brigade's soldiers now live and operate from patrol bases throughout the brigade's AOR instead of within the FOB occupied by the brigade's headquarters. When the surge started and US soldiers began living in the neighborhoods they secured, more Iraqis came forward with information about insurgents and Shiite militiamen. In contrast to Simpson's brigade, the adjoining brigade that secures the sector north of Simpson's brigade still frequently engages Sunni insurgents.

Smith, the brigade S-2, was surprised when he and Simpson were briefed by the brigade S-2 they replaced. The departing S-2 told Smith and Simpson that the neighborhoods they would be securing were changing. Many Sunnis had been driven out by the Jaysh al-Mahdi. Smith and Simpson were also surprised to learn that the S-2 and commander of the old brigade had taken to heart the lessons from an article in the *Military Review* written by Col. Ralph Baker.[1] They had set up a human source network that supplied information they used to capture insurgents and militiamen in the area.

Simpson had heard about the article during an intelligence course at the army's intelligence school at Fort Huachuca, Arizona, before coming to Iraq. The instructors at the intelligence school had been upset about the article, which encouraged field commanders to set up HUMINT source operations. Simpson had learned in his training that anybody other than a member of a Tactical HUMINT Team or HUMINT-trained intelligence officer who used HUMINT sources was committing an illegal act. Nobody at the school had told him why it was illegal.

Smith had the same feelings as Simpson about the source operations. As soon as the old brigade pulled out, Smith and Simpson had briefed the brigade staff and the battalion intelligence officers that they would rely on the THTs for their HUMINT. But the THTs that supported the brigade were only a handful of soldiers compared to the four thousand men and women in the brigade. Many of the soldiers in the THT were young troops who didn't have much experience handling sources. Simpson had become tired of Phillips's criticism of the lack of intelligence. Phillips was an army reservist who had been assigned to the brigade to bring them up to full strength for this deployment. In his civilian career, Phillips was a police officer, and he claimed to know how to handle sources. Even worse, he had come across Baker's article in *Military Review* and had been suggesting the brigade recontact the former brigade's sources.

But Simpson resisted that suggestion, even as the flow of new intelligence dropped off. Smith had confidently predicted that intelligence would increase after the brigade troops became accustomed to their new environment. Lately, Smith had been telling the brigade commander that the drop-off in intelligence and reduction in sectarian violence from the previous year indicated that the number of insurgents in the area had sharply reduced. The brigade operations officer had chuckled and asked if the facts didn't indicate the Shiites had killed or moved all the Sunnis. Smith wasn't amused.

But when Simpson and Smith came to work a couple of days before, they had learned that during the night some special ops soldiers had swooped into their AOR and hit a house and then left with four men. Simpson and Smith weren't sure about the details because the battalion in the area where the raid occurred had helped the task force by setting up the perimeter security during the operation but didn't go into the house. The company that supported the operation didn't have much to report other than four prisoners and a laptop computer were put into the Humvees used by the special ops team before they departed. Simpson's calls to the task force intelligence officer hadn't been returned.

This morning, Smith had walked away from Simpson wondering aloud how he was going to reconcile the task force's raid with his prior claim that insurgent activity was reduced in the area. Simpson began going through his e-mail and came across a classified e-mail from an intelligence officer who asked if tomorrow was a good day for the intelligence officer and an analyst to visit. Shaking his head, Simpson recalled first meeting the intelligence officer.

About two weeks earlier, Simpson had been awakened at 2 o'clock in the morning to learn the brigade had captured some prisoners. One of the brigade's battalions reported that it had been contacted earlier in the evening by an intelligence officer with information about insurgents in their area. Instead of general information about someone named Abu Something who was suspected of being somewhere in the area, this intelligence had been very specific. In fact, the intelligence officer had offered to come point out the specific house. A company from the battalion had a patrol out that evening and it met the intelligence officer about an hour later. The raid had captured three men, some rifles, and a small amount of explosives. The prisoners captured had been brought to the brigade's detention and interrogation facility at its FOB. That's where Simpson met the intelligence officer who had supplied the information about the houses.

The intelligence officer and the men and women with him were dressed in civilian clothes, but they were well armed. They had an Iraqi with them who was wearing a scarf, goggles, and a borrowed army uniform shirt to hide his identity. The Iraqi sat in an LAV, and two of the soldiers clad in civilian clothing kept people away. Even the company's Iraqi interpreter, who had tried to be friendly, had been turned away when he approached the armored Suburban to keep his countryman company. Simpson learned that the Iraqi in the Suburban was a source who had been inside the two houses that had been raided by the brigade's soldiers. The source had pointed out the houses and described the layout of the interiors to the platoon leader and platoon sergeant who led the raid.

Simpson had been put off by the casual air of the people with the intelligence officer and had been irritated because some of the paperwork about the prisoners and the material seized wasn't filled out properly. Of course it wasn't filled out right: The people who provided the information weren't even in the army. Simpson had been a bit embarrassed to learn when he tried to talk down to the intelligence officer that he was talking to a navy lieutenant, so Simpson didn't outrank him. Along with the navy lieutenant, who was a reservist with the Naval Criminal Investigative Service, was an Air Force Office of Special Investigations special agent who Simpson suspected was an NCO. He could tell because the man's eyes seemed to light up while he kept a straight face when the NCIS agent explained who they were. Also, Simpson learned a day later that the AFOSI agent had convinced the platoon leader to let him take a computer and some cell phones that had been seized from the houses.

According to the e-mail Simpson was reading, the NCIS agent wanted to return the computer and cell phones, with a report on the information they contained. Apparently the NCIS agent's intelligence unit had a computer forensics specialist who had examined the equipment. This avoided waiting several days or weeks for the media exploitation specialists at Camp Victory to perform a similar service. The NCIS agent's e-mail stated that he wanted to discuss sharing information with the brigade and find out what the brigade might know that would assist the agent's operations against Sunni insurgents and Shiite militia who were suspected of using explosively formed penetrators in the area. In order to smooth over the flap with the prisoner paperwork, he wanted to bring his unit's deputy operations officer, an army civilian employee who was a military intelligence officer. Simpson had learned what to do by watching his boss. The first step was to ignore such a request, which he had done when he received a similar e-mail three days earlier. Now he would respond to their requests as slowly as possible, hoping they would give up.

Nobody should know more about intelligence in Simpson's AOR than he did, so it wasn't clear how these soldiers, sailors, and airmen who popped into his brigade's AOR could be any help. Besides, Simpson's AOR had experienced only one EFP. Simpson didn't need any help. It was bad enough the brigade had to put up with the special operations task force, but now someone was offering to share information and expecting a similar favor in return. It wasn't the way things were done. Maybe the next step would be to refer the NCIS agent to the division intelligence staff.

To distract himself from the problem of how to respond to the e-mail, Simpson pulled up his checking account online and checked his balance. He noticed his paycheck had been deposited. Here in Iraq, with the weeks running together and not many places to spend money, his balance was beginning to grow, although he would never get rich on army pay. Then he sent an e-mail to his girlfriend back home and began preparing for the rest of the day. Thoughts of his girlfriend lingered. He planned to propose when he returned, which would be in another year. The fifteen-month tours were tougher than the one-year tours. At least that's what he had heard from troops who were on their second or third tours in Iraq.

Simpson thought he would figure out his strategy for handling the request during his visit to the battalion that had allowed this problem to start by using the information to conduct a raid. Simpson began putting on his full "battle rattle," which meant first slipping into body armor followed by his tactical vest bulging with rifle magazines, grenades, first aid kit, and a hydration system that had a water bladder riding on his back with a drinking tube he clipped on his chest so he could suck water from the water reservoir. Then he checked that he had his pistol, M-4 rifle, and helmet.

As Simpson was climbing into a Humvee that would be part of a convoy to the battalion he was visiting that day, a few blocks away Mustafa al-Zamili sipped Chai tea and considered his options. Mustafa was the leader of what the Americans called a "special group" or "secret cell." Originally a follower of Moqtada al-Sadr, Mustafa still professed allegiance to Sadr when it was convenient but had found Sadr to be too indecisive for his taste.

Mustafa's zeal for ruthlessly moving Sunnis out of their homes while cleansing the West Rashid section of Baghdad had been noticed by the Iranian Revolutionary Guards' Qods Force. After being approached to receive advanced training, Mustafa had traveled to Iran. After two months of training in Iran, Mustafa returned to Baghdad and settled back into the al-Jihad neighborhood that was less than two miles from the Green Zone. He now controlled a cell that consisted of himself and four other fighters who had also received training in Iran. While Mustafa and his fighters were in Iran they had been trained by members of the Qods Force and Lebanese Hezbollah in how to use EFPs, rockets, and mortars. They were also trained in collecting intelligence, sniper shooting, and kidnapping operations. Upon the end of the training, Mustafa had been given $10,000 in cash, more money than he had ever seen. That payment was only the beginning of an enriching experience for Mustafa.[2]

Today Mustafa was meeting with an Iranian Qods Force officer who regularly provided cash and weapons. The cash was used to pay

Mustafa and his men and to finance their operations against US forces and other targets suggested by the Qods Force. At this meeting the Qods Force officer was giving Mustafa $25,000. Unlike Simpson, who needed body armor and an armed convoy for travel, Mustafa felt very safe carrying the cash.

In a car nearby were two of Mustafa's men. Even without the men watching over him, only a stranger to the neighborhood would have been foolish enough to accost Mustafa. Although his association with the Qods Force wasn't well known, the neighborhood knew him as a member of the Jaysh al-Mahdi. In addition to the money received from the Qods Force, Mustafa controlled many houses that had been owned by Sunnis who had been killed or chased away. He now received rent from Shiites who lived in the houses and used the furniture and cars that once belonged to the Sunnis.[3]

One of Mustafa's men, Hakim Rashid, had a special aptitude for kidnapping and extortion. The profits from those enterprises, which Hakim shared with Mustafa, added to their wealth. Hakim had been prone to violence before the Americans arrived in Baghdad. He had been among the many criminals released from jail by Saddam before the invasion. Neither man had been educated past high school. Both had been born into families that had suffered from discrimination against Shiites by the Sunnis who ran Saddam Hussein's government. But neither man had warm feelings for all Shiites. In addition to their enmity for the Sunnis who had put down the Shiites who dwelled in slums, both Mustafa and Hakim despised the Islamic Supreme Council of Iraq. They especially despised the ISCI's militia, the Badr Corps.

Many in the ISCI and the Badr Corps came from the ranks of the middle and upper classes of Shiites and had not suffered like the followers of Sadr did. Many in the Badr Corps had joined the Iraqi police and now conducted their sectarian violence and political maneuvering dressed in the uniform of the Iraqi government.

Mustafa found himself pondering future actions. The Iranian Qods Force officer gave him money and told him when to expect the next shipment of EFPs, the armor-piercing roadside bombs that Mustafa's men used against the Americans. While Mustafa's men still placed the bombs and attacked US forces, they also found many who were willing to take the weapons, with instructions where to use them, in exchange for payment. For the more demanding situations that required large arrays of EFPs to be carefully camouflaged, Mustafa's men would use their training and experience and personally carry out the attacks.

But one of Mustafa's men who spoke English and spent much time at an Internet café had showed Mustafa some videos he had downloaded from an American Web site called YouTube. It showed the American devils using airplanes that could see at night attacking warriors who were putting IEDs in place. Mustafa had noticed the attacks were in open areas where it was easy to see what the insurgents were doing. Mustafa assumed the people he watched die in the videos were al-Qaeda Sunni scum and was happy to see them disintegrated by the American machine gun fire.

After seeing that video, Mustafa's men always paid someone else to put EFPs in open areas. The Qods Force did not pay enough to make Mustafa want to take that risk. Mustafa's men were careful to operate as though they were always being watched. Sometimes that meant putting an EFP array in place during the day. Even if local residents saw what they were doing and were suspicious, they knew to keep quiet. By putting their EFPs in place during a time of day when others were around, Mustafa's men didn't draw attention from the airplanes, helicopters, and remote-controlled aircraft that flew so high they couldn't be seen or heard.

In addition to his connections with the Qods Force, Mustafa worked with others as it served him. At times Mustafa would join forces with elements of the Jaysh al-Mahdi. At other times his group would operate independently. Mustafa also joined with criminal gangs that were interested in making money from stealing, robbing, and kidnapping. Mustafa had also paid them to assassinate Badr Corps militiamen who were Iraqi police officers.

Unlike Simpson, Mustafa did not long for the fighting to end or count the days until he returned home. Mustafa was at home and the fighting had given Mustafa power, status, and wealth. Mustafa's savings were very large and kept in cash and a few gold coins he had managed to obtain. Mustafa invested some of his savings in legitimate businesses as a way to prepare for life after the Americans left. His role as a leader of a secret cell also helped protect him and his associates. Tales of his kidnapping and killing helped prevent the same type of misery from visiting his family.

But one of Mustafa's fighters had been captured recently. Kazem al-Yaqubi, who was the best of his group at handling EFPs and other explosives, was taken from his house along with two of Kazem's helpers in the middle of the night. According to Kazem's wife, the soldiers descended upon his house and a house next door, where Kazem had allowed some cousins, including his two helpers, to live. The wife said the Americans had taken a laptop computer and the three cell phones in the house.

Two days later Mustafa and all of his associates had new cell phones to prevent them from being tracked by the Americans. Still, there was probably some record of ownership for at least some of the cell phones that would connect Kazem to some of Mustafa's men. Searching to learn how Kazem was arrested, Mustafa had talked to the translator for the US soldiers who had captured Kazem. Each month, Mustafa paid several translators who worked for US forces as much as the Americans paid the translators in salary to inform Mustafa of what they heard and saw. Luckily, one of those translators had been present when Kazem was captured. Mustafa could have threatened the translator to ensure his cooperation, but the money gave the translator an incentive, and Mustafa told the translator that his spying on the Americans proved his loyalty to Moqtada al-Sadr. The translator was much too scared of what would happen to him and his family to ever disclose his association with Mustafa.

From the translator Mustafa had learned the Americans had a spy in his organization. Mustafa found this odd because he knew that the Americans had decreased their efforts to have sources in this neighborhood. It was one reason why Mustafa operated from the area and usually picked targets outside of the brigade's area of responsibility. The translator told Mustafa he had seen the spy, but the Americans had hidden him in one of their armored SUVs and two of their men sent him away when he tried to get a good look at him. Mustafa regretted that the SUV hadn't been the one his men had attacked last week. An EFP easily penetrated the armor of such vehicles, with devastating results. More concerning to Mustafa, the translator reported that the spy was an Iraqi who worked for a group of Americans who were not part of the soldiers in the area. Mustafa benefited from operating in different areas, and he didn't like the idea of American intelligence trying to track him through different parts of Iraq.

After meeting the translator, Mustafa reflected on the source network he had developed after being trained in Iran. The Iranians and Lebanese recognized the importance of intelligence and had trained him well. Intelligence collection had become a special interest for Mustafa since his return from Iran. Unlike Simpson and the NCIS agent who required much security to travel and who had difficulty meeting someone without being noticed, Mustafa traveled freely through Baghdad while meeting his sources. One of Mustafa's sources had recently helped rid him of a problem.

Some al-Qaeda fighters who had been attacking places where Shiites gathered lived in West Rashid. They had been too well armed to move out of their homes like the other Sunnis the Jaysh al-Mahdi had cleared from the area. The houses in which the Sunnis lived were fortified compounds with high walls and thick doors that were difficult to breach. Because the jihadists had several houses, they were difficult to locate and attack.

Mustafa's source was married to a Sunni, and through her family, who supplied gasoline to the Sunnis, Mustafa had learned where the jihadists were staying. An attack to dislodge the Sunnis would have been difficult, and Mustafa didn't want to fail. Instead of attacking, Mustafa took the information to a Badr Corps soldier he knew who had joined the Iraqi Ministry of Interior two years ago. Despite the ill will between Sadr's followers and the Badr Corps, they sometimes cooperated against a common enemy.

The Badr Corps police officer gave the information to a friend of his in the Ministry of Defense who worked with the American special operations forces. About a week later, the Americans raided the house where the jihadists were staying. Quickly lowering themselves into the compound from helicopters as it was surrounded, the Americans had overcome the light resistance the Sunnis put up. The Sunnis were in prison and Mustafa had not risked any of his fighters to get rid of them.

Although the tale of Mustafa and Simpson is fictional, their stories represent the contrast between the insurgency and the US intelligence effort against the insurgency. As the story illustrates, both insurgents and counterinsurgents require effective intelligence in order to succeed.[4] But the insurgents and the US forces fighting them vary greatly in their operations.

A NETWORK OF NETWORKS

The insurgency is not a single organization or a centrally directed group of organizations. It is a network of networks. Each network has individuals and groups that sometimes work together. But the small size and lack of bureaucracy allows the individuals and groups who oppose the United States to act decisively, to quickly change strategies and tactics, and to carry out high-profile attacks with less chance of detection.

The insurgency in Iraq presents US forces with many possible targets, including the following:

- al-Qaeda in Iraq
- Sunni Islamic extremists who are not affiliated with AQI
- Sunni insurgents who are not Islamic extremists, such as tribal groups opposed to the occupation of Iraq
- Jaysh al-Mahdi
- Other Shiite militias, including Badr Corps and Fadhila
- The "special groups" that operate as an extension of Iran's Qods Force
- Criminal gangs

These forces are arranged in a checkerboard pattern across Iraq and often share the same neighborhoods. The assortment of opponents to the United States is so diverse that two US Army battalions that control adjacent areas may face different insurgent groups.[5] As a result, intelligence officers face not just one war, but several wars against a variety of insurgents with differing interests and reasons for fighting.

Confusing matters further, especially for an intelligence system that was designed to fight the military of a large nation-state instead of an insurgency, the various groups may join together for a single operation that benefits the participants. Even within a particular group, the various cells of insurgents operate in small groups, with little centralized direction of the type found in the armies of Western nations.

The decentralized nature of insurgent groups make them more survivable and, thus, more difficult to defeat. Professor Steven Metz of the Army War College's Strategic Studies Institute has written that no single node of a networked insurgent organization is vital.[6] For example, despite the effort devoted to the manhunt for Abu Musab al-Zarqawi that began in 2004 and culminated in his death in 2006, Zarqawi's network, AQI, continues to operate.

Another aspect of the networked organization of insurgents is that such insurgents are quick to find and use tactics that are most effective with the least cost in terms of money and risk.[7] The tactic that is most effective today is terrorism. As discussed in chapter 3, the publicity surrounding violent acts, not the actual acts of violence, is the weapon that does the most damage to our counterinsurgency efforts. According to Metz, "In terrorism, it matters less how many people were killed than how many people know of and are influenced by the deaths."[8]

Consider AQI's use of chlorine bombs in Iraq during 2007. The fear of injury from chemical weapons captured headlines in the United States and frightened Iraqi residents. The weapons were crude and the chlorine gas released by exploding such bombs was largely ineffective as a weapon to kill Iraqis. The fear of such weapons not only terrorized Iraqis but also caused restrictions in the distribution of chlorine, which had the effect of lowering the already bad water quality in Iraq.

THE BUREAUCRACY—SLUGGISH AND JEALOUS

In contrast to the violent insurgency that is flexible and adaptable because of its networked organization, the intelligence system fighting the insurgency is hierarchal and slow. Many of the practices of the intelligence bureaucracy are more than annoying; they have the effect of detracting from the intelligence effort against the insurgency. The practice that is most harmful to the intelligence war against the insurgency is the failure to share and distribute information, which was discussed in the last chapter. The intelligence bureaucracy results in a practice of passing intelligence information through the hierarchy, which is slow and cumbersome.[9]

The bureaucracy and stovepipes mean that intelligence officers must fight yet another war. This war is an internal struggle that pits one intelligence officer against another. Some are devoted to their protocols, practices, regulations, structure, and the belief in technology as a cure to insurgency. Such intelligence officers believe that adherence to these rules will result in success. But the measurement of success varies: For some, success means making the population safe and taking away support for the insurgency; for others, success is measured in terms of career achievement and defending an organization's turf.

On the other side of this intelligence war are those who believe the current practices and structure are incapable of defeating an insurgency in the limited time the American public will give its leaders in any irregular war. These intelligence officers have no turf to defend. They are the ones who search for ways to succeed despite rules that are designed to preserve the hierarchy instead of defeating the insurgency. Ralph Peters, a writer and retired army officer who served as an intelligence officer, made this observation about the intelligence bureaucracy:

But, then, our intelligence community is, above all, a massive bureaucracy—and bureaucracies discourage risk-taking or excellence that does not match the models of the past. The motto of our vast intelligence establishments is "Play it safe." The mindset may protect careers but does little for our country.[10]

In past chapters I have described the military intelligence bureaucracy at work. Prisoners required a task force replete with rules on who can question them, where they can be questioned, how they can be moved, and so on. Sharing information about what sources were in place and who their targets were was discouraged by passing the request for information to the next level. Reports prepared after hours of source work, analysis, and writing were critiqued by a contractor at Camp Slater who was drawing wages much higher than the military source handler operating in the red zone.

THE CRITICAL ROLE OF ANALYSIS

One vital area of intelligence in the bureaucracy that hasn't been much discussed in prior chapters is intelligence analysis. After HUMINT is received from sources, prisoners, liaison contacts, and investigations, it must be examined for accuracy and compared to other intelligence. The HUMINT is then combined with intelligence from other sources. New intelligence is put into context with what is known and suspected: Does the new information fit with existing intelligence? Does the new information suggest a new tactic or technique used by the enemy?

Intelligence analysts answer those questions. Some of the primary activities of an analyst are reading, researching, writing, and thinking. Traditionally, analysts don't work in close proximity to the people who collect the intelligence they analyze. This is understandable for analysts who study and interpret satellite images or intercepted conversations, but many analysts assigned to HUMINT organizations never have a face-to-face conversation with the person handling the source who provided the information.

There are logistical reasons why analysts don't always operate in the same venue as the collectors. In order to have access to other intelligence collected, an analyst requires a secure high-speed Internet connection, which may not be available where source handlers and other HUMINT personnel are located. Also, a great deal of HUMINT is collected by people in places where more effort and expense to feed, house, and protect them are required. Additionally, analysts benefit from having other analysts to talk with about their projects.

But the principal reason for the separation of analyst and intelligence collector is the hierarchal organization of the military. The intelligence structure was built to feed information to higher headquarters in order for intelligence officers and analysts to use the information to predict the enemy's future actions. This structure made sense when the US Army was preparing to fight a tank battle against the Soviet empire in defense of Western Europe. Much of the intelligence in such a war would have developed from patrol reports, satellite images, and intercepted radio communications.

Compared to a conventional war, a counterinsurgency action is rich in HUMINT. Iraqis offering information approach US checkpoints every day. Soldiers and marines on patrol come in contact with several people on each patrol. Hundreds of new prisoners are interrogated each week. An insurgency provides many opportunities to use human sources to identify and locate insurgents. The increased emphasis on HUMINT elevates the issue of the nature of the relationship between analyst and intelligence officer.

Traditional Analysis

In order to understand the relationship and the need for change, it helps to understand what intelligence analysts do. Intelligence analysts fill different roles at different levels of the US intelligence community. Political and military leaders rely on analysts to provide them an opinion as to the meaning of the intelligence that has been collected. This happens at the national level and at lower levels. The National Intelligence Estimates that are produced to advise the president regarding a variety of topics are examples of this type of analysis.

Some analysts have studied certain topics to the point that they have become the government's leading expert on a certain issue. These experts review all intelligence that is available on their topic of interest and may periodically produce reports or be consulted by other analysts. Nuclear and biological weapons, aircraft technology, spacecraft, and specific geographic areas are examples of topics about which analysts become experts.

At several levels of the intelligence bureaucracy, analysts serve to summarize and report intelligence trends, often on narrow topics such as one terrorist group or activity within a single country. Often these analysts are encouraged by their organizations to publish reports based on that organization's intelligence gathering as a means to demonstrate the value of the organization's intelligence collection and analysis.

A present-day example of the "summarize and report" analytical function can be found in the Combined Intelligence Operations Center of Multi-National Force–Iraq. An analyst may be assigned to a topic or might suggest a topic for a study. The analyst then reviews all of the intelligence information reports and other reporting on that particular topic. For instance, if the analyst were studying an insurgent group, the analyst's report would summarize the history of the group, including the origin of the group's name, the activities attributed to or claimed by the group, and the names of the leaders and prominent members of the group and their backgrounds, including their ethnic group and tribal or religious sect affiliation. The report would probably identify the area of Iraq in which the group operated and the weapons and tactics used. Usually such a report would also contain an opinion as to the group's motivation (religious, sectarian, criminal, or a combination of motives) and a prediction as to future activities.

Such reports help provide an understanding of the nature of the insurgency. Persons desiring to understand more about current operations of insurgent groups in a general sense and their possible connections with other groups find such reports useful. But sometimes such reporting is the classified version of a college term paper: It is interesting to read but doesn't provide the information a commander responsible for securing a sector of Iraq most desires.

Analysts and Source Handlers Can Work Together

The most desired information is actionable intelligence, which is intelligence that is specific enough to allow a military force to identify the insurgent or terrorist causing the most damage and to locate that insurgent in a way that allows US forces to capture or kill him. For instance, knowing that Osama bin Laden is somewhere in western Pakistan, possibly in an area with a large population of supporters of jihad, is not actionable.

In order to avoid the problem of creating classified term papers complete with color charts and graphs that do nothing to find insurgents, the direction I gave to the intelligence analysts at the SCID was simple. I told analysts that if what they were working on did not lead us to a specific house where we could find an insurgent, they were working on the wrong thing.

Using their training and analytical tools to identify the names of insurgents and their associates, their residences and workplaces, and their cell phone numbers and cars was not the level of analysis that many analysts had performed in the past. Not only did the analysts have a goal to locate a specific target, the analysts had to work directly with the SCID agents who were handling the sources or conducting investigations.

This was different and uncomfortable for many of the analysts and the agents. They were not accustomed to working shoulder to shoulder under the same roof. Some analysts and agents took to it better than others. The reason for the discomfort was the prior training and experience of both the analysts and agents.

Most of the analysts at the SCID had been trained by the army in their prior careers as army officers or NCOs. The training and customs of the intelligence community causes friction between analysts and source handlers and does not encourage analysts to orient their analysis to targeting insurgents. Much of the work of analysts is devoted to detecting trends and predicting future tactics by the enemy. Much of that analysis is conducted at the macro level and involves collecting a lot of information and reducing it to statistical data. That does little good in combating an insurgency.

In order to effectively counter an insurgency, US forces must protect the population by reducing violence. Finding the people who are supplying car bombs, EFPs, IEDs, mortars, and rockets will reduce the level of violence. But finding insurgents in urban areas requires a street address, not a four-digit map grid coordinate that narrows the hunt to somewhere within a square kilometer.

HUMINT can provide the detailed targeting information needed to effectively strike the minority of insurgents who are causing the majority of violence. Analysts are needed to review and digest the intelligence collected and to focus the efforts of the intelligence officers collecting HUMINT, whether they are handling sources, interrogating prisoners, or conducting liaison with tribal chiefs and local police officers. Many analysts see themselves as directing the collection of information as they put pieces of a puzzle together. The training provided to many intelligence analysts has taught them that they are the brains of the intelligence operations and that intelligence collectors are to follow their direction.

At times this mindset produces arrogant comments by analysts and taskings that are contrary to the strategy of the source handler. Analysts sometimes communicate in e-mails that seem intended to entertain themselves and their coworkers with their wit at the expense of the source handler or other intelligence collector. The training and bureaucratic structure for analyst-collector communications discourages collaboration and engenders hard feelings that detract from the fight.

But the relationship between analyst and intelligence collector need not be a counterproductive intelligence war. The insight of intelligence analysts can focus and steer an investigation, source operation, or other intelligence collection in the right direction. Unfortunately, the attitude of some analysts, gained from their training or association with other analysts, has been to treat those who collect the intelligence as fungible pieces that can be pushed around a game board at their will. This is an odd approach for analysts to take, because many analysts would find handling a source to be much more troublesome and less of an exact process than they realize. Most analysts don't possess the abilities needed to spot and recruit a source.

On the other hand, many intelligence officers who handle sources and collect intelligence don't approach intelligence collection as methodically and logically as they could. The discipline that comes from an analyst's exhortation to task a source for certain information and the reminder to follow up to collect the information from the source increases the effectiveness of any source handler.

Placing analysts and intelligence officers in the same workplace enhances the effectiveness of a HUMINT operation. Face-to-face discussions often spontaneously occur and allow analysts to extract far more information than what is contained in written reports. Analysts experience firsthand the limitations and potential of sources. Analysts are present when intelligence officers meet with intelligence personnel from other organizations and are able to establish networking contacts that promote the exchange of information. Analysts can demonstrate through link diagrams and other visual aids the connections among suspected insurgents that make clear to the source handlers the information that needs to be collected.

Contracting for Analysis

Pushing analysts to the field level increases the need for analysts. That increased requirement for analysts is part of a larger increase in demand for intelligence professionals of all specialties— including analysts, source handlers, and interrogators—that occurs when fighting an insurgency. The increased demand has created a shortage of qualified analysts that affects our ability to fight an insurgency.

In response to that demand, the military has spent millions in outsourcing analysis work to civilian contractors. Outsourcing intelligence work has several ramifications. Because large amounts of money authorized by Congress in special war appropriations had less scrutiny than normal budget appropriations, outsourcing became a great resource—for contractors.

Following the terrorist attacks on September 11, 2001, military organizations and the intelligence community received billions of dollars to expand and maintain intelligence capability. This spurt in funding had the damnable effect of encouraging stovepipes instead of the sharing of information. Organizations that might otherwise be forced by budget constraints to collaborate and share information and resources were able in the post-9/11 period to build the capability to do what another organization already did.[11] Sadly, the building of more stovepiped intelligence functions took place even as multiple reports, such as the 9/11 Joint Congressional Inquiry Report, cited the lack of collaboration among intelligence organizations as one of the reasons for recent intelligence failures.[12]

The primary beneficiaries of the sudden need for many more intelligence personnel, especially analysts, were companies that contracted with the US government to supply personnel. Others who benefited were the people hired to be analysts, linguists, interrogators, and other intelligence specialists. Individuals with training and experience as an analyst, even only four or five years of experience, were often paid as much as a United States senator if they served in Iraq or Afghanistan. But in exchange for remaining out of the country for a year, the first $80,000.00 of income was received tax free. In addition to their salaries, contractors were provided a place to live and their meals while in Iraq.

That kind of money attracted problems. The organization that supplied the SCID with its intelligence analysts was the Counterintelligence Field Activity, a Defense Department agency. One of the main suppliers of contractors to CIFA was a contractor known as MZM, Inc. In 2006 Mitchell Wade, the CEO of MZM, pled guilty to paying Rep. Randall "Duke" Cunningham, a California congressman who had been a navy fighter pilot during the Vietnam War, more than $1 million in bribes.[13]

Cunningham served on the US House Intelligence Committee and in that position was able to earmark millions of dollars for contracts that would be awarded to MZM. Many of those contracts were for work performed by CIFA. Created in 2002, CIFA's spending exploded as it spent about $1 billion on counterterrorism and counterintelligence projects from 2002 until 2006. The majority of the money was spent for services outsourced to contractors. According to a *U.S. News & World Report* article, MZM gave CIFA employees meals, prime seats for ball games, and invitations to a lavish annual Christmas party. The director of CIFA apparently relied on MZM and its congressional connections to obtain enhanced funding for CIFA.[14]

Given the manner in which CIFA received its funding and selected its contractors, it is remarkable that most of the intelligence analysts CIFA sent to the SCID performed well. Some were outstanding analysts. In addition to the general risk of living in places that were subject to rocket or mortar attacks, some of the analysts exposed themselves to more danger by traveling in the red zone to Camp Victory or other locations.

But then there were others. One such analyst arrived at a time when the SCID received about ten analysts from CIFA within a two-week period. After Don Everest, the SCID's deputy director, interviewed the analysts and learned more about their background, we decided to assign this particular analyst to the SCID team in Basra. Getting to Basra was not easy, especially in June, when this analyst was traveling. Frequent dust storms caused flights to be canceled. The easiest way to get the analyst to Basra was to take him to the BIAP, where he would wait for a flight—a wait that might take a few days.

Fortunately, the National Guard platoon that served as the SCID's security element was part of a brigade reconnaissance team that was headquartered at Camp Slater at the BIAP. The team commander and his staff frequently assisted the SCID by billeting and transporting people awaiting flights or who were stuck overnight at Camp Victory or Camp Slater. The analyst was waiting at the team office in a palace at Camp Slater for a flight to Basra. The analyst stepped out of the office into a hallway near the front door of the palace, where an army lieutenant colonel spotted him.

"You!" The officer followed his shout with a loud verbal assault. The lieutenant colonel later explained to Don Everest that he had been the analyst's boss about two months earlier when the analyst was working at the MNF–I intelligence directorate at Camp Slater. One day the analyst didn't show up for work. Because none of the analyst's coworkers knew where he was, the intelligence directorate had to consider the possibility the analyst had been kidnapped or been involved in an accident.

A few days later the lieutenant colonel learned the analyst had left Baghdad after finding a different contractor job that he preferred. The analyst didn't bother to tell anyone he was leaving a war zone. The new job was at the SCID. If the analyst hadn't been assigned to Basra and been standing around a palace waiting for a flight, he might have served his one-year tour at the SCID without incident.

But his streak of bad luck continued. The lieutenant colonel who discovered the missing analyst happened to be the officer who controlled access to the classified intelligence databases needed in order to perform duties as an analyst. Ten minutes after the lieutenant colonel returned to his office, the analyst's access to all classified systems in Iraq was revoked. This meant he was worthless to the SCID. No more big salary. Fortunately, his bags were already packed and he was at the airport. He was able to catch a flight out of Baghdad the next day.

THE FAILURE TO WORK TOGETHER

A stifling bureaucracy demanding strict allegiance to its rules, analysts and intelligence collectors not working together, and contractors taking our tax dollars to supply intelligence personnel are some of the battles among intelligence officers. These internal conflicts reduce our ability to fight our insurgent opponents. In earlier chapters I described the disagreement in 2005 among intelligence officers as to whether Iran's importation of EFPs and other activities constituted a threat worthy of our attention. As the war has progressed, there can be no question Iran's intervention in Iraq has killed many American servicemen and detracted from our ability to face the Sunni insurgency. Iran's activity—and our ignoring that activity—has prolonged our time in Iraq.

But at least the dispute among intelligence officers as to the degree and nature of the Iranian threat was based on opinions that legitimately differed. The other wars among intelligence officers have no legitimate purpose and hurt only ourselves. The intelligence bureaucracy is filled with rules jealously guarded by people who have spent a career learning and enforcing the rules regardless of their effect. Stovepipes and the resistance to sharing intelligence they encourage are caused by many factors, including competition among intelligence organizations, arrogance, and the lack of a single entity in charge of intelligence operations in an insurgency. Analysts and source handlers are two types of intelligence officers that are both vital to defeating any enemy. But the failure to work together drastically reduces the amount and quality of HUMINT our sources produce.

Skirmishes among intelligence officers may never end, but the war among intelligence officers must end—or the next war may result in catastrophe.

NOTES

1. Ralph O. Baker, "HUMINT-Centric Operations: Developing Actionable Intelligence in the Urban Counterinsurgency Environment," *Military Review*, March–April 2007, p. 12.

2. Although this is a hypothetical account, see Mark Kukis, "Signs of Iran's Hand in Iraq," *Time*, March 18, 2008, http://www.time.com/time/world/article/0,8599,1723301,00.html (accessed March 29, 2008), for an account of a Jaysh al-Mahdi fighter sent to Iran for similar training.

3. Joshua Parlow, "Mahdi Army, Not Al-Qaeda, Is Enemy No. 1 in Western Baghdad," *Washington Post*, July 16, 2007, p. A1.

4. Kyle Teamey and Jonathan Sweet, "Organizing Intelligence for Counterinsurgency," *Military Review*, September–October 2006, p. 24.

5. Ibid., p. 25.

6. Steven Metz, "Rethinking Insurgency," Strategic Studies Institute, June 2007, p. 13, http://www.strategicstudiesinstitute.army.mil/Pubs/display.cfm?pubID=790 (accessed March 31, 2008).

7. Ibid., p. 48.

8. Ibid., p. 14.

9. Teamey and Sweet, "Organizing Intelligence for Counterinsurgency," p. 27.

10. Ralph Peters, *Beyond Terror: Strategy in a Changing World* (Mechanicsburg, PA: Stackpole Books, 2002), p. 197.

11. Sebastian Abbot, "The Outsourcing of U.S. Intelligence," News21: A Journalism Initiative of the Carnegie and Knight Foundations, July 28, 2006, http://newsinitiative.org/story/2006/07/28/the_outsourcing_of_u_s_intelligence (accessed March 31, 2008).

12. Douglas Hart and Steven Simon, "Thinking Straight and Talking Straight: Problems of Intelligence Analysis," *Survival*, Spring 2006, p. 51, http://www.cyberneutics.com/publications/SurvivalFeb06.pdf (accessed March 30, 2008).

13. Chitra Ragavan, "Capitol Crooks," *U.S. News & World Report*, September 25, 2006, pp. 54–66.

14. Ibid.

Chapter 9

THE NEXT WAR

What kind of war and what type of opponent will the United States next face? The answer to that question should guide how our military and the rest of our government prepare to fight the next war. Knowing what type of war is likely in the future should also guide our intelligence community in its preparation for war and in its actions between wars.

North Korea and Iran possess or seek to build nuclear weapons and routinely issue bellicose threats against the United States. China and Russia are former cold war foes that have the industrial base and military tradition that could compete with the United States. In order to face those nations, the United States must have a strong military that can fight a third-generation war of maneuver using armor, infantry, artillery, and airpower.

But after the convincing defeats of Saddam Hussein's armies in the 1991 Gulf War and the 2003 invasion of Iraq and the rapid defeat of the Taliban in Afghanistan in 2001, it is unlikely that any nation will be quick to take on the United States in a conventional war.[1] In analyzing the nature of the next war our nation will face, we should recognize certain characteristics of war in the early twenty-first century.

The ability of the United States to fight and win wars that utilize massive firepower, bombs directed by GPS or lasers, and well-equipped armor and infantry forces is unparalleled. Because our opponents can't match this high-intensity combat, the United States achieves quick victories. But the speedy advances that decapitate a regime also allow enemy forces to go underground largely intact. The irregular war that follows such a nominal victory forces our military to stay in place for longer periods of time.[2]

The high-intensity combat made possible by the US military's increased reliance on high-tech weapons reduces our casualties. The prospect of low casualties while achieving a military victory makes the use of military force more likely. This is especially true if our political leaders don't recognize the difference between achieving a military victory and political goals. But at the same time that our superiority in conventional warfare encourages our use of force, our superiority pushes our opponents into relying on irregular warfare.[3] The enemies of the United States see the difficulty, if not futility, in a conventional war with our country, and they also note that unconventional fourth-generation wars are the only wars the United States has lost.[4] Even foes with significant conventional war capabilities appreciate the advantage gained by a large power using an insurgency to bleed its opponent. During the US war in Vietnam, the Soviet Union and China trained and supplied the North Vietnamese army. A few years later the United States reversed roles when it supplied Afghan rebels in their fight against the Soviet Union. More recently, Iran has diverted a significant portion of the US effort in Iraq by supplying and training Shiite militias that inflict casualties on US forces.

In addition to the imbalance of conventional military power

guiding our foes to the use of unconventional warfare, there is another cause that results in the same effect. Many of the areas of the world that affect our national interests are in Asia. For the foreseeable future our nation's economy will be highly influenced by the price and availability of oil. Many of the countries that possess nuclear weapons—including India, China, Pakistan, North Korea, and Israel—are in Asia. Add to that list the country of Iran, which seems intent on gaining such weapons.

With the exception of Israel, these Asian countries have an Eastern world tradition. The Eastern world differs from the Western world in many respects, including the tradition of war. The second- and third-generation wars described by William Lind and T. X. Hammes have been the foundation of the Western style of war historically fought by European and American forces. In contrast, the Eastern style of war practiced for centuries in China, Persia, and Arab lands relies on indirectness, deception, attrition, and protraction. These characteristics, espoused by Sun Tzu and Mao Tse-tung, cause the Eastern style of war to be more irregular, unorthodox, and asymmetric than the traditional war preferred by Western countries.[5]

The proliferation of terrorism and the deterioration of smaller nation-states provide ample locations where terrorism can take root. Professor Steven Metz has written that the insurgencies fought in today's world are competitions for uncontrolled space. Metz believes today's insurgencies are similar to the small irregular wars fought on the peripheries of declining empires such as the Roman Empire and the Ottoman Empire.[6] Transnational groups such as criminal gangs and al-Qaeda ignore national borders and act in their own interest. Even strong nations have trouble resisting the corrosive effect of such transnational groups.

Nations with weak economies, enemies on their borders, or cultures rife with graft and corruption will find resisting such transnational groups much harder. A lack of law and order found in such places encourages transnational groups to settle.[7] The horn of Africa (Somalia, Ethiopia, Eritrea), the "stans" (Kyrgyzstan, Uzbekistan, Turkmenistan, Tajikistan, Kazakhstan), and even Mexico and Central America are all places that could become engulfed in insurgencies.

If terrorists use these contested areas as bases from which to launch terrorist attacks against the United States, our nation will respond. The war in Afghanistan was started to kill or capture Osama bin Laden and other al-Qaeda members responsible for the September 11, 2001, attacks and to deprive al-Qaeda of its base in Afghanistan. US forces invaded Iraq with the stated intention of preventing the use of weapons of mass destruction against the United States. These two wars make clear the United States will act either in response to terrorism or preemptively to protect itself from a significant threat.

Not all would agree with the above prediction of what to expect in the next war. Despite the experiences of Vietnam, Afghanistan, and Iraq, some believe that irregular war is a distraction from preparing for war with a peer state such as China or Russia. This reasoning holds that if the United States reconfigures its military forces to deal primarily with fourth-generation warfare, the results could be catastrophic. Proponents of this theory point to Russian moves to reestablish a sphere of influence in the space of the former Soviet Union.[8] Such a battle with China or Russia would be the high-technology war for which the US military has traditionally prepared. Proponents of this reasoning may see an emphasis on fourth-generation warfare as a possible threat to acquiring new weapons needed for a future high technology war such as reconnaissance satellites that can survive attacks and air support that can survive intense surface-to-air missile threats.

But conventional war and counterinsurgency operations are not parts of an either/or proposition. The United States must be prepared for both conventional war with a well-equipped and technologically adept enemy *and* fourth-generation war with an unconventional opponent. Conventional war is likely to be relatively short compared to the Iraq War, and, conversely, any future unconventional opponent will seek to prolong the war as long as possible. But both types of war will be expensive. Contrary to the prewar belief of some in the Bush administration that revenue from Iraq oil production could be used to finance the postwar reconstruction of Iraq and that US troop levels could be drastically reduced after the capture of Baghdad, the Iraq War has cost US taxpayers hundreds of billions of dollars. This level of expenditure complicates our ability to defend against a conventional war because dollars spent for operations in Iraq and Afghanistan have not been available to fund aircraft, ships, and ground equipment that would normally have been procured.

The dispute over whether to prepare for an insurgency or a high intensity conventional war centers on how to equip, organize, and train our military. Some of the resistance to preparing for counterinsurgency operations arises from those who have an interest in what weapons and equipment are purchased for our military. Although forces that fight an insurgency require lighter and more mobile equipment than forces fighting a conventional war, the true change required does not center on the procurement of weapons. The change that is needed is one of attitude and culture. Across the military, the United States must institutionalize the lessons of Afghanistan and Iraq.

If the military succeeded in creating an institutional memory of how to fight an insurgency and changed its organization and training to incorporate those lessons as part of military doctrine and culture, that change would be a monumental success. The history of the US military suggests change of that significance is unlikely. The US Army and Marine Corps have fought a series of irregular wars— and after each one they forgot the lessons that were learned at a high cost. The wars against the Native Americans in the late nineteenth century, the Philippine Insurrection of 1899–1902, a series of small wars in Latin America in the early twentieth century, and the Vietnam War all preceded the Iraq War. Despite that considerable experience, the US military had to learn again in Iraq how to fight an unconventional war.

If the US military were to face an unconventional war two years after significantly reducing operations in Iraq, there would be plenty of personnel still in the force who would recall the lessons of Iraq. But if the United States does not undertake a large counterinsurgency effort for another ten years, the US military will be relearning the lessons of irregular war if those lessons are not institutionalized into its training and operational methods.

A massive cultural change will be required to convince the leadership of the US military that counterinsurgency is not an aberration; it is instead one of the primary missions of our military. Large-scale warfare in which a division fights against a division in operations with tanks and jets is the aberration. Since the end of World War II, the US Army has experienced only about six hundred hours of that type of war.[9]

Because the past leadership of the army and other military services have never incorporated the lessons of past unconventional wars into military doctrine, I have little hope the current leadership will succeed. I believe that left to their own counsel, the leaders of the Defense Department and the military services will not even attempt to make the changes necessary to successfully fight what is likely to be the next war.

The only people who can make the changes required are soldiers, marines, sailors, and airmen who have another ten or fifteen years left in their military careers. Unfortunately, the deck is stacked against the military officers and NCOs who would champion such change because the military leaders of today will select their successors based upon who shares the opinions of the current leadership. That is why America's political leaders must force the change in the military's culture. In order to make such a change, our representatives, senators, and president must become aware of the problem and the cultural shift that is necessary.

CHANGE THE INTELLIGENCE CULTURE

Another cultural shift is also necessary. We must change our intelligence operations undertaken to fight terrorists, insurgents, and other 4GW opponents. Changing our intelligence community will benefit our nation in several ways.

The changes outlined below can have immediate effect in fighting terrorism. Our country will gain immediately and won't have to wait until the next counterinsurgency operation to see the benefit. There is another benefit to changing the intelligence culture. In the event the rest of the military fails to incorporate the lessons from its experiences in Afghanistan and Iraq, an improved intelligence system will cushion the impact of that failure.

Recognize the Value of HUMINT

The first priority in changing the intelligence community is to recognize the value of HUMINT and to improve our ability to collect HUMINT. Improving HUMINT will save the lives of US servicemen and women fighting the next war. Improving HUMINT will also save the lives of US citizens at home and abroad. There is no substitute for having a source in the room when an insurgent or terrorist discusses his plans. Even if the source isn't in the room, if the source is close enough to identify the key players and reports clues as to their intentions, such information is extraordinarily valuable.

Effective HUMINT can slow or reduce the impact of an insurgency. The new counterinsurgency manual published by the army and Marine Corps adopts the principle that in order to defeat an insurgency, one must win the battle for the population by reducing violence and restoring order. Reduced violence translates into an improvement in the daily life and commerce of the population. Much of the dissatisfaction with the United States in Iraq arises because of several reasons, including a lack of jobs; the daily random attacks in markets, cafés, and government offices; unreliable electricity; poor water quality; and a shortage of gasoline. All of these reasons to oppose the United States arise out of the lack of security.

Good HUMINT is remarkably humane. The troops that go to an insurgent's residence still have the familiar orders to "kill or capture" the insurgent. But good HUMINT results in fewer unintended injuries to neighbors and less harassment of the population through cordon-and-search operations. "Precision" air strikes conducted in a city don't always have precise results. True precision results from knowing where an insurgent can be found at a particular time. Accurate HUMINT allows US forces to be more discriminating in their use of force. In turn, this reduced use of force encourages acceptance and support for the US counterinsurgency operations. When the population supports the local government, the insurgents' days are numbered.

Counterinsurgency operations using the new strategy force US troops to accept more risk as they live and work among the population they seek to protect. Well-coordinated HUMINT operations can reduce the risk to troops by identifying and capturing insurgents responsible for violence against US troops and the indigenous population.

In order to realize the full potential of HUMINT in an unconventional war, the military must commit to making HUMINT a full partner in the intelligence community. That means promoting officers who have devoted significant portions of their careers into intelligence leadership positions. An officer pursuing an intelligence career who has demonstrated the potential to achieve high rank (called a "fastburner") should have at least one tour of duty as a HUMINT officer. There is a world of difference between memorizing the steps to recruiting and handling a source and actually doing so.

Enlarge the HUMINT Force

The size of the HUMINT force should be enlarged to allow significant numbers of HUMINT personnel, especially those likely to be handling sources and liaison operations, to become proficient in languages and area studies. There is no substitute for an intelligence officer who is able to express himself, even with only rudimentary skill, in the language of the person he is meeting. Second only to the ability to speak the local language is a deep knowledge of the customs and culture of the area. Intelligence officers who have to use a translator can still ingratiate themselves with local officials using their knowledge of the area's history, politics, and religion.

When fighting an insurgency, the need for trained and experienced intelligence officers, especially source handlers, will exceed what is available in the active duty and civilian staff of military intelligence organizations. The military must have the ability to increase the numbers of competent intelligence personnel and avoid, to the extent possible, being forced to rely on contractors. Military reservists and National Guardsmen who are law enforcement officers in their civilian careers can easily make the transition to intelligence operations. Counterinsurgency operations and operations against terrorists increasingly require the skills of criminal investigators. Reservists and guardsmen who have actually handled criminal sources are ideal candidates to handle intelligence sources. As reserve and guard personnel perform law enforcement duties in their civilian careers, they constantly gain and renew experience in the key skills of intelligence operations such as recruiting and handling a source, conducting investigations, and meeting with other law enforcement or security personnel.

If intelligence billets are not available to maintain reservists and guardsmen in intelligence organizations during peacetime, the military services should survey reservists and guardsmen to identify law enforcement officers who could be cross-trained in the event of counterinsurgency duty. Military intelligence organizations should establish shortened courses that teach the basics of the military intelligence system.

Embed Analysts in HUMINT Operations

In order to maximize the production of human sources and other HUMINT operations, intelligence analysts should be placed in HUMINT organizations that are operating in counterinsurgency operations. Embedding analysts in intelligence organizations, as was done at the SCID, can improve the organization's source operations. To be effective, however, the fusion of source handler and analyst must be managed by a leader devoted to making it work. The different backgrounds and skill sets of analysts, on one side, and investigators and source handlers, on the other, can lead to conflict.

Analysts can be the corporate memory of an intelligence organization. Because most analysts serve only a year at a particular assignment in a war theater, experience with a particular group of insurgents or location must be constantly replenished. At the SCID, many of the contract analysts worked at the Counterintelligence Field Activity either before or after their assignment in Iraq. After they returned from Iraq, some were available to provide assistance on projects that required researching databases or doing other work that could be done in the United States.

An improved solution for the SCID and other intelligence organizations would be to dedicate three analysts to a single analytical position at the SCID. Two of the analysts would remain in the United States but would exclusively work on projects at the SCID (or another intelligence unit that used this system) and would be in communication with analysts in Iraq every day. The analyst who was in Iraq would have to pass on information from source reports, meetings with other agencies, and information from investigators and source handlers.

Analysts who are deployed to Iraq develop a deeper knowledge of insurgent groups, weapons and tactics of insurgents, sectarian conflict, the economy, and the overall country environment. This learning occurs in part because people deployed to Iraq work harder and longer than their counterparts in the United States. With few distractions and plenty to do, twelve- and fourteen-hour workdays are common. Weekends are a chance to work on a project without having to respond to telephone calls or e-mails from counterparts in the United States, who are home with their families. For most in Iraq, duty carries on seven days a week.

When the analyst in Iraq completes a tour of duty, one of the other analysts would go to Iraq, and the analyst who had just left Iraq would return to the analytical cell that supported the SCID. The returning analyst's knowledge of the area would be invaluable in briefing others and continuing to work on projects that supported source operations and other intelligence missions in Iraq. Eventually the third analyst would go to Iraq in a similar rotation. The tours of duty in Iraq could be one year, but in order to keep fresh minds and bodies in the theater, the analysts could perform shorter tours of four or six month tours.

Under this proposed system, the analysts who work in the United States could also conduct liaison with other intelligence units in the United States to develop information that would assist the projects in Iraq. The key to making such a system effective would be to ensure the analysts were devoted to the work of the unit in Iraq. At times, analysts at CIFA headquarters who we attempted to use for SCID projects were diverted to work on projects that seemed important to bosses based in the United States. To make the system work, the attitude of all the analysts must be that they are assigned to the unit in Iraq and just happen to work at some building inside the Washington Beltway.

MAKE THE RULES FOR INTELLIGENCE RATIONAL

Adopting a system for rotating analysts in HUMINT organizations to the war theater would be a change. But change is not a process welcomed in most organizations, including in the intelligence community. The army's intelligence bureaucracy has developed a complicated set of rules about many issues. Many of the personnel in the army's intelligence organizations are comfortable with the rules.

They have developed expertise at following the rules—and adopting practices that give the appearance of following the rules while pursuing a more practical solution.

One example of such self-deception is the army's prohibition on telling a source that has not been formally recruited what information to obtain. Tasking a person who has demonstrated willingness to become a source in order to test his or her ability to obtain information and follow instructions is common in other intelligence and law enforcement organizations. It is also common in the army, but the army disguises its tasking of a potential source by using a semantics exercise. Instead of tasking a potential source, army intelligence personnel "sensitize" a potential source by telling the potential source what interests the source handler without giving specific instructions as to what information to get and how to obtain it. The process of sensitizing, especially conducted through a translator who is not a trained intelligence officer, gives less specific instruction to the source and creates a more dangerous situation for the source. The very purpose for not tasking a source that hasn't been formally recruited is to prevent harm to the source. The army's practice of sensitizing a source doesn't protect the safety of the source; instead, it allows the army the false modesty of claiming it didn't task the source in the event some harm comes to the source. It is a practice that serves only to shield the army from criticism.

You might wonder why an air force officer is so concerned about army practices. I am concerned because the army's rules and practices are routinely adopted as the practices that govern intelligence operations when the military services are combined into a single operation. These "joint" operations are how most military operations are conducted. Operation Iraqi Freedom—the invasion of Iraq and the continuing occupation—is not an army operation. It is an operation mounted and directed by US Central Command, a unified combatant command. The commander of CENTCOM reports directly to the secretary of defense.

Because CENTCOM and the other combatant commands have components from all of the services, it is not difficult for CENTCOM to task the air force or navy to supply personnel that are needed for an operation conducted by CENTCOM. For this reason, air force personnel have gone to Iraq and Afghanistan to perform duties they don't normally perform, such as being the ground escort force for convoys of trucks delivering supplies throughout Iraq, interrogating prisoners, and serving in intelligence units that principally serve ground forces.

Reforming the army's intelligence bureaucracy may exceed the army's will or ability. Similar to integrating the lessons for fighting an insurgency into the army's doctrine and training, the best hope for reform is with midlevel officers who have served in Iraq and who move into higher positions. But the chances of reform by that process are even lower in the army's intelligence organization than in the army at large. Many of the reforms needed are focused on HUMINT, and senior intelligence officers who have risen through the ranks of technologically driven intelligence disciplines such as signals intelligence have little interest or understanding of HUMINT.

INTELLIGENCE SUPREMO

My suggestions are not intended to single out the army's intelligence system. There are inefficiencies and problems in the intelligence operations of the other military services, but those problems don't affect our ability to fight insurgencies and terrorists to the extent the army's problems do. The problems of the army, however, affect all of the services. Army intelligence officers are joined in Iraq by intelligence personnel from the Marine Corps, navy, and air force. CENTCOM and the Defense Intelligence Agency have also deployed intelligence personnel to Iraq. Civilian intelligence and law enforcement agencies that have representatives in Iraq include the CIA, National Security Agency, FBI, and the Department of Homeland Security.

In chapter 7 I mentioned the lack of a single intelligence officer who was in charge of all intelligence in Iraq. Neither the CIA's chief of station nor the senior military intelligence officer work for the other. One of the characteristics of a successful counterinsurgency campaign is a competent police force and HUMINT gathering organization under a single authority.[10] British forces came to the same conclusion based on their experiences in Northern Ireland.

From 1969 to 1983, nearly twenty organizations that collected intelligence in Northern Ireland were formed or evolved from existing organizations. Initially the operations of the various intelligence organizations were not coordinated by a single leader. The British found that their intelligence efforts were inefficient and created the potential for a source to sell the same information to different intelligence agencies. Eventually the British centralized control for security activities and appointed an intelligence supremo to run the intelligence war.[11]

For US intelligence to work effectively in a counterinsurgency, there must be a single intelligence officer in charge of all intelligence. This will be a difficult pill to swallow for any organization that perceives it is losing control. The military could argue that during a military campaign, especially an invasion or other active military action, only a military intelligence officer should be in charge. Others have argued that once a US ambassador has been appointed, the ambassador should control the counterinsurgency operation because much of the counterinsurgency effort depends on US agencies and contractors outside the control of the military.[12] Following the logic of that arrangement, the CIA's chief of station, who is part of the ambassador's country team, could function as the lead intelligence officer.

Placing the CIA in charge of all intelligence operations in counterinsurgency would probably not be a good use of the talents of that agency. Philip Zelikow, the counselor to the state department, found during his visits to Iraq that the CIA was not involved in the major aspects of counterinsurgency intelligence, at the tactical level. Instead, the CIA had focused on al-Qaeda and the technical side of intelligence, communication intercepts, and aerial photography.[13]

Perhaps the intelligence supremo in a counterinsurgency should be an intelligence officer selected by the director of national intelligence after the completion of the initial military action, when military forces have transitioned from invasion to static security of occupied lands. The overall leader could be a military intelligence officer, a senior CIA officer, or a member of the Office of the Director of National Intelligence. Rotating the responsibility among different elements of the intelligence community would be useful. The origin of the intelligence leader is not important. The most important criteria for filling such a position are the ability to lead and the willingness to focus on accomplishing the mission. Persons seeking to create a new bureaucracy to encompass all of the smaller bureaucracies of the intelligence agencies operating in the counterinsurgency operation should not be considered.

NETWORK LIKE LAW ENFORCEMENT

In addition to the appointment of an intelligence leader for the counterinsurgency, the US intelligence community must adopt networking. This culture change should be modeled after law enforcement's battle against violent criminal gangs that operate across borders. Gang experts have observed the appearance of a new type of criminal gang, a third-generation gang that is identified by three characteristics. Third-generation gangs adopt some degree of political activity that for some sophisticated gangs includes using the political process to achieve their goals or even destabilizing a government. The second characteristic of these gangs is their international reach; they are transnational organizations. The third characteristic is a higher level of sophistication. This can take the form of advanced infantry tactics for ambushes, the use of computers, and the creation of networks with other gangs.[14]

As a result, the transnational criminal gangs resemble transnational terrorist groups such as al-Qaeda in many ways. In addition to operating across borders, both gangs and terrorist groups practice indiscriminate violence and intimidation. Transnational gangs, like transnational terrorists, pose significant threats to national security.[15]

Confronting these third-generation gangs are the law enforcement agencies of the United States and other countries. Although law enforcement organizations such as the FBI, city police departments, sheriff's offices, and state law enforcement agencies are hierarchal, they have been forced to cooperate with each other as criminals expand their geographic reach. The United States has no national police force. An FBI agent who appears at a city police department must ask for help and has no authority to demand it. (Many local law enforcement officers will grin as they tell stories of FBI agents who thought otherwise.)

Despite the natural jealousy and interpersonal conflicts that arise from any human endeavor, law enforcement agencies have developed the ability to operate in networks that exceeds the experience of intelligence and military organizations. Law enforcement networking is not perfect. John P. Sullivan is a lieutenant with the Los Angeles County Sheriff's Department who has extensively studied and written about transnational gangs. The advice he has given about dealing with the threat posed by networked gangs is critical to the security of the United States in the coming years:

> To combat groups evolving along this path requires that police, security agencies, and other government offices quickly recognize the threats that can be posed by internetted adversaries, and thus craft networks of their own. Police, military, and security forces must learn to integrate network forms into their hierarchical structures to enable rapid, robust, and flexible response across organizational and political boundaries. Otherwise, networked adversaries may exploit the gaps and seams between government organizations. These must be filled through innovative, multilateral, interagency collaboration.[16]

Sullivan's advice for police and military forces to develop networks of their own to defeat a networked enemy is crucial.

Hierarchal organizations such as armies do not respond quickly to a rapidly changing enemy that is a network of networks. On the other hand, our government is necessarily hierarchal, and that hierarchy serves many useful purposes. The solution to marshaling our intelligence forces to detect, locate, and neutralize insurgents or terrorists is a combination of a hierarchy and network. Organizations that combine the task effectiveness of a hierarchy and the flexibility of a network maximize their ability to perform their missions.[17]

Some military intelligence officers who have studied counterinsurgency have envisioned networking among intelligence organizations similar to the networking that Sullivan has suggested. Kyle Teamey, the lead author for the portions of the new counterinsurgency manual that address intelligence, envisions ad hoc intelligence sharing by intelligence officers using e-mail, chat rooms, and the telephone.[18] To that list of communication methods, I add one that I found to be the most effective: Intelligence officers who make an effort to meet and work with their counterparts in other agencies achieve more than those who prefer to remain inside their stovepiped organizations.

Although conferences are useful for meeting colleagues, the most effective method for building relationships is one-on-one interaction between intelligence collectors who are working together on the same project. A single successful project often leads to more joint projects. The relationships that are built during these task-oriented meetings become conduits for information. As intelligence officers work with each other, they become aware of each other's interests and talents. Even if friendships don't arise, the self-interest of both parties and their supervisors helps continue the exchange of information.

Network relationships are fragile because they depend on interpersonal relationships. A new supervisor in one organization can cause good information conduits to be turned off. Most intelligence managers have spent a career working within stovepipes. Many are satisfied to continue with a system they have mastered well enough to achieve promotion to manager. Selecting leaders who are more interested in results than organizational turf is the only antidote to an attitude that kills networking among intelligence and law enforcement agencies.

The status quo is hard to change. Most of the people I met in intelligence organizations were good people. Analysts, source handlers, investigators, and career intelligence officers sought to defeat the insurgency. Most were frustrated with stovepipes and rules that hamstrung them. But they learned to live with the way things were.

The status quo is dangerous. Professional journals within the military and intelligence communities have decried stovepipes for years. Commissions have identified the lack of information sharing as a critical cause of intelligence failures. For decades politicians and writers have expressed chagrin about our nation's limited ability to collect HUMINT as billions of dollars have been invested in technologically based intelligence gathering.

The status quo will result in more American deaths unless our military, intelligence, and political leaders act. As a nation we must reject the inertia that leaves stovepipes in place and HUMINT at the bottom of the intelligence food chain.

NOTES

1. T. X. Hammes, *The Sling and the Stone: On War in the 21st Century* (St. Paul, MN: Zenith Press, 2006), p. 254.

2. Jeffrey Record, "Why the Strong Lose?" *Parameters*, Winter 2006–2006, p. 27, http://carlisle-www.army.mil/usawc/Parameters/05winter/record.pdf (accessed April 5, 2008).

3. Ibid., pp. 28–29.

4. Hammes, *The Sling and the Stone*, p. 3.

5. Robert M. Cassidy, *Counterinsurgency and the Global War on Terror: Military Culture and Irregular War* (Stanford: Stanford University Press, 2008), p. 3.

6. Steven Metz, "Rethinking Insurgency," Strategic Studies Institute, June 2007, p. 11, http://www.strategicstudiesinstitute.army.mil/Pubs/display.cfm?pubID=790 (accessed March 31, 2008).

7. Ibid., p. 9.

8. George Friedman, "Beyond Fourth Generation Warfare," *Officer*, September 2007, pp. 57–60.

9. Cassidy, *Counterinsurgency and the Global War on Terror*, p. 101.

10. David J. Clark, "The Vital Role of Intelligence in Counterinsurgency Operations," U.S. Army War College Strategy Research Project, March 15, 2006, p. 14, http://www.strategicstudiesinstitute.army.mil/pdffiles/ksil309.pdf (accessed April 6, 2008.)

11. Brian A. Jackson, "Counterinsurgency Intelligence in a 'Long War': The British Experience in Northern Ireland," *Military Review*, January–February 2007, p. 76.

12. Thomas X. Hammes, "An Oversight Hearing on the Planning and Conduct of the War in Iraq," Senate Democratic Policy Committee Hearing, September 25, 2006, http://democrats.senate.gov/dpc/hearings/hearing38/hammes.pdf (accessed April 6, 2008).

13. Bob Woodward, *State of Denial* (New York: Simon & Schuster, 2006), p. 397.

14. John P. Sullivan, "Gangs, Hooligans, and Anarchists—Vanguard of Netwar in the Streets," in *Networks and Netwars: The Future of Terror, Crime, and Militancy*, ed. John Arquilla and David Ronfeldt (Santa Monica, CA: RAND Corporation, 2001), pp. 101–102, http://rand.org/pubs/monograph_reports/MR1382/MR1382.ch4.pdf (accessed April 6, 2008).

15. Gary I. Wilson and John P. Sullivan, "On Gangs, Crime, and Terrorism," Defense and the National Interest, February 28, 2007, p. 9, http://www.d-n-i.net/fcs/pdf/wilson_sullivan_gangs_terrorism.pdf (accessed April 6, 2008).

16. Sullivan, "Gangs, Hooligans, and Anarchists," p. 120.

17. Metz, "Rethinking Insurgency," p. 12.

18. Kyle Teamey and Jonathan Sweet, "Organizing Intelligence for Counterinsurgency," *Military Review*, September–October 2006, p. 28.

INDEX